No-Load Stocks

Other McGraw-Hill Books by Charles B. Carlson

BUYING STOCKS WITHOUT A BROKER

FREE LUNCH ON WALL STREET

No-Load Stocks

How to Buy Your First Share and Every Share Directly from the Company—With No Broker's Fee

Charles B. Carlson, CFA

Editor, *Dow Theory Forecasts*

McGraw-Hill, Inc.

New York   San Francisco   Washington, D.C.   Auckland   Bogotá
Caracas   Lisbon   London   Madrid   Mexico City   Milan
Montreal   New Delhi   San Juan   Singapore
Sydney   Tokyo   Toronto

Library of Congress Cataloging-in-Publication Data

Carlson, Charles B.
   No-load stocks : how to buy your first share and every share
directly from the company—with no broker's fee / Charles B. Carlson.
     p.   cm.
   Includes bibliographical references and index.
   ISBN 0-07-011187-1 (pbk. : alk paper)
   1. Stocks. 2. Investing. I. Title.
HG4661.C328 1995
332.63'22—dc20   94-36446
                                                       CIP

7 8 9 0 QBP/QBP 9 0 9 8 7 6

ISBN 0-07-011187-1 (PBK)

*The sponsoring editor for this book was David Conti, the editing supervisor was
Virginia Carroll, and the production supervisor was Donald Schmidt. It was
set in Palatino by North Market Street Graphics.*

Printed and bound by Quebecor-Book Press

McGraw-Hill books are available at special quantity discounts to use as
premiums and sales promotions, or for use in corporate training programs.
For more information, please write to the Director of Special Sales,
McGraw-Hill, Inc., 11 West 19th Street, New York, NY 10011. Or contact
your local bookstore.

This publication is designed to provide accurate and authoritative information in regard to the subject matter covered. It is sold with the understand-
ing that the publisher is not engaged in rendering legal, accounting, or
other professional service. If legal advice or other expert assistance is
required, the services of a competent professional person should be sought.
                *—from a declaration of principles jointly adopted by a committee
                    of the American Bar Association and a committee of publishers*

This book is printed on recycled, acid-free paper containing a
minimum of 50% recycled de-inked fiber.

To Amber, Anthony, Christina, Christopher,
Joshua, Meghan, and Sarah;
To their tired parents, grandparents,
and great-grandparents;
and, of course, to Auntie Dee.

Contents

Author's Note

This book is a comprehensive guide to what I call No-Load Stocks. These are stocks that you never need to purchase through a broker. Your *first share* and *every share* can be bought *directly* from the company that issued the stock.

While I have tried to give accurate and up-to-date information concerning no-load stock programs, readers should understand that companies frequently change aspects of these programs. It's likely that certain features of programs discussed in the book have changed since the book's publication. A program discussed in this book may have been suspended or even eliminated. Fortunately, it's more likely that new no-load stock programs have been implemented since these pages left the printer. Because of frequent plan changes, it is always best to read the company's plan prospectus, which provides all of the details of the program, before investing.

Because of my work in this area, I maintain a list of no-load stocks that is updated continuously. As a service to readers, this updated list of all no-load stocks and their telephone numbers is available free of charge by writing Dow Theory Forecasts, Inc., 7412 Calumet Avenue, Hammond, Indiana 46324-2692. Use the code words "No-Load Stocks" when making requests. Please include a business-size, self-addressed stamped envelope.

Preface

No-load mutual funds have become the investment of choice for millions of small investors—for good reason. Mutual-fund investing is *easy*. No brokers. No commissions. No hassles. No big minimum investments. Just request an application via a toll-free number, fill it out, return it with your check, and that's all there is to it. What could be easier? Certainly not stock investing!

Well, the fact is that there are a growing number of stocks in which you can buy your *first* share and *every* share directly, without a broker and without brokerage commissions, just like a no-load mutual fund. Better still, these *no-load stocks*™, as I call them, possess other attractive features usually associated with mutual-fund investing:

- Automatic cash investments via electronic funds transfers from an investor's savings or checking account
- IRA investing, with the company providing the custodial services
- The ability to sell stock, in some cases over the phone, for little or no commissions

Despite the many benefits of no-load stocks, it's possible that you may never have known that such stocks exist. That's not surprising. The companies operating no-load stock plans aren't permitted, under mandate from the Securities and Exchange Commission, to advertise aggressively the programs. And stock brokers, who are often the only source of investment information for individual investors, aren't likely to extol the virtues of no-load stocks, for obvious reasons. Thus, the reason for this book: to make individual investors aware that there is an increasingly viable investment alternative to no-load mutual funds, one combining the best elements of both stocks and mutual funds.

Many Wall Street purists regard no-load stocks as an investment having only limited appeal for a limited segment of the investing public. I disagree. The last decade has seen an explosion in the number of do-it-yourself investors who feel comfortable making their own investment decisions and want to invest directly, without a broker. I know these investors would love to invest directly in individual stocks if such direct-purchase programs were widely available. Furthermore, my position as editor of *Dow Theory Forecasts* and *DRIP Investor* investment newsletters keeps me in touch with literally thousands of individual investors, and rarely a week goes by without one of my subscribers inquiring as to what companies permit direct investment for initial purchases.

Need more evidence that investors want no-load stocks? Exxon, one of the more prominent no-load stocks, implemented its program in March 1992. In the first month of the program, the company received 50,000 phone calls and opened 25,000 new accounts. In the first year of its no-load stock program, Exxon opened 187,000 new accounts. Those are big numbers, especially when you take into account that Exxon had to remain relatively closemouthed about the program to avoid the wrath of the SEC. Who knows how many individuals would have invested directly with Exxon had they known about the program?

Despite the naysayers—many of whom are "gatekeepers" who make a living providing investors with access to the markets—who feel that no-load stocks are nothing more than a passing oddity, several forces are at work which should push the number of no-load stocks sharply higher in the months and years ahead. But investors don't have to wait to get started investing in no-load stocks. Indeed, many quality companies offer the programs today. To find out which ones, read on.

I think you'll be glad you did.

Charles B. Carlson

Acknowledgments

I would like to thank the readers of *DRIP Investor* and *Dow Theory Forecasts* investment newsletters for their comments concerning no-load stocks. Their interest in the subject was one of the driving forces that caused me to write this book. I would also like to thank Jim Volpe of First Chicago Trust Corporation of New York and Robert Smith of Houston Industries for their unique insights.

Special thanks go to my editor at McGraw-Hill, David Conti, for his suggestions, criticisms, and, most of all, patience.

I would be remiss if I didn't thank the entire staff of Dow Theory Forecasts, Inc., especially Avis Beitz, for assistance on this project. Monica Taylor also deserves special mention for her research efforts, not only on this book but also on my previous two.

Finally, I'd like to thank two good friends of mine, Jeff Kallay and his wife Jean, for their continuing support and counsel.

No-Load Stocks

Introduction

In a perfect world, investors would be able to do the following:

- Go to a McDonald's and buy two Big Macs, two orders of fries, two Cokes, and two shares of McDonald's stock.
- Shop at Wal-Mart Stores for bug spray, suntan lotion, and light bulbs and pick up five shares of Wal-Mart stock at the checkout counter.
- Buy a new Jeep Grand Cherokee, as well as 15 shares of Chrysler stock, from your local Chrysler/Jeep dealership. (Better still, the dealer gives you the 15 shares as its way of saying "Thanks.")
- Purchase a Reese's peanut butter cup and return the coupon inside for a 3 percent discount on purchases of Hershey Foods stock directly from the company.
- Fill out the application form on the back of the Kellogg's Cocoa Krispies box and return it along with your money to buy 10 shares of Kellogg stock for the kindergarten capitalist in your family.

In short, a perfect world for investors would be one in which you could invest directly with the company of your choice.

No broker.

No commissions.

Just you and the company.

Unfortunately, as most of you know, stock investing isn't nearly that easy. In fact, buying stock is like attending your high school prom—you can't get in until you pass the chaperone, who makes sure you pay your admission fee and agree to abide by the house rules. Of course, in the case of the stock market, the chaperone is the broker, who charges what amounts to an admission fee every time you buy or sell stock. However, many of us didn't believe we needed a chaperone at the prom, and I'm sure many of us feel the same way about investing in the stock market. We can do it ourselves, thank you.

On the other hand, investing in no-load mutual funds is pretty close to a perfect world for investors. You invest directly, with no sales fee, and usually in amounts that don't break your piggy bank.

To be sure, mutual funds have their downsides relative to individual stocks, such as "hidden" costs in the way of annual management expenses, redemption penalties, and 12b-1 fees, not to mention the potential for unwanted tax liabilities due to capital gains distributions. Furthermore, the performance of most mutual funds, to put it kindly, has been mediocre.

What if an investment existed that combined the best elements of no-load mutual funds with the best elements of individual stock investing? In other words, what if there were no-load *stocks*?

Well, guess what—no-load stocks do exist, and they're the subject of this book.

What exactly is a no-load stock? As you'll read in Chapter 1, no-load stock programs permit investors to buy their first share, and every subsequent share, directly from the company, without a broker.

Shares are purchased in much the same way as shares are purchased in a no-load mutual fund:

- Investors call the company, usually via a toll-free number, to request an application form and a plan prospectus.
- The company mails the materials directly to the investor.
- Once the investor receives the materials and completes the application, he or she makes the initial investment directly by returning the application and a check to the company.
- Once the initial investment has been made, investors are free to make subsequent purchases directly with the company.

In addition to direct investing, no-load stocks share other attributes with no-load mutual funds, such as monthly automatic cash investments and IRA investing. Best of all, investors pay no brokerage commissions when investing in no-load stocks.

Of course, just because an investor is able to buy stock directly from a company doesn't make the stock a worthwhile investment. The overriding factor to consider with any investment is its quality and long-term total-return prospects. For guidance when investing in no-load stocks, Chapter 2 provides a number of strategies to help you incorporate no-load stocks into your investment program.

By now, I'm sure some of you are saying that, while no-load stocks are interesting, they still don't match the attraction of no-load mutual funds. Certainly, no-load mutual funds merit their place in nearly any investment program. However, I believe that individual stock ownership, perhaps via no-load stocks, is an excellent way to round out a diversified investment portfolio. Furthermore, I maintain that while the mutual-fund industry has done a masterful job of portraying all the benefits of mutual-fund investing, there are several downsides to mutual-fund investing—negatives which are lessened or eliminated when investing in no-load stocks. These mutual fund "myths" and how no-load stocks stack up against no-load mutual funds in terms of cost and performance are explored in Chapter 3.

I wish this book had twice or three times as many pages as it does. That would mean that hundreds of no-load stocks exist today. Unfortunately, that's not the case. However, while the number of no-load stocks is small compared to the thousands of stocks on the various exchanges, the increase in no-load stock programs in the last two years has been impressive. Furthermore, major changes are in the works which will speed up the SEC approval process for companies wishing to implement no-load stock programs. The ability of corporations to derive several benefits from offering these plans is another driving force behind the implementation of no-load stock programs. Thus, the number of no-load stock programs should grow sharply over the next several years. I examine the reasons why more no-load stocks are on their way in Chapter 4.

The book includes a complete review of all no-load stock programs in Chapter 5. Addresses, telephone numbers, stock symbols, program details, business profiles, statistical histories, and performance ratings are provided for all no-load stocks.

If you think about it, a company doesn't have to stop at letting investors buy just its stock directly. Why couldn't companies sell corporate bonds directly to investors? Or preferred stock? Or convertible bonds? And why couldn't a foreign company whose American Depositary Receipts (ADRs) trade in the United States sell ADRs directly to United States investors? And why couldn't a school or highway authority sell tax-exempt bonds directly to investors? Expanding the concept of no-load stocks to other investments is examined in the Epilogue.

Many of you may see similarities between no-load stocks and dividend reinvestment plans (DRIPs), programs which I discussed in depth in my first book, *Buying Stocks Without a Broker* (McGraw-Hill, 1992). However, it's important to understand that no-load stocks are not merely extensions of companies' DRIP plans, but much more. No-load stocks represent a whole new way of investing in stocks, a way which provides choices and options heretofore not available to the small stock investor.

History tells us that most revolutions start slowly, building momentum over time until a critical mass of support is reached. At that point, change begins to occur, not incrementally, but exponentially. Revolutions in the financial markets are no different. Just look at no-load mutual funds. In the early years, the flow of money into mutual funds was a trickle rather than a flood. However, over time, as the merits of mutual-fund investing became more widely recognized, huge amounts of money began to pour into these once "obscure" investments. Today, there's no mistaking the revolutionary impact mutual funds have had on the investment landscape.

Could no-load stocks be the next revolution on Wall Street? Let's hope so.

1

What's a No-Load Stock?

What does Texaco, the big oil company, have in common with Fidelity mutual funds? Or Exxon, another leading oil company, with T. Rowe Price mutual funds? Or Dial, the consumer products company, with Vanguard funds? Or U S West, one of the seven regional Bell telephone companies, with Janus funds?

On the surface, it appears that these companies have nothing in common with these no-load mutual funds, especially when it comes to making purchases in these two types of investments. No-load mutual funds allow you to deal directly with the fund family, without using a broker or paying commission. On the other hand, stocks such as Texaco, Exxon, Dial, and U S West require you to use a broker to make your purchases, right?

Well, you might be surprised to learn that Texaco, Exxon, Dial, and U S West are just four of the growing number of publicly traded companies in which investors may buy their first share and every share of stock *directly from the firm*—without using a broker. Texaco, Exxon, Dial, and U S West are what I call *no-load stocks*.

What's a No-Load Stock?

No-load stocks share many of the features that are usually associated with no-load mutual funds.

Direct Investing—with No Brokerage Commission

The most obvious common trait of no-load mutual funds and no-load stocks is that both are purchased without using a broker or paying brokerage commissions. In both cases, investors deal directly, via the mail.

The process for buying no-load stocks is the same as buying no-load mutual funds:

- *Call for information.*   Investors must first contact the company to obtain an application form and a plan prospectus. The plan prospectus describes in great detail all of the aspects of the no-load stock program—what the minimum is for the initial investment, when the funds will be invested, how investors may sell shares through the company, and any other features the plan offers. In most cases, companies have toll-free telephone numbers to handle inquiries, which is similar to the toll-free numbers provided by no-load mutual funds.

- *Fill out the application form.*   Once you've received the material in the mail, read the prospectus and fill out the application form. Texaco's application form is shown in Figure 1-1.

- *Cut a check.*   To make your initial investment, make out a check to the company or its transfer agent. Instructions will be given on the application form. Make sure that your initial investment falls within the parameters for the minimum and maximum investment.

- *Mail it to the company.*   Put your check and application form in an envelope and return it to the company. In some cases, the company will include a return envelope in the application material.

And that's it.

In most cases, your initial investment will automatically enroll you in the company's dividend reinvestment plan and/or stock purchase plan. With these programs, you can have your dividends reinvested as well as make additional cash investments to purchase more shares.

Low Investment Minimums

A big reason mutual funds are so popular with small investors is that they don't require huge investments to get started. Most mutual funds have minimums of $1000 to $2000 and usually lower the minimum for investments in an individual retirement account. Some mutual funds have minimums as low as $100. A few mutual funds even waive the minimum investment if you agree to invest $100 or more a month. Investing in such

IMPORTANT
Return this application together
with your check in the enclosed
envelope or send to:
TEXACO INC.
P.O. Box 10818
Newark, NJ 07193-0818

APPLICATION FORM

PLEASE **PRINT** CLEARLY

MAKE CHECK PAYABLE TO:
TEXACO INC.
AMOUNT OF INVESTMENT

Citizenship: ☐ U.S.   ☐ Foreign
SOCIAL SECURITY NO.
(TAXPAYER I.D. NUMBER)

($250 MINIMUM - $120,000 MAXIMUM)

(OF ACCOUNT TO BE OPENED)

ACCOUNT REGISTRATION (See Information on Reverse Side)

DIVIDEND REINVESTMENT

Participants must select either
100% or 0% (zero percent)
dividend reinvestment.

NAME (1)

NAME (2) (If applicable)

Please check the
appropriate box.

NAME (3) (If applicable)

☐ 100% Dividend
Reinvestment

STREET ADDRESS (P.O. BOX)

☐ 0% (Zero Percent)
Dividend Reinvestment

CITY   STATE   ZIP CODE

NOTE: If you are registering a living trust, the above registration must include the name of the trustee(s) and date of the
trust agreement.

GIFTING

Does this enrollment represent a gift to a third party?   ☐ Yes   ☐ No

If you answered yes, please indicate the complete address of the individual to whom you wish the gift certificate to be sent.
If you do not provide an address in the space below, the gift certificate will be mailed directly to the first party indicated above.

NAME

STREET ADDRESS (P.O. BOX)

CITY   STATE   ZIP CODE

ACKNOWLEDGEMENTS AND AUTHORIZATIONS

I acknowledge receipt of the prospectus describing the details of the Investor Services Plan (the "Plan") and hereby request
that the above account be enrolled in the Plan. Enclosed is a check or money order for the amount indicated above to be
applied toward the purchase of shares for the above account. I understand that the account's participation is subject to the
Terms and Conditions of the Plan as set forth in the prospectus that accompanied this Application Form, and that enrollment
may be discontinued at any time by written notice to Texaco Inc., Investor Services Plan, 2000 Westchester Ave., White Plains,
New York 10650.

I further understand that all dividends paid on the shares held in the account will be automatically reinvested unless I select
the 0% (zero percent) dividend reinvestment option. I hereby appoint Texaco Inc. as agent for applying dividends as payment
for any such shares purchased for the above account under the Plan.

Under penalties of perjury, I certify that the Social Security Number (Taxpayer Identification Number) indicated above is true
and correct and that I am not subject to back-up withholding per the Internal Revenue Code. Please note that if a Social Security
Number (Taxpayer Identification Number) is not provided, back-up withholding tax will be withheld from dividend payments.

Signed _____   Date _____

OTHER INFORMATION

Please provide daytime telephone number where you may be contacted in the event additional information is
required: (_____)_____

Figure 1-1. Texaco's application form for its direct-purchase program.

GENERAL GUIDELINES FOR COMMON FORMS OF STOCK REGISTRATION

The manner in which stock may be registered is governed by various state laws. The following are intended as general guidelines indicating some of the more common forms of stock registration. If you have any questions regarding a specific form of registration, we suggest that you consult with an attorney.

OWNERSHIP OF STOCK BY A MINOR

It is not common practice to register stock in an individual minor's name, since it may require court action to sell or transfer the shares prior to the minor attaining his/her age of majority. Custodial registration of an account, usually by a parent or an adult family member of the minor, does not require court action. The two forms of custodial registration most commonly used are:

Jane Wilson Custodian	Jane Wilson Custodian For
For Mary Ann Wilson Under	Mary Ann Wilson [Name of State]
The Uniform Gifts to	Uniform Transfer to
Minors Act [Name of State]	Minors Act

Please include the Social Security Number of the <u>minor</u> when opening an account. For your convenience, we will register the custodial account to the appropriate state of residency per the above examples.

OWNERSHIP BY AN INDIVIDUAL

The given name of an individual must be used, exclusive of titles such as "Dr.," "Mr.," "Rev."
A woman should use her first name not that of her husband. For example:

"JANE WHITNEY WILSON" **NOT** "MRS JOHN W WILSON"

OWNERSHIP BY TWO OR MORE INDIVIDUALS

Most states recognize the registration "As Joint Tenants with Right of Survivorship and not as Tenants in Common." This form of registration, shown as "JT TEN" following the names, provides for sole ownership to pass to the surviving owner upon the death of the other. For example:

"JOHN H WILSON & JANE W WILSON JT TEN"

The conjunction "OR" **cannot** be used in registering stock ownership. Other forms of multiple tenant registration, such as Tenants in Common, may also be used but may not provide for survivorship benefits. Should you have any questions about the appropriateness of the registration you wish to use, we suggest you consult with an attorney.

Inquiries concerning the
Plan may be directed to our
TOLL FREE number 1-800-283-9785

Monday-Thursday 9:00 am-12:00 pm &
1:00-3:00 pm EST
Friday 9:00 am - 12:00 pm &
1:00-2:00 pm EST

Figure 1-1. (*Continued*)

small increments is appealing to investors with limited pocketbooks. Fortunately, no-load stocks have taken their cue from the mutual-fund industry and have made their minimum initial investments quite affordable. Indeed, in the case of Regions Financial, a leading bank in the Southeast, the minimum initial investment is just $20. Dial requires a minimum initial investment of just $100. Kerr-McGee, a chemical and natural resources concern, has the highest minimum investment of all no-load stocks at $750—still well below the minimums of many mutual funds. What's nice about such low minimums is that an investor can diversify among several no-load stocks with very little money. In fact, Chapter 2 will show you how to build a "mini" portfolio of four quality no-load stocks with an initial investment of less than $300.

Following is a list of all no-load stocks that have open enrollment (available to investors in nearly all 50 states) along with their initial investment minimums:

American Recreation Centers ($100)

Arrow Financial ($300)

Atlantic Energy ($250)

Barnett Banks ($250)

Comsat ($250)

Dial ($100)

DQE ($100)

Exxon ($250)

Houston Industries ($250)

Interchange Financial Services ($100)

Johnson Controls ($50)

Kellwood ($100)

Kerr-McGee ($750)

Mobil ($250)

Regions Financial ($20)

SCANA ($250)

Texaco ($250)

U S West ($300)

Following is a list of no-load stocks that have certain restrictions on enrollment along with their initial investment minimums:

American Water Works Company, Inc. ($100)

Bancorp Hawaii, Inc. ($250)

Carolina Power & Light Co. ($20)

Cascade Natural Gas Corp. ($250)

Centerior Energy Corp. ($10)

Central Hudson Gas & Electric ($100)

Central Maine Power Co. ($25)

Central & South West ($100)

Central Vermont Public Service Corp. ($50)

Connecticut Energy Corp. ($250)

Dominion Resources, Inc. ($20)

Duke Power Co. ($25)

Florida Progress Corp. ($100)

Hawaiian Electric Industries, Inc. ($100)

Idaho Power Co. ($10)

Interstate Power Co. ($50)

Minnesota Power & Light Co. ($10)

Montana Power Co. ($10)

National Fuel Gas Co. ($200)

Nevada Power Co. ($25)

New Jersey Resources Corp. ($25)

Northern States Power Co. ($10)

NUI Corp. ($125)

Oklahoma Gas & Electric Co. ($25)

Philadelphia Suburban Corp. ($250)

Pinnacle West Capital Corp. ($10)

Puget Sound P & L Co. ($25)

San Diego Gas & Electric Co. ($25)

Southwest Gas Corp. ($100)

Union Electric Co. (no minimum)

United Water Resources, Inc. ($25)

Western Resources, Inc. ($20)

WICOR, Inc. ($100)

Wisconsin Energy Corp. ($25)

And not only do no-load stocks make it easy to get started by having low investment minimums for the initial purchase, they make it even easier to continue accumulating stock over the long term. For example, in the case of Dial, once you have made your initial purchase and have enrolled in the stock purchase plan, subsequent investments may be made for as little as $10 at a time. In general, investment minimums for subsequent purchases in no-load stock programs are $10 to $100—much lower than the minimums in most no-load mutual funds. The beauty of such low minimum requirements is that you can add to all of your no-load stock holdings with a relatively small investment each month. In Chapter 2, I'll show you how to make monthly contributions to nine no-load stocks for a total of just $265.

If you have deeper pockets, no-load stocks are still an attractive investment option. Like mutual funds, which permit huge investments, most no-load stocks have maximum investment amounts that will be adequate for nearly every investor. For example, Exxon permits annual investments of up to $100,000. Several no-load stock programs have annual investment maximums of $50,000 or more. And remember—other than a no-load mutual fund, where else can you invest such large sums of money and pay no brokerage commissions?

Following are the minimum and maximum investments permitted by no-load stocks once you've enrolled in their stock purchase plans:

American Recreation Centers ($25–$5,000 per month)

American Water Works Co., Inc. ($100–$5,000 per month)

Arrow Financial ($50–$10,000 per quarter)

Atlantic Energy (up to $100,000 per year)

Bancorp Hawaii, Inc. ($25–$5,000 per quarter)

Barnett Banks ($25–$10,000 per month)

Carolina Power & Light Co. ($20–$2,000 per month)

Cascade Natural Gas Corp. ($50–$20,000 per year)

Centerior Energy Corp. ($10–$40,000 per year)

Central Hudson Gas & Electric ($25–$10,000 per quarter)

Central Maine Power Co. ($10–$40,000 per year)

Central & South West ($25–$100,000 per year)

Central Vermont Public Service Corp. ($50–$2,000 per month)

Comsat ($50–$10,000 per month)

Connecticut Energy Corp. ($50–$50,000 per year)

Dial ($10–$5,000 per month)

Dominion Resources, Inc. (up to $50,000 per quarter)

DQE ($10–$60,000 per year)

Duke Power Co. ($25–$20,000 per quarter)

Exxon ($50–$100,000 per year)

Florida Progress Corp. ($10–$100,000 per year)

Hawaiian Electric Industries, Inc. ($25–$25,000 per quarter)

Houston Industries ($50–$120,000 per year)

Idaho Power Co. ($10–$15,000 per quarter)

Interchange Financial Services ($25 per month minimum, no maximum)

Interstate Power Co. ($25–$2,000 per month)

Johnson Controls ($50–$15,000 per quarter)

Kellwood ($25–$3,000 per month)

Kerr-McGee ($10–$3,000 per quarter)

Minnesota Power & Light Co. ($10–$10,000 per quarter)

Mobil ($10–$7,500 per month)

Montana Power Co. ($10–$15,000 per quarter)

National Fuel Gas Co. ($25–$5,000 per month)

Nevada Power Co. ($25–$25,000 per quarter)

New Jersey Resources Corp. ($25–$30,000 per year)

Northern States Power Co. ($10–$10,000 per quarter)

NUI Corp. ($25–$60,000 per year)

Oklahoma Gas & Electric Co. ($10–$5,000 per quarter)

Philadelphia Suburban Corp. ($25–$10,000 per year)

Pinnacle West Capital Corp. ($10–$5,000 per quarter)

Puget Sound P & L Co. ($25–$100,000 per year)

Regions Financial ($20–$10,000 per month)

San Diego Gas & Electric Co. ($25–$25,000 per quarter)

SCANA ($25–$36,000 per year)

Southwest Gas Corp. ($25–$25,000 per year)

Texaco ($50–$120,000 per year)

Union Electric Co. (up to $60,000 per year)

United Water Resources, Inc. ($25–$3,000 per quarter)

U S West ($25–$100,000 per year)

Western Resources, Inc. ($20–$60,000 per year)

WICOR, Inc. ($100–$10,000 per month)

Wisconsin Energy Corp. ($25–$8,000 per month)

Regular Statements/Record-Keeping Assistance

Another way no-load stocks and mutual funds are similar is in the regular statements each sends to their investors. Figure 1-2 shows a statement from Exxon. Companies with no-load stock programs send a statement to investors after every investment. The statement shows the number of shares purchased, the purchase price, the total number of shares held in the account, and, in some cases, the total value of the shares. Companies also provide a year-end statement to assist you at tax time. My experience has been that statements from firms offering no-load stocks are far easier to

CURRENT DIVIDEND PERIOD			DIVIDENDS PAID IN CASH	
RECORD DATE	11/12/93		SHARES	
PAYMENT DATE	12/10/93		GROSS DIVIDEND AMOUNT	
RATE PER SHARE	$0.72		TAX WITHHELD	
			CASH PAID	

SHARE POSITION ENTITLED TO DIVIDEND		DIVIDENDS REINVESTED	
HELD BY YOU IN CERTIFICATES		SHARES	26.603
HELD BY US FOR SAFEKEEPING	26.603	GROSS DIVIDEND AMOUNT	$19.15
TOTAL SHARES	26.603	TAX WITHHELD	
		AMOUNT REINVESTED	$19.15

TRANSACTION RECORD (shares held by us for safekeeping) as of: 12/10/93

TRANSACTION/ SETTLEMENT DATE	TRANSACTION DESCRIPTION	TRANSACTION AMOUNT	PRICE PER SHARE	SALES FEE	TRANSACTION SHARES	SAFEKEEPING SHARE BALANCE
1/01/93	BEGINNING BALANCE					6.124
1/07/93	CASH PURCHASE	$100.00	$62.024		1.612	7.736
2/11/93	CASH PURCHASE	100.00	62.491		1.600	9.336
3/10/93	DIVIDEND PURCHASE	5.57	64.149		0.087	9.423
3/11/93	CASH PURCHASE	200.00	63.701		3.140	12.563
6/10/93	CASH PURCHASE	300.00	66.826		4.489	17.052
6/10/93	DIVIDEND PURCHASE	9.05	65.946		0.137	17.189
7/01/93	CASH PURCHASE	300.00	65.692		4.567	21.756
8/26/93	CASH PURCHASE	100.00	66.176		1.511	23.267
9/10/93	DIVIDEND PURCHASE	15.66	65.077		0.241	23.508
9/23/93	CASH PURCHASE	200.00	64.625		3.095	26.603
12/10/93	DIVIDEND PURCHASE	19.15	62.528		0.306	26.909

IN ORDER TO ENSURE ACCURATE DELIVERY, PLEASE USE THE ENCLOSED COURTESY ENVELOPE WHEN SENDING OPTIONAL CASH DEPOSITS OR MAKING A REQUEST. THANK YOU.

CURRENT MARKET VALUE INFORMATION AS OF: 12/10/93

CERTIFICATE SHARES	SAFEKEEPING SHARES	TOTAL SHARES	MARKET PRICE PER SHARE	TOTAL MARKET VALUE
0	26.909	26.909	$62.875	$1,691.90

EXXON CORPORATION

STATEMENT #
PLEASE RETAIN THIS RECORD FOR TAX PURPOSES

Figure 1-2. Exxon direct-purchase statement.

decipher than typical brokerage statements. Another benefit is that companies and their transfer agents provide an excellent source for assistance in
piecing together historical trading information. This information is especially important when determining a stock's cost basis for tax purposes.

Direct Ownership

When you buy shares directly from a no-load mutual fund, you are the
registered owner of the fund shares. That's not always the case when
investors buy stock. Indeed, although this may surprise you, most stock
investors are not the registered shareholders of the companies in which
they invest. In fact, it's possible, indeed likely, that your company has no
record of you as a shareholder. How can that be?

The fact is that, unbeknownst to many investors, their shares are held in
"street" name or, in other words, in the name of the brokerage firm that
purchased the shares for you.

There are two ways to own stock: in street name or as a registered shareholder on the books of the corporation. The identity of street-name
investors is withheld from the company. All correspondence between the
investor and the company goes through the brokerage firm.

The reason many investors end up with street-name accounts is because
this is the method of ownership that brokers push. To be sure, holding
shares in street name has certain advantages, primarily ones of convenience. The amount of paperwork is reduced because brokerage houses
act as custodian of your funds, providing regular consolidated statements
that help in record keeping and tax preparation. In street-name accounts,
investors don't have to worry about storing certificates. Street-name ownership also makes selling easier because the shares are immediately available to the brokerage firm to sell.

The benefits of street-name ownership, however, carry a price. What
you gain in convenience with a street-name account, you lose in control
and flexibility. For example, want to sell your shares? If the stock is held in
street name, the odds are that you'll sell through the broker who bought
your shares. Thus, street-name ownership greatly reduces your ability to
shop for the cheapest commissions; you are, in effect, locked in to paying
the commissions of the brokerage firm where your shares are held. Sure,
you can always re-register the shares in your own name, take ownership
of the stock certificates, and sell the shares through any broker you'd like.
However, many brokers charge dearly to register shares in the investor's
name, and the re-registration process can drag on forever.

In addition to locking up an investor's assets, brokers like street-name
accounts because they can earn fees from lending street-name shares to
short sellers and other investors. It's perfectly legal for a brokerage firm to

lend your shares if you have a margin account, just as it's perfectly legal for a bank to loan your money. And, like the bank which receives interest on loans made with your money, brokerage firms earn fees on your shares that they lend to investors.

Another cost of having stock registered in street name is that it precludes you from enrolling in company-sponsored dividend reinvestment and stock purchase plans (DRIPs). In nearly every case, companies with DRIPs require participants to be registered shareholders. Investors who want to buy stock directly from a company cannot do so if their stock is held in street name.

Another potential problem of owning shares in street name is that it may be difficult to receive quarterly and annual reports from the company. A number of companies, such as Disney (Walt) and Browning-Ferris Industries, have stopped sending quarterly and annual reports to brokerage firms to disseminate to street-name accounts. More companies are expected to follow suit due to high clerical, printing, and postage costs. In many cases, unless you're a registered shareholder, you could be cut out of the information flow from the company.

Missing out on special shareholder perks and discounts is another potential cost of having stock registered in street name. Many companies provide special discounts, freebies, and giveaways to their shareholders. For example, Wrigley, Wm., Jr., the chewing gum company, sends each shareholder 20 packs of gum every year around Christmas. Brown-Forman, the spirits and consumer products company, has made available in the past to shareholders 50 percent discounts on Lenox china and Hartmann luggage. In many instances, the perks are available only to registered shareholders, not street-name holders. (For further information on shareholder perks and freebies, let me plug my book, *Free Lunch on Wall Street: Perks, Freebies, and Giveaways*, published by McGraw-Hill and available by calling 219-931-6480.)

Fortunately, when you buy no-load stocks, you automatically become a registered shareholder with the company, the same as if you bought mutual-fund shares directly from the fund company. As a registered shareholder, you have control over the shares. If you want to take possession of stock certificates in order to sell through a broker of your choice, notify the company and certificates will be sent immediately. And, as a registered shareholder, you're assured of receiving all quarterly and annual reports.

Safekeeping Services

When you purchase shares in a mutual fund, you are not sent share certificates. Rather, your holdings are recorded in book-entry form. No-load stock programs have adopted a similar system of recording ownership. Shares purchased in no-load stock programs are registered in book-entry form. There are no physical certificates. However, if a shareholder wants to take possession of the stock certificate, all he or she has to do is notify the company or its transfer agent, and a certificate will be created and sent to the investor. Such safekeeping services are attractive because they relieve investors of having to store stock certificates. Any of you who have gone through the hassle of getting a replacement certificate because your certificate was lost, stolen, or damaged know the value of having the shares held by the company in book-entry form.

Fractional Shares

When you invest, say, $1000 in a no-load mutual fund, all of your money is invested, regardless of the net asset value of the mutual fund. In other words, a $1000 investment in a mutual fund with a net asset value of $23.50 will buy 42.553 shares, and the mutual fund will carry the investor on its books with an investment of 42.553 shares, fractional shares and all.

It's a different story when you buy individual stocks. Let's say you want to invest $1000 in McDonald's, and the stock is trading at $53.25 per share. Even though your $1000 is worth 18.779 shares of McDonald's, no broker is going to sell you fractional shares. What this forces investors to do is invest not on their own terms, but on those offered by the broker. Want to invest a full $1000 per month in a stock, regardless of the price? You can't if you go through a broker. You'll have to invest amounts that buy whole shares.

I know some of you are probably thinking I'm making a mountain out of a molehill, but I disagree. The mutual-fund industry understands that small investors don't necessarily think in terms of how many shares they can buy each month in a stock or mutual fund; they think in terms of the number of dollars they can squeeze out of their monthly budgets to invest. The mutual-fund industry accommodates small investors by giving them an opportunity to invest their entire budgeted investment each and every month, regardless if the investment buys whole shares or fractional shares; the brokerage community does not.

Fortunately, no-load stocks have parted ways with traditional stock investing by allowing an investor's entire investment to go toward whole and fractional shares. An excellent example is Regions Financial. At the time of this writing, the stock was selling in the $30s. Yet, the initial minimum investment permitted by Regions Financial in its no-load stock program is just $20, an amount less than the price of one share of stock. In other words, Regions Financial will allow you to buy a fractional share even with your first investment. Try getting a Charles Schwab or Merrill

Lynch broker to do that for you. And no-load stocks will also allow you to purchase fractional shares with subsequent monthly purchases once you've enrolled in their stock purchase programs.

Frequent Purchases

Mutual funds will accept money from investors anytime. Of course, so will brokers, but they'll also take their cut each time. One drawback of no-load stocks is that the opportunities to purchase stock each month are limited. Most no-load stocks invest money only once a month. However, that situation is changing. No-load stocks are realizing that investors want the flexibility to make more frequent purchases, especially if a stock drops in price. Thus, several no-load stock programs have instituted more frequent purchases. Exxon and U S West, for example, will buy shares once a week for investors in the stock purchase program. Look for more no-load stocks to institute weekly, and perhaps even daily, purchases over the next few years.

Frequent Sells

Selling a mutual fund is easy—it requires just a phone call in many instances. And in most cases, no fees are charged for selling mutual-fund shares. Selling stock through a no-load stock program, unfortunately, is not as easy. In most cases, the companies require a sell notice in writing, and it may take 5 to 10 business days to sell the shares and additional time to remit the funds to the investor. In addition, most no-load stocks charge fees to sell shares for investors, although these fees are still smaller than those of traditional brokerage commissions. Fortunately, the situation is improving. For example, Dial permits investors to sell stock through its no-load stock program with just a phone call, and Dial picks up all of the fees for selling the shares. As no-load stock programs become more mainstream and companies become more comfortable with adding enhancements to the programs, look for improvements in the speed and cost of selling shares through the programs.

Dividend Reinvestment

Mutual funds give investors the option of receiving cash dividends and capital distributions or having them reinvested in the fund. As a rule, mutual funds don't charge investors to reinvest dividends. Having dividends reinvested in additional shares is an excellent way to build your investment over time. No-load stocks also give investors the option of having their dividends reinvested, and most of the firms charge no fees for providing this service.

IRA Investing

Most no-load mutual funds permit investors to place their mutual-fund investments in an individual retirement account (IRA), and the fund acts as the custodian for the account. Because of this feature, mutual funds offer one of the easiest ways to save for retirement. Unfortunately, including individual stocks in an IRA is not as simple in many cases. In order to do so, you must have a custodian for the account. Brokerage firms are the usual custodians for IRAs that hold individual stocks. The problem with this arrangement is that investors incur large commissions any time they buy or sell stock in the IRA. Fortunately, a number of no-load stocks provide an option for investors to include their investments in an IRA, and the company or its agent provides custodial features. No-load stocks which offer an IRA option include Barnett Banks, Connecticut Energy, Exxon, and Mobil.

The IRA feature is one of the newer wrinkles among no-load stocks, but it is one that is expected to grow over time for a variety of reasons. First, having an IRA in a no-load stock program provides an avenue for a company to gain a piece of the trillion-dollar retirement investing market. As the population continues to age, this investment segment will continue to grow in importance. A company that wants to snare retirement money for its own equity base will be more competitive if it offers an IRA program to investors. Also, a secondary benefit of the IRA option is the nature of the relationship between investor and corporation. As discussed in Chapter 4, companies like a stable shareholder base, one focused on long-term investing. Such a base means that the stock will be less vulnerable to the erratic trading that sometimes occurs in stocks controlled by institutional investors, who are more short-term oriented than individual investors. IRA investing implies investing for the long haul. An IRA program brings more long-term investors to the shareholder base, which is seen as a positive by many companies.

Another reason IRAs will be more commonplace in no-load stock programs is because individual investors want them. First Trust Corp., a Denver-based firm which provides custodial services for retirement plans, conducted a survey examining three IRA programs. The study found that, while investors choose a particular direct-purchase program because of expected financial returns, they also want greater investment choices and flexibility. IRAs offer an additional choice for investors, and the study showed that, all things being equal, firms offering IRAs in their direct purchase plans were perceived as more attractive by individual investors than companies that didn't offer IRAs.

If there is a drawback to IRAs offered by no-load stocks, it's the fees. There is a trend in the mutual-fund business to eliminate fees on IRAs, although some mutual funds require that investors have at least $10,000 in an IRA before the fee is eliminated. On the other hand, the fees in no-load stocks, although not onerous, could add up over time. Exxon and Mobil charge a $20 administrative fee per year for participants who invest in their IRAs; Connecticut Energy, approximately $55; Barnett Banks, $35. While these are not huge fees, they could add up if you have two or more IRAs provided by these firms. As IRA programs grow in popularity and the firms have a larger number of accounts in them, economies of scale could help to lower the annual fees. Also, I wouldn't be surprised to see firms lower or eliminate the annual administrative fees once an investor's IRA exceeds some minimum amount, which is similar to mutual funds.

Automatic Investment Programs

Most mutual funds offer automatic investment programs. These services allow a mutual fund to withdraw electronically a predetermined amount of money each month from an investor's savings or checking account to make regular investments in the mutual fund. Investors like such programs because they simplify the investment process, save time, reduce postage costs, and ensure that investors will invest regularly in their mutual funds.

For example, let's say you own the Fidelity Magellan fund. Fidelity will set up a system whereby the firm withdraws a minimum of $100 per month from your checking account to purchase fund shares. The beauty of this arrangement is twofold. First, you don't have to worry about forgetting to invest each month in your fund, nor do you have to pay the postage to send your payment to Fidelity. In addition, automatic investment services provide an excellent way to *dollar-cost average* in the fund. Your $100 investment will buy fewer fund shares when the fund is expensive and more shares when the fund is cheap. While dollar-cost averaging doesn't ensure a profit, it does ensure that the average cost of your investments will always be less than the average selling price of the stock or mutual fund at the time your purchases were made.

While dollar-cost averaging in stocks can be done if you're a disciplined investor, it can be expensive. Buying increments of stock every month, especially with amounts as small as $50 or $100, will expose you to huge commission charges. In fact, depending on your broker, your $50 monthly investments could be all but chewed up by an equal amount in commission costs.

Fortunately, several no-load stock programs offer automatic investment programs for investors. Barnett Banks and U S West offer monthly automatic cash investments for just a $25 minimum. DQE, an electric utility in the western part of Pennsylvania, has an automatic investment option for a minimum $10. Exxon offers monthly automatic investments with a minimum $50. Automatic investment services have been one of the faster-growing enhancements to no-load stocks and should be more prevalent in the future.

The Evolution of No-Load Stocks

NYSE's Monthly Investment Plan

The roots of no-load stocks stem back as far as the 1950s and the New York Stock Exchange's Monthly Investment Plan. This may seem hard to believe, but at one time the New York Stock Exchange not only encouraged small investors to own stock, but the exchange also made it incredibly easy to do so. The Monthly Investment Plan, sponsored by New York Stock Exchange member firms, provided a simple and economical way for individuals to invest as little as $40 every three months to buy shares in some 1200 NYSE stocks, common and preferred. An investor could sign up for the program at any member firm. All trades went through the brokerage firm, which received a small fee. The commission, according to a 1961 brochure, was a flat 6 percent of the investment when the amount invested was $100 or less. For the minimum $40 investment, the charge was $2.26. For investments of over $100, the 6 percent commission gradually decreased until investments of $1000—the monthly maximum investment permitted in the plan—was $14.85, or 1.5 percent of the amount invested. Investors could make simultaneous payments into a number of stocks with a single check. For example, with a single $100 payment to the broker, you could designate that $47.17 (after commission) be invested in a chemical company and $47.17 be invested in a utility. Another feature of the program permitted participants to have their dividends reinvested for additional shares. Participants were also able to sell their shares through the plan for a small fee. There were no contracts or start-up fees, nor did participants have to agree to contribute every month or every quarter. It was easy to enroll. Investors could either contact a brokerage firm or use an enrollment form which was included in the introductory brochure (Figure 1-3).

Despite what sounds like a perfect program for small investors, the Monthly Investment Plan died out over time. Although the individual with whom I spoke at the New York Stock Exchange couldn't remember why, my guess is that member firms got tired of taking such small orders for small fees and stopped supporting the plan.

Figure 1-3. *(Courtesy New York Stock Exchange Archives)*

On MIP transactions the commission is a straight 6% when the amount invested is $100 or less. Over $100 the charge is progressively less than 6%, as shown in the following table, with a minimum of $6 for each transaction. The same charges apply to sales. Of course, the more you invest at one time, the lower the rate of commission. For example, here are some typical transactions:

PAYMENT	AMOUNT INVESTED AT ODD-LOT PRICES	COMMISSION* AMT.	%
$ 40	$ 37.74	$ 2.26	6.0
60	56.60	3.40	6.0
80	75.47	4.53	6.0
100	94.34	5.66	6.0
200	194.00	6.00	3.1
300	293.14	6.86	2.3
500	490.10	9.90	2.0
1000	985.15	14.85	1.5

*In some cases the commission may be less. For instance, on an investment of $980, in a stock selling at $140, the minimum commission would be $10.50, because where the amount of money involved is $100 or more, the minimum charge shall not exceed $1.50 per share.

There are no opening or starting fees, no dues, assessments or custody fees.

After the broker's commission is deducted from your payment, the exact number of shares your dollars will buy is figured to four decimal places. It's like buying $5 worth of gasoline. For example, $50 will buy 2.6206 shares of a stock selling for $18 a share, and 0.2621 of a share of a $180 stock.

Figure 1-3. (Continued)

If you wish, you may have several MIP's, making payments either simultaneously or at alternating dates. Let's suppose you want to make one monthly payment for two stocks, a chemical and a utility. A payment of $100, after deducting commissions, would buy $47.17 of each stock.

Or perhaps you might want three quarterly Plans, with a payment due each month. You could buy, let's say, an oil stock in January, April, July and October; a steel stock in February, May, August and November; and a food stock in March, June, September and December.

You can receive your full shares whenever you request them, or when you terminate your Monthly Investment Plan. There is no charge for delivery on termination of the Plan, or when you request 50 shares or more. If your request is for less than 50 shares, *and you do not terminate the Plan,* there will be a C.O.D. handling charge of $1 plus mailing costs. When you take delivery of shares, your name will be registered on the company's books as a stockholder, so your dividends on those shares can no longer be reinvested automatically in your MIP account.

After each of your purchases, you will be mailed a confirmation showing the amount of money received, number of shares bought, price, commission paid and total shares held for your account at that time—together with a reminder of your next scheduled payment. Since you do your investing by mail under this convenient Plan, there's no need to visit your broker's office to make payments.

Figure 1-3. (*Continued*)

The 50 STOCKS most popular with investors using the
MONTHLY INVESTMENT PLAN

Symbol	In Order of Popularity as of November 24, 1961	Year Consecutive Annual Dividend Payments Began	Latest 12 Months Cash Dividends (Incl. Extras)	Price Per Share 12/1/61	Yield**
GM	General Motors Corp. Cars, trucks, appliances	1915	$2.00	$55	3.6%
IBM	Int'l Business Machines Corp. Sells, leases bus. machines	1916	2.20a	579	0.4*
T	American Tel. & Tel. Co. Bell telephone system	1881	3.45	133⅛	2.6*
GE	General Electric Co. Electrical equip., jet engines	1899	2.00	80⅝	2.5
MMM	Minnesota Mining & Mfg. Co. Adhesives, abrasives	1916	0.63	73½	0.9*
DOW	Dow Chemical Co. Industrial chemicals	1911	1.45	75⅜	1.9*
TY	Tri-Continental Corp. Closed-end investment co.	1945	1.47	51¾	2.8
J	Standard Oil Co. (N.J.) Petroleum products	1899	2.25	48½	4.6
GEN	General Telephone & El. Corp. Tel. hldg. co., electronics	1936	0.76	25⅜	3.0
PFE	Pfizer (Chas.) & Co. Drugs, chemicals	1901	0.80	50	1.6
SY	Sperry Rand Corp. Electronic controls, bus. mach.	1934	0.19a	22¾	D
RCA	Radio Corp. of America Electronics, TV, radio brdcast.	1940	1.00a	52⅜	1.9*
SA	Safeway Stores, Inc. Chain grocery stores	1927	1.50	62⅛	2.4*
P	Phillips Petroleum Co. Petroleum products	1934	1.70	59	2.9
EK	Eastman Kodak Co. Photo equip., synthetic fibers	1902	2.25	108¾	2.1
SD	Standard Oil Co. of Calif. Petroleum products	1912	2.00	55	3.6
MTC	Monsanto Chemical Co. Chem., synthetic fibers	1925	0.98a	52⅝	1.9*
S	Sears, Roebuck & Co. Mail order, retail stores	1935	1.40	84½	1.7*
GO	Gulf Oil Corp. Petroleum products	1936	1.02a	40¾	2.5*
LEM	Lehman Corp. Closed-end investment co.	1930	0.53e	34⅜	1.5
CG	Columbia Gas System, Inc. Natural gas pipelines	1943	1.10	28⅝	3.8
ACY	American Cyanamid Co. Pharmaceuticals, chemicals	1934	1.60	45	3.6
UK	Union Carbide Corp. Chem., plastics, metal alloys	1918	3.60	128¾	2.8
AL	Aluminium Ltd. Aluminum	1939	0.70t	27	2.6
IT	Int'l Tel. & Tel. Corp. Electronic & communic. equip.	1951	1.00	58⅛	1.7

**Yield based on dividends paid in latest 12 months (including extras) and December 1 price.
a—Adjusted for stock dividends and splits.
e—Excludes dividends paid from security profits

12

Figure 1-3. (*Continued*)

Under the Monthly Investment
Plan there are some 1200 stocks
on the New York Stock Exchange
from which to choose.
Here's the latest list of the
50 most popular with MIP buyers.

Symbol	In Order of Popularity as of November 24, 1961	Year Consecutive Annual Dividend Payments Began	Latest 12 Months Cash Dividends (Incl. Extras)	Price Per Share 12/1/61	Yield**
DD	duPont de Nemours (E. I.) & Co. Nylon, chemicals	1904	$6.75	$239½	2.8%
WX	Westinghouse Electric Corp. Elec. equip., atomic energy	1935	1.20	39¾	3.0
RLM	Reynolds Metals Co. Aluminum producer	1942	0.50	37¼	1.3
MRK	Merck & Co., Inc. Medicinal chem. drugs	1935	1.60	89½	1.8
GD	General Dynamics Corp. Aircraft, missiles, submarines	1936	0.50	27	D
MAD	Madison Fund, Inc. Closed-end investment co.	1939	0.60e	29⅞	2.0
OLM	Olin Mathieson Chemical Corp. Chemicals, drugs, metals	1926	1.00	39¾	2.5
LIT	Litton Industries, Inc. Electronic equip., bus. mach.	—	—	155¼	—
BS	Bethlehem Steel Corp. Steel, shipbuilding	1939	2.40	41⅛	5.8
BC	Brunswick Corporation Bowling equip., pleasure boats	1937	0.40a	53⅜	0.7*
ELG	El Paso Natural Gas Co. Natural gas pipelines	1936	1.30	25⅞	5.0
AC	American Can Co. Cans & containers	1923	2.00	48⅛	4.2
PCG	Pacific Gas & Electric Co. Operating public utility	1919	2.75	105¾	2.6*
UGC	United Gas Corp. Natural gas system	1944	1.50	41	3.7
X	U. S. Steel Corp. Basic & finished steel, cement	1940	3.00	79	3.8
TXN	Texas Instruments, Inc. Electronic devices	—	—	109½	—
TX	Texaco Inc. Petroleum products	1903	1.49a	54¼	2.7*
AMF	American Machine & Foundry Co. Recreational eq. indust. mach.	1927	0.85a	37⅛	2.3*
AA	Aluminum Co. of America Aluminum	1939	1.20	57⅜	2.1
AV	Avco Corporation Aircraft parts electronics	1957	0.58	25¼	2.3*
WIN	Winn-Dixie Stores Inc. Chain grocery stores	1943	0.77	39½	1.9*
LLT	Long Island Lighting Co. Operating public utility	1950	1.48	57½	2.6*
M	Montgomery Ward & Co., Inc. Mail order, retail stores	1936	1.00	31⅜	3.2
GT	Goodyear Tire & Rubber Co. Tires, rubber, chem. prods.	1937	0.88a	44¾	2.0*
NP	Northern Pacific Ry. Co. Railroad	1943	2.20	43	5.1

*—Dividend rate increased since December 2, 1960.
D—Dividend rate decreased since December 2, 1960.
†—Subject to tax withheld by a state, territory or foreign government.
Sources: Wall Street Journal; Standard & Poor's Dividend Record.

13

Figure 1-3. (Continued)

MONTHLY INVESTMENT PLAN
of
Members New York Stock Exchange

PURCHASE ORDER

.................................19......

....
(Name of Member Firm to be filled in)
Gentlemen:

IT IS MY PRESENT INTENTION TO INVEST WITH $.............. ☐ monthly ☐ quarterly

PAYMENTS IN .... LISTED ON THE
(fill in name of stock)

NEW YORK STOCK EXCHANGE, COMMENCING WITH AN INITIAL PAYMENT OF
$.................. FOR WHICH MY CHECK OR MONEY ORDER IS ATTACHED.

Each remittance for my account ($40 minimum), less your commission, will be applied by you, as my broker, to the purchase of full shares of the stock named above and/or a fractional interest in such a share. Purchases will be made at the first odd-lot price established after the day the payment is credited to my account. See Terms and Conditions #2, #3 and #4.

Cash dividends, and proceeds from the sale of rights or special distributions are to be automatically reinvested in my account, unless you are otherwise notified by me in writing with respect to future cash dividends and proceeds.

I reserve the right to cancel this order at any time, without penalty or charge, by written notice to you. You also may cancel this order at any time by written notice to me. Purchases made before the receipt of a cancellation notice will not be affected by such notice.

THE TERMS AND CONDITIONS SET FORTH ON THE
REVERSE SIDE ARE PART OF THIS PURCHASE ORDER.

Mr.
Mrs. ....
Miss   (Print Full Legal Name)   (Legal Signature)

....
     (Street Address)   (Business or Occupation)

....
     (City, Zone and State)   (Citizenship)   (Social Security No.)

FOR OFFICE USE ONLY

....
(Member Firm Identifying   (Name of Member Firm)   (Authorized Initials for
Number—Not Over 4 Digits)   Opening a New Account)

CUT ALONG THIS DOTTED LINE

How to fill in your MIP Purchase Order—

1. Remove the purchase order from the back cover of this book (opposite pages). Fill in name of the Member Firm with whom you wish to open your account in the space above the word "Gentlemen". Date the order. A separate purchase order is needed for each stock you decide to buy. If you want more than one Plan, additional purchase order forms are available from your Member Firm office.

2. Fill in dollar amount of payments you plan to make—$40 minimum—and cross out either Monthly or Quarterly, whichever doesn't apply.

3. Fill in name of company LISTED ON THE NEW YORK STOCK EXCHANGE whose stock you want to buy. You may make your selection from some 1200 such stocks.

4. Indicate amount of payment accompanying purchase order. You may start your Plan with any amount from $40 to $1000. Many investors start their plans with an initial payment larger than the amount planned for later regular purchases, thus getting their accounts off to a good start.

5. Print your full legal name, not initials, your address, occupation, and citizenship. A married woman should use her given and maiden names in addition to her married name, and give her husband's occupation.

6. Sign the application.

7. Attach your check or money order, make payable to your Member Firm. This payment must accompany the purchase order. Instructions for subsequent payments will be sent you with your confirmations of purchases. NEVER MAIL CASH!

8. To be eligible to have an MIP account, you must be at least 21 years of age. In addition, you must be a U.S. citizen, or a resident alien filing a U.S. income tax return, or a resident of Canada.

9. Before you mail the purchase order to your Member Firm, be sure: ■ All spaces are filled in and all questions answered ■ You have used your legal signature in signing the purchase order ■ You have enclosed a check or money order made payable to your Member Firm.

Figure 1-3. (*Continued*)

DRIPs

The next step in the evolution of no-load stocks was the development of corporate dividend reinvestment plans (DRIPs). DRIPs have been around for more than two decades—AT&T offered one of the first prominent DRIP plans in 1973—and are going strong today. The programs, sponsored by some 900 publicly traded corporations, allow investors to buy stock directly from the companies. Shares are purchased in two ways: with dividends that the firm reinvests in additional shares and with optional cash payments permitted in most plans.

The concept of DRIPs was similar to the concept of its predecessor, the Monthly Investment Plan, with one big difference. DRIPs represented a way for investors to deal directly with companies to purchase stock—a revolutionary development within the context of how financial markets work. Prior to DRIPs, the only avenue to invest in stocks was through the brokerage community. Even the NYSE's Monthly Investment Plan, with all of its attractions, required a broker to make the transaction. DRIPs were different. Now, investors could deal directly with companies, without an intermediary, to buy stock.

DRIPs took direct investing to a new level, but there was a catch. In order to enroll in most DRIPs, investors must be registered shareholders of at least one share. Unfortunately, getting that first share can present all sorts of problems. Many brokers won't even handle a one-share purchase, and those that do charge dearly to do so. Thus, in order to take advantage of all that DRIPs have to offer, you still have to use a broker to buy the first share.

The First No-Load Stocks

It wasn't until the early 1980s that companies decided to take their DRIPs the final step and allow even initial purchases to be made directly. Pioneers of this no-load stock concept were Citicorp, Control Data, and W.R. Grace. One impetus for the programs was a perceived need by the firms to broaden their shareholder bases to include individual investors. As discussed in Chapter 4, companies benefit in a variety of ways from offering DRIPs and no-load stock programs. Diversifying the shareholder base is one way to limit corporate control by institutional investors while bringing on board more small investors, who tend to be more loyal and long-term oriented.

Over time, more companies adopted no-load stock programs, adding various features along the way. Perhaps the programs most responsible for the continued evolution of no-load stocks were those introduced by Exxon and Texaco. Both programs expanded the types of services offered in a no-load stock program. The fact that both firms were popular names with investors, as well as components of the widely followed Dow Jones Industrial Average, helped spur interest in no-load stocks among investors as well as corporations.

Do-It-Yourself Investor

The evolution of no-load stocks has been greatly impacted by the growth of the do-it-yourself investor. I don't think there's any question that individuals are more sophisticated now about stocks and investing than they've been in the history of the stock market. One reason is the explosion of inexpensive and available information. Financial magazines, newspapers, newsletters, and television and radio shows have helped to demystify the financial markets for millions of investors. And with computers and inexpensive software and databases, even individuals with modest means have the ability to store, analyze, and manipulate huge amounts of data to improve investment decision making.

The end result is a more informed investor who wants to call his or her own investment shots while saving money in the process. In the era of fixed commissions, there was little incentive to educate yourself concerning investments. You were going to pay the same high brokerage rates regardless if you or your broker selected your investments.

The SEC changed everything when it eliminated fixed commissions on "May Day"—May 1, 1975. May Day gave birth to a new player on the financial scene: the discount broker. Investors were now faced with the option of either using a full-service broker—and paying top dollar in commissions for his or her expertise and resources—or using a discount broker and saving a bundle on commissions. Practically overnight, the value of becoming a self-reliant investor jumped dramatically. Consequently, over time, more and more investors began educating themselves on stocks and investing in general. The growth of the do-it-yourself investor produced a bonanza for the discount brokerage community. Indeed, Charles Schwab, the leading discount broker, saw its total revenues increase roughly 256 percent from 1986 to 1993. Over that same time frame, Merrill Lynch, the top full-service broker, saw revenues grow by only 73 percent.

No-Load Mutual Funds

Charles Schwab doesn't work for free, however, which means do-it-yourself investors still pay a fee to gain access to the market. Wouldn't it be great to buy investments and pay no fee? Enter no-load mutual funds.

The Investment Company Institute, a mutual-fund trade group, credits the Scudder fund family with starting the first no-load mutual fund way back in the 1920s. However, it wasn't until more than five decades later that no-load funds truly came into prominence. Just as discount brokers benefited from the growth of the do-it-yourself investor in the 1980s, no-load mutual funds benefited from investors' desire to shave or even eliminate transaction costs.

Was it the professional money management available with mutual funds that spurred demand? The ability to diversify with limited funds? Certainly these two factors contributed to the growth of mutual-fund investing. Still, it's difficult to discount just how important convenience and commission-free investing played in the growth of no-load mutual funds. Little wonder that Exxon and other pioneers in no-load stocks incorporated features from the no-load fund industry into their no-load stock programs. Clearly, no-load mutual funds had a huge role in shaping today's no-load stock programs and cultivating demand for direct investment of stocks.

Who Needs a Middleman?

When you strip everything away, stock brokers are middlemen who bring buyers and sellers together. What's been happening to middlemen in today's business world?

- Wal-Mart Stores, the retailing giant, no longer deals with middlemen. The firm goes directly to suppliers to purchase products, saving the distributor's 3 to 5 percent cut.

- Factory outlets, mail-order catalogs, "category-killing" retailers, and warehouse clubs are making middlemen an endangered species in a variety of consumer markets.

- It's estimated that about one in five homes is sold each year by their owners, without the help of a real-estate broker.

- Individuals can now buy such financial products as insurance and treasury securities without using a broker.

- On-line services such as Prodigy, CompuServe, and America Online are acting as agents, allowing individuals to buy anything from clothes to airplane tickets—all without going through a middleman.

Why the death of the middleman? Information and communication are much cheaper today than they were even a decade ago. It's not surprising that the elimination of the middleman would make its way into the financial markets. A broker's biggest weapons—contacts and knowledge—are less proprietary. Stockbrokers are some of the best-paid middlemen in the business world—the nation's stockbrokers earned an average of $128,000 in 1993, according to *The Wall Street Journal*—which provides extra incentives for the buyer and seller to find a way to do without their services. No-load mutual funds are perhaps the most obvious example of the trend toward the elimination of the middleman in the financial markets. No-load stocks are the next logical step.

Investing in No-Load Stocks

Now that you know what no-load stocks are and how they've evolved over time, you're no doubt wondering:

- *What companies offer no-load stock programs?*   To learn more about specific no-load stock programs, see the comprehensive reviews of all no-load stocks in Chapter 5.

- *How does an investor incorporate no-load stocks into an investment program?* Investment strategies using no-load stocks are discussed in the next chapter.

2

Investment Strategies Using No-Load Stocks

There are literally hundreds of different investment strategies used by investors with varying degrees of success. There are those investors who buy stocks only when the P-E ratio (the stock's price per share divided by 12-month earnings per share) is below the market average. There are investors who buy only stocks which yield at least 4 percent and have paid higher dividends annually for at least a decade. Some investors buy only stocks that trade below book value. And still other investors buy shares in companies where earnings have risen in each of the last five quarters and whose price performance is strong relative to its competitors.

What's the best investment strategy? There really is no one answer to that question, and that's what makes stock investing so interesting and challenging. Any investor, from the novice to the expert, can achieve excellent results using widely different investment approaches.

I would argue, however, that while no single way of investing ensures success, profitable investment strategies, whether investing in mutual funds, stocks, or no-load stocks, often have a number of common elements:

- *Focus on the long term.* As editor of *Dow Theory Forecasts,* I see thousands of portfolios every year. Those investors who have achieved the most success have focused on long-term performance. What's long term? Ask three investors, and you'll get three different answers. Some investors believe "long term" is until lunch time; others believe it's a lifetime. I'm somewhere in between. Long-term investing to me is investing with a time horizon of at least 5 years and more likely 10 to 15 years.

Why do I think long-term investing is so important? A 1991 study by two college professors, P. R. Chandy and William Reichenstein, shows that the biggest risk associated with stock investing is not being in the market at the wrong time, but being out of the market at the right time. The professors looked at monthly market returns from 1926 through 1987. What they found was that if the 50 best monthly returns were eliminated, the S&P 500's 62-year positive return disappears. In other words, if you had chosen the absolutely wrong 50 months to be out of the market but were invested in the market the remaining 93.3 percent of the time, your return would have been nil. The study went on to find that if an investor missed the 26 best monthly stock returns, his or her return would have been roughly equivalent to the return on treasury bills over the same time frame.

T. Rowe Price, the mutual-fund company, conducted a study examining stock purchases at the exact worst time each year from 1969 to 1989. In the study, $2000 was invested each year in the S&P 500 index at the annual peak, and dividends were reinvested quarterly. The study found that even if an individual invested at the market's high point each year, his or her account value at the end of the 20-year period would have been more than four times his or her cumulative investment during that time.

Ibbotson Associates, a Chicago-based research firm, found that investors who held stocks for five years would have lost money in only seven of 60-plus five-year periods since 1926, and four of those seven periods encompassed the 1929 crash. And in every 15-year period dating back to 1926, the S&P 500 index produced a positive return.

True, a few investors are quite successful at timing the market and trading stocks. However, those investors, judging from the reams of studies conducted, are the rare exception. (See Figure 2-1 for a look at 25 years of stock market history.)

Another reason that a long-term approach is preferable is that it holds down trading costs. Frequent trading generates commissions which eat away at a portfolio. Frequent trading also creates potential tax liabilities. Every time an investment held outside of a retirement account is sold, a potential tax liability is created. Currently, gains on stocks held for less than a year are taxed as ordinary income. For investors in the highest tax bracket, that means Uncle Sam takes nearly 40 percent of the profit. Gains on investments held for more than a year are taxed at only 28 percent, which provides an incentive to invest with a time horizon of at least one year. And investors who never sell stock defer taxes indefinitely.

- *Disciplined approach to investing.* Another common trait of successful investors is a disciplined approach to investing. The director of the T. Rowe

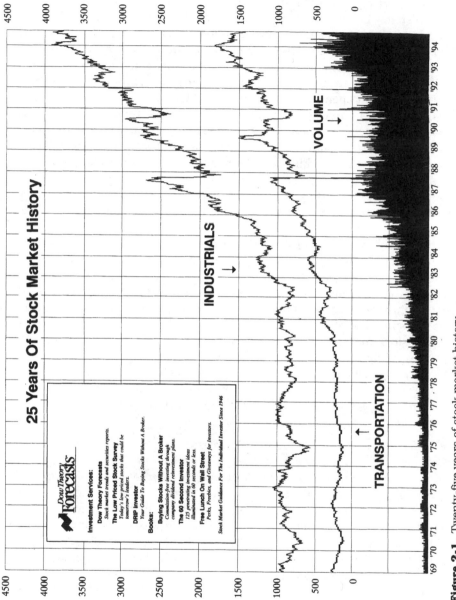

Figure 2-1. Twenty-five years of stock market history.

Price study previously cited stated, "For those with a long-term investment horizon and the discipline to stay the course, the commitment to invest may be more important than the timing of the investment."

Disciplined investing has a number of facets. First, a disciplined investment approach means adherence to an investment strategy over time. Too often, investors adopt the "investment strategy of the week" approach to their portfolios. This week, they focus on value investing; next week, momentum investing; the week after, high-dividend stocks. Unfortunately, investors who change approaches frequently often do so at exactly the wrong time. When value stocks are out of favor, that's the time to invest if you're a long-term investor, not when they are on every broker's buy list. Sticking to a particular investment strategy provides some ballast to a portfolio during volatile market periods.

Disciplined investing also means staying the course and not shifting gears depending on short-term developments. I've seen many long-term investors become short-term traders when their holdings registered a quick 25 percent gain. Conversely, I've seen traders become long-term investors when a position went against them but they refused to take a loss. If you are a long-term investor, be a long-term investor. If you determine that you want to trade stocks, be a trader. Know what you are going to do with your investments before you invest, and stick to your strategy.

Finally, disciplined investing often means going against the crowd. The stock market is perhaps the only market in the world where merchandise becomes more sought after the more expensive it becomes. "Buy low, sell high" is everyone's favorite cliché, but few investors have the nerve to buck the crowd and buy when stocks are out of favor. However, being a disciplined investor means stepping up to buy or sell when the herd is going in the opposite direction.

- *Diversify—to a point.* Successful investors realize the importance of diversification. However, proper diversification doesn't necessarily mean that you have to own 40 stocks, 10 mutual funds, bonds, real estate, precious metals, coins, baseball cards, and an ostrich farm. In fact, investors may often be too diversified across investments.

  Surprisingly, research has shown that a stock portfolio of roughly 15 to 20 issues can provide adequate diversification, especially if this portfolio is combined with other investments, such as corporate bonds, treasury securities, and foreign investments. More on diversification across investments as well as diversification across time periods is discussed later in the chapter.

- *Limit transaction costs.* A hard fact of investing, but one overlooked by many investors, is that transaction costs erode the value of your investments. If you pay a broker $100 in commissions, that's $100 that will never return a dime to you this year or any year. If you pay a mutual fund 2 percent on your $25,000 holding, that $500 will never make you any money. Herein lies the real impact of transaction costs: not only do you lose the use of the money in the year you pay for the transaction, but in every year after. Paying $500 in mutual-fund fees in one year is bad enough. But the loss isn't just $500—it's $500 plus interest in year 2, 3, 4, and so on. What's $500 in 20 years at 8 percent interest per year? $2330. And that's just one year's commission. Pay $500 each year for 20 years at 8 percent, and your total loss is $24,711.

Another way of looking at fees is in terms of annual portfolio performance. For example, let's say your stock portfolio climbs 15 percent before commissions, and your buddy's is up only 13 percent. It seems your portfolio did better, right? But if your trading costs amounted to 3 percent of the value of your portfolio, and your friend's trading costs were less than 1 percent, your friend actually did better for the year.

Low costs are one of the major drivers behind the success of the Vanguard family of mutual funds. Vanguard is the second-largest fund family in the country with $128 billion under management. Vanguard's mutual funds have achieved impressive performances for the most part. One reason is that Vanguard traditionally has among the lowest fees in the business. This difference is especially significant when comparing performance of Vanguard's money-market and fixed-income funds versus the competition. Vanguard has learned the secret that, if you keep costs down, your investments don't have to work as hard to produce good results.

I'm sure some of you are saying that fees don't matter—it's performance that counts. That's usually the rationale given by investors who've enjoyed 15 to 20 percent annual portfolio gains over the last decade and don't mind paying 1 or 2 percent a year in fees. One problem with the bull markets of the '80s and '90s is that they desensitized investors to the impact of fees. "Who cares about a 2 percent load fee when I'm earning 20 percent on my money?" "How much can that 3 percent wrap fee or that 2 percent commission charge hurt me when my portfolio is rising 18 percent per year?" The problem is that the returns of the last decade have been extremely atypical. It may surprise some of you, but the average annual return on stocks since 1926 is just over 10 percent. And that's before inflation. When you take into account inflation plus annual trading fees, the return shrinks dramatically. What if the next decade sees below-average market returns? That 1 or 2 percent annual fee could be the difference between a winning and losing portfolio.

Moral of the story: Successful investors understand the impact of transaction costs on a portfolio and take that into account when devising an investment strategy. Smart investors limit trading activity, watch commissions and fund fees, and invest directly whenever possible. Remember, a portfolio's risk and return are inseparable. The only way to increase returns without taking on more risk is by lowering transaction costs. Read that statement again:

The only way to increase returns without increasing risk is to cut transaction costs.

Investing in No-Load Stocks

If you look again at the four keys to investment success—invest for the long term, maintain a disciplined approach, diversify, and control trading costs—it's no wonder that no-load mutual funds have become so popular. Indeed, no-load funds, via automatic investment services and low investment minimums, provide an easy way to invest regularly for long-term gains; funds provide diversification; and no-load funds provide a relatively low-cost investment alternative. However, for each of the reasons mutual funds make sense for investors, no-load stocks work as well or better.

Long-Term Investing in No-Load Stocks

No-load stocks provide excellent vehicles for long-term investing. First, investment minimums are quite low in most no-load stocks—usually $100 to $250 to get started and $50 or less for additional investments. Thus, it's easy to maintain an investment program over time, even if your financial situation changes due to a new baby, college tuition, or even a job layoff.

Second, and perhaps most importantly, investing for the long term means investing in no-load stocks with good potential over the next 5, 10, 20, or even 30 years. Fortunately, a number of no-load stocks are what I consider to be excellent long-term investments. These companies, which include such blue chips as Dial, Exxon, Regions Financial, and U S West, have the strong market positions, healthy finances, and favorable sales and earnings growth prospects that should produce solid capital gains over the long term. For guidance as to the best no-load stocks for long-term investing, refer to the performance ratings which appear with each no-load stock review in Chapter 5.

A final reason that makes long-term investing in no-load stocks easy is that several programs have set up mechanisms to promote long-term investing. One of these mechanisms is the automatic investment service which is offered by a few no-load stocks. This system makes monthly investing a "no-brainer," because money is withdrawn automatically from your checking or savings account. Another mechanism is the emergence of IRA options in certain no-load stock programs. IRAs represent the essence of long-term investing, and no-load stocks offering an IRA feature provide an excellent avenue to maintain a long-term investment program.

Disciplined Investing with No-Load Stocks

One of the keys of disciplined investing is establishing an investment program that is free from the dangerous emotions that can kill portfolio performance. Admittedly, freeing the investment process from emotions is easier said than done, especially when it comes to making rational, disciplined decisions during extremely volatile market periods. One strategy that strips the investment process of emotion is dollar-cost averaging, which was discussed briefly in Chapter 1.

In a nutshell, dollar-cost averaging entails the regular investment of a fixed amount of money on a regular basis, either every month or perhaps every quarter. For example, let's say you own the Fidelity Magellan fund. Dollar-cost averaging says that you invest the same amount of money every month, perhaps $200. When Fidelity Magellan's net asset value is, say, $50, your $200 investment buys four fund shares. When the fund's net asset value is, say, $47.50, your $200 buys 4.21 shares. Herein lies the beauty of dollar-cost averaging. By making the same $200 investment, you buy more shares in the fund when Fidelity Magellan is down and fewer shares when it is up in price.

No-load stocks are excellent vehicles for dollar-cost averaging for much the same reasons as mutual funds are. First, no-load stocks will invest all of your money into both whole and fractional shares. That is, all of your monthly $200 investment will go toward stock. Being able to invest dollar amounts makes it easier to establish a dollar-cost averaging program. Second, because there are little or no fees when buying no-load stocks, making monthly purchases doesn't cost a fortune in commissions as it would when buying stocks through a broker. Finally, the automatic investment service provided by several no-load stocks makes it easier to maintain a dollar-cost averaging strategy since your investments don't depend on you remembering to send a check each month to the company.

Variations of dollar-cost averaging based on the stock's current price, the 52-week price range, dividend yield, or P-E ratio have been developed in an attempt to give more leverage to the strategy. For example, let's say that your valuation model indicates that the stock or fund is undervalued. Instead of making your customary $200 investment, you decide to invest

$250. Conversely, perhaps your valuation model indicates the stock is overvalued by 20 percent. You may decide to lower your monthly investment to $150.

Intuitively, modified dollar-cost averaging is appealing, as you leverage your investments on the downside while limiting investments on the upside. However, the problem with such a program is that you are injecting timing into the equation based on your perceptions of value—the very thing that you were trying to avoid with dollar-cost averaging. Perhaps your valuation model is flawed. You may be buying ever-decreasing dollar amounts of a stock in a company that becomes a huge star. Under straight dollar-cost averaging, you would still be protecting yourself from buying too many shares at the top, but at least you'd be buying larger dollar amounts. The other problem with modified dollar-cost averaging based on valuation models is that you are buying greater dollar amounts as the stock drops than you would under basic dollar-cost averaging. While this strategy will pay off when the stock turns around, it is especially disastrous if the stock continues to fall. Still, if you are daring and want to leverage a dollar-cost averaging strategy by applying certain valuation models, you can still do so using no-load stocks.

Value Averaging

Another form of dollar-cost averaging that can be employed using no-load stocks is value averaging. Value averaging says that, instead of making the same investment each month in a stock or mutual fund, you vary the amount invested so that the value of the portfolio increases by a fixed sum or percentage each interval.

For example, let's say that, instead of investing $500 each month, you want the value of your investment to rise by $500 each month. In month one, the value of your investment rose $200. Under value averaging, you would add $300 to the investment to achieve your plan of having the investment increase $500 each month. Now, let's say that the investment rose $600 in a given month. Since you want the investment to rise only $500 under value averaging, you would sell $100 worth of the investment. Conversely, let's say the value of the investment dropped $200 in a given month. Since you want the value of the investment to rise $500 each month, you would have to contribute $700 for that month—$200 to offset the loss plus $500 to increase the value of the portfolio.

An easy way to compare value averaging with basic dollar-cost averaging is to think in the following terms:

- With dollar-cost averaging, you know how much you'll invest, but you don't know what the value will be at the end of your investment horizon.

- With value averaging, you know how much your portfolio will be worth at the end of your investment horizon, but you don't know how much it will cost out of your pocket.

When examined in these terms, it's easy to see that value averaging is a more aggressive strategy than dollar-cost averaging. The total amount you invest is not constrained, as it is under dollar-cost averaging. Another negative of value averaging compared to dollar-cost averaging is that the strategy could create more transaction costs since you may have to sell shares to stay within your parameters. The selling also creates tax consequences. Finally, value averaging requires more monitoring than a basic dollar-cost averaging program.

Still, studies have shown that returns from value averaging compare favorably to dollar-cost averaging. Michael Edleson, who popularized value averaging with his book *Value Averaging: The Safe and Easy Strategy for Higher Investment Returns* (International Publishing), ran 50 computer simulations over a variety of five-year market periods. More than 90 percent of the time, value averaging outperformed dollar-cost averaging.

Which method is appropriate, especially for investors in no-load stocks? I think it depends to a large extent on how much time you want to spend monitoring your portfolio, how aggressive you want to be (remember that value averaging is more aggressive since there is no cap on how much you invest to maintain the system), and how much you can afford to invest. If you invest $25 or $50 in a particular no-load stock each month, it's easier to dollar-cost average. However, if you invest $1000 or more a month, value averaging may be more attractive to you.

Diversify with No-Load Stocks

Diversification in a portfolio is critical to controlling risk while maximizing returns. Most investors think of diversification only in terms of the number of stocks held in a portfolio. However, diversification has more than one face.

I've already talked about two forms of diversification and how they apply to investing in no-load stocks. Long-term investing is really a form of time diversification. The potential risk, as measured in volatility, of stock returns in any given year is relatively high. However, volatility of portfolio returns is considerably less over a longer holding period. The reason is simple: Time can make up for a multitude of portfolio sins. The longer you hold a portfolio, the better your chances that poor performance in a given year is offset by strong gains in subsequent years.

Another way of looking at diversification across time is in the following example: A 75-year-old and a 30-year-old each owns an index mutual fund. An index mutual fund tracks the performance of a popular stock market index, such as the Standard & Poor's 500. Even though both investors have the exact same investment, the 75-year-old faces much greater risk owning the index fund since the 75-year-old doesn't have much time to make up for a bad year. On the other hand, the 30-year-old who plans to buy and hold the fund for the long term faces much less risk owning the index fund since chances are that a poor return in one year will be offset by gains in the future. In a nutshell, time diversification works because rates of return across time are not correlated; what the market does this year or next has no bearing on its performance 5 or 10 years from now.

Another form of time diversification that I've already discussed is dollar-cost averaging, or any other investment strategy that requires steady buying over an extended period of time. When investors dollar-cost average, they are spreading their purchases out over time. This diversification of investment assures that an investor doesn't invest all of his or her money at the absolute peak of the market.

A third form of diversification is across securities, which is best described in the familiar maxim, "Don't put all of your eggs in one basket."

In academic terms, portfolios are affected by two types of risk: *systematic* and *unsystematic*. Systematic risk, also called market risk, is the volatility that affects all securities. Systematic risk cannot be eliminated by diversification. However, unsystematic risk, or firm-specific risk, can. Examples of unsystematic risk include lengthy labor strikes, the death of the CEO, lawsuits, or any other risk which specifically affects a firm's investment potential. This form of risk can be reduced or even eliminated through proper diversification.

The concept of correlation, which is important in time diversification, is also critical in diversification across securities. For example, let's say that an investor has a portfolio consisting solely of 25 electric utilities (by the way, I've seen portfolios like this). Is such a portfolio diversified merely because it holds 25 different companies? Of course not, since the return on each electric utility in the portfolio will likely be closely correlated with every other one. Conversely, a portfolio of 25 stocks spanning a variety of industries could have very little or even no unsystematic risk.

This simple example brings up an important point. Too often, investors associate diversification with holding many stocks—50, 100, 200, or more stocks, just like the mutual funds own.

One reason investors are under the misconception that proper portfolio diversification requires many stocks is because that view of the investment world is pushed so strongly by the mutual-fund industry. A main selling point of mutual funds is the ability for investors to spread a modest investment across hundreds of stocks in a single portfolio. But before accepting what mutual funds tell you about diversification, it's important to look at the facts. Academic studies have shown that in order to have adequate, albeit imperfect, portfolio diversification, investors need to own roughly 15 to 20 stocks in a portfolio. Of course, these stocks must not have a high degree of correlation. After 20 stocks, unsystematic risk in a portfolio is reduced very little by adding additional stocks to the mix.

So why do some mutual funds hold 100 or even 1000 stocks? Because they have to in order to invest their funds. In the case of Fidelity's Magellan fund, the fund's assets of $34 billion are spread over more than 550 stocks, which means that the average investment per stock is a whopping $61 million. If Magellan held only 50 stocks, the average investment per company would be a staggering $680 million. The bottom line is that Magellan doesn't own over 550 stocks because owning that many enhances portfolio diversification; it owns over 550 stocks because it cannot afford to have any larger sums of money in any one stock. It's hard enough for Magellan to get in or out of a stock without affecting its price when the fund owns $61 million of the stock; it would be impossible with a much smaller number of stocks.

Admittedly, the Magellan fund is an extreme example of why mutual funds own a lot of stocks. Still, it indicates that many mutual funds may have little choice but to own a lot of stocks, and it has nothing to do with proper portfolio diversification.

Perhaps a more telling point is reflected in the diversification approach by billionaire Warren Buffet, arguably the greatest investor of our time. Buffet runs Berkshire Hathaway, a publicly traded company which is basically an investment vehicle for Buffet. How many holdings does Buffet have in his multibillion dollar investment portfolio? Less than 20.

Which brings me to diversification across assets and no-load stocks. I'm sure some of you are saying that the limited number of no-load stocks makes it virtually impossible to achieve proper portfolio diversification. I agree that a portfolio consisting solely of no-load stocks may have limitations in terms of proper diversification. However, that isn't enough to disqualify no-load stocks from consideration. In fact, I think that a selected portfolio of no-load stocks will afford a reasonable level of diversification. Furthermore, when held with bonds, mutual funds, and other investments, no-load stocks can enhance a portfolio's diversification.

No-Cost Investing
with No-Load Stocks

The fourth key to a successful investment strategy is limiting transaction costs. We've already touched upon the importance of keeping transaction costs low, but it bears repeating. Brokerage commissions, load fees, redemption fees, and wrap fees all come right out of your pocket. You may never actually see these fees. Chances are, you don't even know when you pay them since, at least in the case of mutual funds, you rarely write a check to cover the fees. They're just taken from your account each year. Nevertheless, their impact on portfolio performance is very real.

Fortunately, no-load stocks offer an excellent way to hold down transaction costs. Indeed, like no-load mutual funds, most no-load stocks do not charge a sales fee on initial and subsequent investments. But no-load stocks go one step further than mutual funds in that there are no annual management or administrative fees associated with no-load stocks. It's not uncommon for some no-load mutual funds to charge 1 to 2 percent annually to manage and administer your fund. While those percentages may seem small, over time their impact can be huge.

With no-load stocks, those annual management and administrative fees and brokerage commissions vanish. All of your money is working for you each and every year.

Focus on Quality

You probably noticed that not one of my four keys to investment success mentioned picking "value" stocks or stocks showing rising earnings momentum. While these and other strategies can be successful, investment philosophies are really a matter of personal preference and investing style. The following is a brief discussion of my approach to investing.

I regard my stock investments as long term—*extremely* long term. Indeed, I look at stock investing with 10- to 15-year time horizons at a minimum. Thus, my portfolio focuses on quality companies that meet the following criteria:

- *Longevity.* If I'm investing for 15 years in a company, I need that company to be around for that long. One way to ensure survival is by maintaining a rock-solid balance sheet, with minimal long-term debt and ample cash flow.

- *Strong track records.* "Past performance is no guarantee of future success," as the mutual-fund sales literature often states. Such is the case with stock performance. A company that has done well in the past may miss industry changes which hurt market share and profits. IBM is an example of a company that lost its way after years of success. Nevertheless, I think that, in certain industries, a company's track record is important in evaluating future prospects. How has the company weathered recessions in the past? What competitive moves has the company made to guard market share? What has been its earnings-growth history? Does the firm usually raise its dividend every year? If a firm has a history of making the right decisions, your chances increase that its positive performance will continue into the future.

- *Stability/growth prospects of the industry.* If you have read my first book, *Buying Stocks Without A Broker* (McGraw-Hill), you know I'm not a huge fan of most cyclical companies. Sure, there are times when cyclical stocks capture Wall Street's attention and skyrocket. However, since I'm not trying to trade stocks, I prefer to invest in companies which operate in industries that are stable and have discernible long-term growth prospects.

- *Defensible market positions.* I prefer companies that have defensible market positions due to strong brand names, proprietary products, or competitive advantages, such as being a low-cost producer.

Of course, by following these criteria, I've missed my share of stocks which fell outside these parameters but did extremely well. However, I believe a focus on quality will serve the average investor quite well over the long term. Fortunately, as shown in the reviews in Chapter 5, a number of no-load stocks meet my criteria for investing. That's why my own portfolio includes such no-load stocks as Exxon and Regions Financial.

Model Portfolios Using No-Load Stocks

There are a number of ways to incorporate no-load stocks into an investment portfolio. This section examines a variety of ways to be your own mutual-fund manager by building a portfolio using no-load stocks.

No-Load Stock Index Portfolio. One popular investment strategy that has evolved over the last decade is index investing, or buying a portfolio of stocks that simulates one of the popular market indexes, such as the Standard & Poor's 500. Index investing has gained prominence due to the large body of literature indicating that it is very difficult to outperform the market year in and year out. Thus, if you can't beat the market, why not become the market by investing in a fund that mimics the market's movement. Index funds have another attribute in that, since changes to the popular indexes occur rather infrequently, trading costs are minimal. In addition, since there is no real stock-picking skill in an index fund—you just buy the stocks in the particular index that is being copied—management and administrative fees are quite low.

Investors could apply an index approach to no-load stocks by investing in each no-load stock for which they are eligible.

Let's look at a possible no-load stock index portfolio featuring 15 no-load stocks which are open to nearly all investors. (Price data were not available for Arrow Financial, Interchange Financial Services, and U S West, which are the remaining three no-load stocks with open enrollment.)

No-Load Stock Index Portfolio

American Recreation Centers

Atlantic Energy

Barnett Banks

Comsat

Dial

DQE

Exxon

Houston Industries

Johnson Controls

Kellwood

Kerr-McGee

Mobil

Regions Financial

SCANA

Texaco

As is the case with any portfolio, before investing you want to know two things:

- *How much would it take to invest in the portfolio?*   In the case of our no-load stock index portfolio, the initial fee in order to invest the minimums for each of the companies would be $3220—not a small amount, but well within the pocketbooks of many investors. And remember, all of that money goes to work for you in the companies.

- *What are the expectations for portfolio performance?*   This one is tough to answer since such an "index" portfolio has never existed. But if you permit me a few liberties, we might get some insight into how this portfolio might perform.

While past performance is no indication of the future (where have I heard that before?), the performance of this no-load stock index portfolio—assuming a $1000 initial investment in each of the 15 stocks—would have provided outstanding returns over the decade ending December 31, 1993. Indeed, that $15,000 would have grown to nearly $61,000 with dividends reinvested. That represents a gain of more than 306 percent. How does that stack up against the market? The Standard & Poor's 500, which is the yardstick by which many mutual funds measure performance, rose 301.4 percent over the same time period. And how did the no-load stock index fund perform relative to the average equity fund? Very well. According to Lipper Analytical Services, a monitor of mutual-fund performance, the average performance of general equity mutual funds was roughly 235 percent in that time period.

Do these results mean that investing in this portfolio is a "can't miss" proposition? Of course not. However, I think they indicate that you don't necessarily have to sacrifice performance when investing in no-load stocks.

Portfolios for the Financially Challenged.   Let's face it, for many of us money is so tight that investing in anything except the essentials is almost a laughable concept. Oh sure, if you're real careful with your money, you might end up with an extra $75 or $100 each month. But what can you do with that piddling amount, other than put it in the bank?

How about no-load stocks?

Indeed, with just $70, you can invest in a couple of no-load stocks, and with a little bit more, you can build positions in several no-load issues.

Following are portfolios based on their minimum initial investments:

$70 Portfolio

Johnson Controls

Regions Financial

Comments: Is this portfolio properly diversified? Of course not. Is this an example of putting all of your eggs in one basket? Perhaps. But it's a start, and it's tough to overstate the importance of getting started in any investment program. So many times individuals with limited funds never get into the game because they feel they never have enough to start. That's not the case with no-load stocks. It is better to start with just two companies, build up your holdings, and diversify as your funds grow than never to start at all. Furthermore, with just your $70 investment, you're buying into two pretty good companies. Regions Financial is one of the top regional banks in the country. Johnson Controls has leading positions in control systems for buildings. If you want to maintain a regular investment program in these two issues, it'll cost you just $70 a month.

$270 Portfolio

Dial

Kellwood

Johnson Controls

Regions Financial

Comments: If you have a few more dollars to invest, you can add two more quality no-load stocks to the portfolio. Since a number of no-load stocks have $100 minimums, you have a variety from which to choose. My two favorites in this price range are Dial and Kellwood. Dial is a leading producer of such consumer products as Dial soap, Lunch Bucket microwaveable meals, and Armour Star canned meats. The firm also operates Premier cruise lines and has a variety of service businesses. Kellwood markets apparel, home furnishings, and recreational products. The largest unit is apparel, which makes brand-name and private-label goods. Products are in the budget to the moderately priced categories. Both Dial and Kellwood have good market positions and favorable long-term growth prospects. The total amount you need to make minimum monthly investments in each of these four companies is just $105.

$520 Portfolio

Dial

Exxon

Johnson Controls

Kellwood

Regions Financial

Comments: With an additional $250, you could add Exxon to your portfolio. Exxon is one of the top no-load stocks in the market. The issue combines worthwhile growth potential with an attractive yield. Exxon also offers a number of appealing options in its no-load stock program, such as an IRA and automatic investments. How much would you need to invest in each of these companies on a monthly basis? Just $155.

$720 Portfolio

American Recreation Centers

Dial

DQE

Exxon

Johnson Controls

Kellwood

Regions Financial

Comments: For investors with slightly deeper pockets, you can add a leisure company and electric utility to your portfolio. American Recreation Centers operates bowling alleys, primarily in California and Texas. Profits have been erratic through the years, as has been stock's performance. American Recreation represents one of the more speculative no-load stocks. However, the issue has reasonable potential. DQE is the parent company of Duquesne Light, an electric utility in the western part of Pennsylvania. DQE has improved its competitive position in recent years. The stock provides an acceptable holding in the utility sector. A monthly investment program in all of these stocks would cost $190.

$1020 Portfolio

American Recreation Centers

Dial

DQE

Exxon

Johnson Controls

Kellwood

Regions Financial

U S West

Comments: The addition to this portfolio is U S West, one of the seven regional Bell companies resulting from the breakup of AT&T. The company's service region spans 14 Great Plains, Rocky Mountain, and Pacific Northwest states. In addition to local telephone services, the company provides mobile communications, advertising, directory publishing, and international cable operations. The firm has an alliance with Time Warner Entertainment to build full-service networks providing interactive services, such as video-on-demand, home shopping, banking, and various information services. A communications stock provides a nice complement to the rest of the portfolio. What is the minimum amount needed to invest in each of these eight companies each month? $215.

$1270 Portfolio

American Recreation Centers

Comsat

Dial

DQE

Exxon

Johnson Controls

Kellwood

Regions Financial

U S West

Comments: The addition to this portfolio is Comsat, a provider of satellite communications and information services. Comsat provides the portfolio with inroads into a number of exciting growth markets, such as interactive entertainment and information services. A monthly investment program in all of these stocks would cost $265.

What I hope these "poor person's portfolios" show is that it doesn't take $5000 or more to start investing in stocks. With as little as $70, you can begin investing in good, sound stocks. And with a little more than $1000, you can create a surprisingly diversified portfolio of nine companies as well as add to the portfolio each month with a relatively small amount of money.

"Sector" Portfolios.   "Sector" funds allow investors to diversify investments within a single industry. Leading purveyors of sector funds include Fidelity, which has more than 30 sector funds specializing in such areas as leisure, energy, precious metals, software, and health care; and Vanguard, which offers sector funds in such industries as utilities and energy.

While building sector portfolios using no-load stocks has limitations, there are a few groups that are well represented. The following are some ideas for sector portfolios using no-load stocks.

Energy Portfolio

Exxon

Kerr-McGee

Mobil

Texaco

Comments: It's interesting that oil stocks are so well represented among no-load stocks. One reason may be that oil companies understand the importance of building loyalty with consumers, and one way to turn a consumer into a customer is by making him or her a shareholder. Oil stocks tend to run in and out of market favor as oil prices rise and fall. However, many oil stocks provide healthy yields and reasonable upside potential. This portfolio includes some blue chips in the industry, particularly Exxon. Minimum initial investment in this portfolio: $1500.

Utility Portfolio

Atlantic Energy

DQE

Houston Industries

SCANA

U S West

Comments: Utilities are another group that is well represented among no-load stocks. Not only do these five utilities allow investors in nearly every state to buy initial shares directly, but there are several more water, electric, and natural gas utilities throughout the country (these utilities are reviewed in Chapter 5) which allow either their utility customers or residents in the states in which they operate to buy initial shares directly. Thus, it is quite possible, depending on the state in which you live, to invest in eight or more no-load utilities.

Keep in mind, however, that a portfolio consisting exclusively of utilities is not properly diversified. Remember, these are sector portfolios and are not meant to be all-encompassing portfolios. Too often individuals, especially those interested in income, invest exclusively in utilities. Unfortunately, when interest rates rise, as they did at the beginning of 1994, utilities fall sharply. Investments in a sector portfolio, be it utilities, energy, or whatever industry, should be balanced with investments in other areas. You might notice that one of the suggested holdings is U S West. Since the company's largest business is regulated local telephone services, the firm is an appropriate holding in our utility portfolio and provides some diversification. Minimum initial investment in this portfolio: $1150.

Banking Portfolio

Arrow Financial

Barnett Banks

Interchange Financial Services

Regions Financial

Comments: This portfolio contains two blue-chip banks and two aggressive holdings. Arrow Financial is the bank holding company for banks in New York and Vermont. Profits have been erratic over the years. Interchange Financial operates banks in Bergen and Passaic counties, New Jersey. The firm has put together a few years of higher per-share earnings. Still, given its relatively small size, these shares have to be considered relatively aggressive. Barnett Banks is a major bank in Florida. The firm's position in a growing area of the country is a plus. Regions Financial is a major force in the Southeast. Annual earnings growth has been impressive over the last decade. This issue is my favorite among the no-load bank stocks. Minimum initial investment for this portfolio is $670.

Blue-Chip Portfolio

Investors who buy only "name" stocks should find no shortage among the list of no-load stocks. The following stocks represent well-known companies that have established dominant positions in their national or regional markets:

Barnett Banks

Dial

Exxon

Mobil

Regions Financial

Texaco

U S West

Comments: This portfolio contains names familiar to most investors. Indeed, two oil issues, Exxon and Texaco, are components of the Dow Jones Industrial Average, and Mobil is another highly regarded oil issue. Dial's stable of top brand names are well known to investors and consumers alike. U S West is one of the largest telephone companies in the country and provides a way to play the development of the "information highway." Barnett Banks and Regions Financial dominate their regional banking markets. This portfolio, although heavy on oils, nevertheless would be a nice start for an investor who is building a portfolio of 15 to 20 good blue-chip issues. Minimum initial investment: $1,420.

Retirement Portfolio. Given their long-term appeal, no-load stocks make an excellent investment for a long-term, tax-preferenced account such as an IRA. Unfortunately, putting no-load stocks in an IRA is not as easy as it appears.

The key for including no-load stocks in an IRA is to find a custodian to oversee the account. Brokerage firms, except in rare instances, won't provide custodial services for investors who want to hold no-load stocks in a self-directed IRA. The reason is that, in order to participate in a no-load stock program, the shares must be registered in the name of the investor, not in street name. However, brokers will only provide custodial services for accounts in which securities are held in street name. Chances are, if you approach a broker about providing custodial services for an IRA with no-load stocks, he or she will try to convince you to have the stock reregistered in street name. Keep in mind, however, that you'll be unable to participate in a company's no-load stock program if the shares are held in street name.

Also be aware that the broker may try to sell you on his or her firm's "dividend reinvestment plan." A number of brokerage firms have developed what amounts to a synthetic dividend reinvestment plan. These programs allow investors to have their dividends reinvested for little or no fees. The brokerage firms also allow these stocks to be included in IRAs on which they provide custodial services.

When investigating these brokerage-sponsored "DRIP" plans, it is important to realize that these plans are different from company-sponsored no-load stock and dividend reinvestment plans. First, in order to participate in the broker's plan, the shares must be held in street name, which automatically eliminates you from participating in the company's no-load stock and dividend reinvestment plans. Furthermore, the ability to buy additional shares directly from the company for little or no commission is lost. If you want to buy additional shares, you'll pay the brokerage firm's full commission rates of perhaps $30 or more. When a broker tells you that his or her firm offers a plan similar to your no-load stock program and that you can include these investments in an IRA, the plan may not be as attractive as it sounds.

One possible option for a custodian is your bank. Try your local bank's trust department to see if it would be willing to provide custodial services for an IRA holding no-load stocks.

Another option is to contact one of the companies that specializes in providing custodial services. One firm that provides custodial services for IRAs with no-load stocks is First Trust (800-525-2124). Contact the firm for information and a fee schedule.

Once you've secured a custodial agent, you could include any no-load stock in a retirement portfolio. No-load stocks especially appropriate for a retirement account are Exxon, Regions Financial, and U S West.

One last way to include no-load stocks in a retirement account is by investing in those firms that offer an IRA option as part of their no-load stock programs. Exxon has an attractive IRA plan open to all investors. Yearly administrative fees are just $20. For further information, call (800) 252-1800.

Another no-load stock with an IRA option is Connecticut Energy. Unfortunately, only utility customers may buy initial shares directly. However, for customers who buy direct and noncustomers who join the company's dividend reinvestment plan after securing the initial shares from a broker, Connecticut Energy offers an interesting plan. The firm allows investors to hold other issues in the IRA account in addition to Connecticut Energy stock. For example, if you own Connecticut Energy plus five other stocks and would like to have all of them in an IRA, an agent of Connecticut Energy will provide custodial services. For further information about this plan, call (800) 826-4172.

Problems with No-Load Stock Investing

Up to this point, I've addressed mostly the positives of investing in no-load stocks and ways to incorporate no-load stocks into a well-rounded portfolio. However, I would be remiss if I didn't point out some of the shortcomings of no-load stocks as well as provide ways to deal with potential problems.

Diversification Concerns

One problem that has already been discussed is the limited diversification of a portfolio investing exclusively in no-load stocks. Even though the number of no-load stocks is growing, and there are a variety of ways to build "miniportfolios" from no-load stocks, the fact is that the number of no-load stocks, when compared to the thousands of stocks listed on the exchanges, is rather small. But, I think it's important to realize that, for reasons discussed in Chapter 4, the number of no-load stocks will increase dramatically over the next few years. With a larger pool of no-load stocks from which to choose, diversification opportunities will improve.

Also, just because you may not be able to invest in 20 or 30 no-load stocks doesn't mean that you cannot incorporate a few into a portfolio consisting of bonds, stocks, and mutual funds in order to enhance diversification. One of the questions I receive all the time is "Should I invest in stocks or mutual funds?" Quite frankly, I've never figured out how stocks and mutual funds became an either/or issue. I personally own both stocks and mutual funds and am pleased to say that both can exist profitability in a portfolio. While I believe that individual stocks have a number of advantages over mutual funds (these advantages are discussed in-depth in Chapter 3), I'm not so provincial that I ignore the benefits of mutual funds. That's why I have both in my investment portfolio. The point I'm trying to make is that, even if you own a number of stocks and mutual funds already, you still may be able to take advantage of all that a no-load stock gives you while enhancing the diversification of your existing portfolio.

Bottom line: It may be difficult, in certain circumstances, to diversify properly by investing solely in no-load stocks. But no-load stocks can go a long way toward enhancing diversification of an existing portfolio, especially for investors with limited investment capital.

Speed of Execution on the Buy and Sell Sides

One of the major benefits of investing via a broker is speed of execution. You can buy or sell stock almost instantaneously if you are willing to transact at prevailing market prices. Such execution speed gives you ample control over the price at which you buy or sell stock.

Unfortunately, transaction speed is slowed when investing in no-load stocks. Remember the process for investing in no-load stocks: Call the company for information, wait for the application to arrive, fill out the application, cut a check, and return the forms to the company. This process can take three weeks or more from the time you make the phone call to the time your funds are invested by the company. In that time, the stock price could have fluctuated significantly. There's a chance that the stock could have moved higher and out of what you perceive to be a good buying range. The flip side is that the stock could have fallen into an even more desirable buying range. These potential fluctuations also occur with monthly investments. Most no-load stocks buy shares once a month, which means there could be a time lag between when your funds are received and when they're invested.

Because of these lags, no-load stocks are not trading vehicles. However, over the long term, such price fluctuations should wash out and not have a major effect on a portfolio.

The time lags on the buy side also apply to the sell side. Let's say you want to sell your shares. Most no-load stocks will permit you to sell the stock directly through the plans. The advantage of selling through the company is that commissions are usually much cheaper than if you sold through the broker. The downside to selling through the company is that it may take 5 to 10 business days before your transaction is made and additional days for the funds to be remitted to you. This time lag leaves the door open for price fluctuations prior to the execution of your sell order. However, there's always the possibility that the stock will rise and your sale will be executed at a higher price than you expected. Again, such fluctuations probably wash out over the long term, but they can make a big difference on a short-term basis.

What are some ways to deal with the time lags when buying and selling no-load stocks? One strategy is to send your money to the company as close as possible to the investment date (investment dates are listed in the plan's prospectus). In this way, your money is not sitting around for weeks without earning interest (companies don't pay interest on funds awaiting investment in their stock purchase plans). Also, you can have a better idea of the price range at which you'll be buying shares if you wait until close to the investment date.

Another way to improve the buy process is by taking advantage of the company's automatic investment services, if such services are available. These services assure that you won't miss an investment date and help to get your funds to the company at the proper time.

A way to deal with the time lag on the sell side is to put yourself in the position to sell stock quickly if need be. All no-load stock plans will issue certificates to investors upon request. Let's say that, over time, you've built up a holding in a particular company of 500 shares. There's nothing stopping you from contacting the company and requesting that it send you certificates representing, say, 200 shares of stock. With certificates in hand, you now have the ability to go to any broker and immediately sell your holdings. Keep in mind that to get quicker transaction speed, you'll probably pay considerably more in commissions. Still, for investors who want greater flexibility, taking possession of certificates representing a portion of your holdings in the plan is definitely a way to speed up the process when you want to sell.

As mentioned in Chapter 1, a number of no-load stocks have been addressing the time-lag issue by improving the buy and sell processes. For example, Exxon and U S West make investments on a weekly basis rather than monthly. Dial has taken measures to improve things on the sell side. Even though most firms require sell instructions in writing, Dial allows its no-load stock investors to sell stock with just a phone call, and Dial picks up all of the costs for selling. Look for more no-load stocks to implement procedures which streamline the buy and sell processes.

Record-Keeping Headaches

One criticism I often hear about direct-purchase plans is that they're a nightmare when it comes to keeping records. These record-keeping headaches usually occur when shares are sold and a cost basis needs to be determined for tax purposes.

Certainly, any investment in which there's frequent buying of small— sometimes fractional—amounts of stock presents challenges for investors. But these challenges aren't necessarily intrinsic to no-load stocks. The challenges exist when using a dollar-cost averaging program or, for that matter, any program that makes regular investments to buy whole and fractional shares. If you buy mutual-fund shares every month, you're faced with the same challenges in determining your cost basis as buying shares in a no-load stock every month.

Fortunately, companies provide an excellent source of information to ease the record-keeping hassle. First, companies send statements after each investment. Second, at the end of the year, companies provide a 1099 form to show the amount of dividends that you received or had reinvested. (Remember: Dividends that are reinvested still count as income for tax purposes.) These statements are similar to the statements you receive from your broker or mutual fund.

Now, let's say you want to sell shares in a no-load stock. It's critical that you have records indicating the price at which you bought the shares. This determines your cost basis, which will determine whether the sell transaction generates a gain or loss. If you've kept good records, you can use the specific shares method, which means you can pick which shares you are selling and use the appropriate purchase price. If you don't have good records, you'll have to use the first-in, first-out method, which means the cost basis is the purchase price of the first shares purchased. This method will likely lead to bigger taxes since it's more likely that the first shares purchased have the largest gains. Determining a cost basis with no-load stocks, especially if your investments were buying fractional shares, is extremely difficult without proper records. Companies and their transfer agents may be able to help you piece together your buying history. However, it's always best to keep and record information that the company provides in the regular statements. If this is done, record-keeping headaches are limited.

Conclusion

This chapter has covered a lot of ground in terms of investing in no-load stocks and pitfalls to avoid. Remember that merely because a company has a no-load stock program doesn't make it a good investment. Investors need to do their homework when considering any investment, including no-load stocks.

3

No-Load Stocks versus No-Load Mutual Funds

To say that mutual funds have become the investment of choice of investors is an understatement. Indeed, money in mutual funds now totals over $2 trillion. Perhaps an even more telling statistic reflecting investors' insatiable appetite for funds is the fact that there are now more mutual funds than stocks listed on the New York and American Stock Exchanges.

A big reason for the growth in mutual funds was the development of the "no-load" concept. Not only did no-load mutual funds eliminate the sales fee, but they also changed the way investors interact with funds. Load funds are sold by brokers; no-load funds are sold directly, without an intermediary. Making it possible for small investors to deal directly with mutual funds via the mail was a key factor in their popularity.

An example of the drawing power of no-load funds is the Skyline Special Equities Fund. This mutual fund had a stellar record since its inception in 1987. However, despite its strong performance, assets in the fund grew to only $62 million in July 1992. What was the problem? From its origin in 1987 to July 1992, the fund charged a 3.85 percent load fee. In August 1992, however, the fund dropped the load fee. What happened? Assets soared to $172.4 million by the end of 1992—a 178 percent increase in less than five months. The fact that the fund's performance continued to be strong was one factor boosting fund assets. Nevertheless, insiders at the fund say that a big catalyst for the increase in assets was the elimination of the load fee. Eliminating the sales fee made it cheaper to invest in the fund. Even more importantly, becoming a no-load fund made investing in the fund easier because individuals could go directly to the fund.

Mutual Fund Myths

The mutual-fund industry has done a masterful job at selling no-load funds as the only investment that makes sense for small investors. However, what the fund industry doesn't tell you is that mutual funds have their own imperfections that need to be considered by investors. Indeed, the attraction of no-load mutual funds—often at the expense of ownership of individual stocks—may not be all it's cracked up to be. This chapter explores common myths surrounding mutual-fund investing and examines aspects of mutual-fund investing relative to investing in no-load stocks.

Myth 1: Mutual Funds Are Safe Investments

Contrary to what many investors believe, mutual funds, including money-market mutual funds, are not federally insured investments. Even mutual funds sold by banks are not federally insured, although a study by the American Association of Retired Persons showed that less than 20 percent of those surveyed understood that mutual funds bought at a bank are not federally insured. And if you use the word *safe* to mean that mutual funds are immune to sharp downturns, you're wrong as well. Just ask holders of the Steadman Oceanographic fund, who saw their investment decline 62 percent for the 10-year period through 1993. Or the holders of the DFA Japanese Small Company fund, who saw the value of their holdings drop nearly 17 percent in the five-year period through 1993. Or the Frontier Equity fund, which posted a nearly 25 percent decline in 1993. Remember that mutual funds are only as safe as the securities in which they are invested.

From a No-Load Stock (NLS) Perspective. *Are mutual funds safer than no-load stocks? I won't attempt to argue that diversification doesn't matter in limiting downside risk, and diversification is easier to achieve with no-load mutual funds than no-load stocks. Still, investors who choose no-load mutual funds over a portfolio of no-load stocks or stocks in general may be surprised to see how unsafe these funds are during declining markets.*

Myth 2: I Can Expect Above-Average Performance from My Mutual-Fund Investment

You can expect above-average performance, but you probably won't get it. In any given year, it's not unusual for at least two-thirds of all mutual funds to underperform the market as measured by Standard & Poor's (S&P) 500. For the 10-year period ending 1993, only funds specializing in international, financial-services, and health-care equities outperformed the S&P 500. General equity funds in that period posted an average gain, including reinvested dividends, of 234.6 percent versus the return on the S&P 500 of 301.4 percent.

Several factors account for the lackluster performance of most funds. First, many academics argue that the market is so efficient—in other words, stock prices reflect all that is known about a stock and discount information so quickly that finding mispriced stocks is very difficult—that it is extremely difficult to outperform the market on a consistent basis. Many practitioners in the investment field hold that markets are not as efficient as academics believe. Still, you probably won't find too many fund managers who won't acknowledge the difficulty in beating the market.

But even if you believe that it's possible to beat the market regularly, how many mutual-fund managers have the skill to do so? Very few. And the number of mutual-fund managers who truly add value is being spread thinner over an always increasing number of mutual-fund offerings. Indeed, there are now more than 5,000 mutual funds. Are all of these funds being managed by fund managers who add value? Of course not. Furthermore, performance may be even bleaker over the next decade if the financial markets turn more difficult. After all, it wasn't too hard to show double-digit gains during the last decade when stocks in general were rising at such a rapid rate. However, in an environment where market returns are more in line with historical averages of roughly 10 percent per year for stocks, the disparities between the few effective fund managers and the huge number of mediocre ones will be even more evident.

Also affecting mutual-fund performance is that, in some instances, a mutual fund may have little incentive to go for above-average performance. For example, a fund that accumulates, say, $2 billion in assets may have much more of an incentive to maintain the status quo by focusing on conservative investments. That's because, with $2 billion in assets, fees to the mutual fund could be anywhere from $20 to $40 million every year, even if the fund doesn't make a dime for its shareholders. Thus, preservation of capital rather than aggressive asset appreciation may be the primary objective of the fund manager.

One final factor causing subpar mutual-fund returns has been the huge amounts of money flowing into funds in recent years. In many cases, such huge inflows have created problems for fund managers, who are pressured to put these funds to work in stocks. However, especially during periods when stocks are high, huge inflows may force fund managers to abandon investment strategies that were successful when the mutual fund was small or to invest in stocks that may be overpriced and not offering the best upside potential. Some funds have closed their doors to new participants when they perceived fund assets were overwhelming the fund manager's strategy, but the temptation to take in more money because of the annual management fee has caused a number of mutual funds with stellar track records to join the ranks of mediocre performers. Bottom line: Keep your expectations in check when investing in mutual funds. That way you won't be too disappointed when your fund comes up short.

From an NLS Perspective. *I won't say that no-load stocks, as a group, will outperform no-load mutual funds over time. I will say that investors who ignore no-load stocks for no-load mutual funds may be overlooking some attractive long-term capital-gains performers while relegating their investment funds to subpar performance.*

Myth 3: My Mutual-Fund Manager Will Protect Me from Bear Markets by Timing the Market

This may be one of the biggest myths of the mutual-fund industry. If you think outperforming the market by picking the best stocks is difficult, it's even more difficult to time the market properly on a sustained basis. Investors who believe their mutual-fund manager can pick stocks *and* time the market need a reality check. First, it's unlikely that your fund manager will successfully call market tops and bottoms over time. But even in the extreme case when a fund manager may have some ability to call market turns, his or her hands may be tied for a variety of reasons. It may be that the fund's policy is to be fully invested at all times, regardless of market conditions. Many mutual funds take the approach that their fund holders invest in order to have exposure to stocks. It's not the job of the fund manager to allocate assets in cash and stocks in order to deal with bear markets. Asset allocation is the job of the fund holder; investing in stocks is the job of the fund manager.

Another reason why your fund manager may not try to protect you from a bear market is that it may hurt his or her compensation. Fund managers are often paid a base salary and a performance bonus. A manager who turns bearish too early and moves money to cash could hurt the fund's performance and, therefore, his or her bonus. The fund manager's risk of turning bearish and being wrong may outweigh the reward of turning bearish and being right.

From an NLS Perspective. *Since you're the "fund manager" with your no-load stocks, you make the decisions whether to turn bearish or not. While* *there's a good chance you'll be wrong if you choose to time the market with your no-load stock investments, at least you're following your own agenda and not the agenda of your fund manager.*

Myth 4: Investing in No-Load Mutual Funds Is "No-Cost" Investing

Much of the popularity of no-load funds is the fact that they can be bought without a sales fee. However, to say that investing in no-load funds is "no-cost" investing is simply not true. In many cases, the costs of investing in no-load mutual funds are greater than the costs of investing in individual stocks, especially no-load stocks. The problem is that most investors don't realize it since funds deduct expenses from your holdings, which means you never actually write a check to pay expenses. This may be less obvious, but it is no less painful to portfolio performance.

The sales, or "load," fee is only the tip of the fee iceberg in terms of the costs of investing in mutual funds. I've already discussed fees in Chapter 2, but some of the material bears repeating, given the huge impact fees have on investment results.

No-load funds have a variety of fees at their disposal to take money from your pockets:

- *Annual management and administrative fees.* These are the fees that all no-load funds charge to manage and administer the assets. Rates differ from one fund group to another and across types of funds. However, it is not uncommon for equity funds, especially those investing in foreign securities, to have annual management fees of well over 1 percent and more than 2 percent in some instances. Administrative fees may include such things as account setup fees, annual account maintenance fees, telephone redemption fees, wire redemption fees, IRA annual maintenance fees, account closeout fees, and check redemption processing fees.

- *12b-1 fees.* A number of no-load mutual funds charge 12b-1 fees to help defray expenses. These fees have become more regulated in recent years, although 12b-1 fees can still consume up to 0.75 percent of your assets.

- *Back-end loads.* Since mutual funds realize that investors don't like up-front load fees, they have become adept at building less conspicuous fees into the system. One such fee is a "back-end" or redemption fee. Most back-end load fees apply if a fund holder sells shares within five years. The fees decline the longer the fund shares are held and usually disappear if the fund is held for longer than five or six years.

When you add all of these fees together, it's quite possible that a no-load mutual fund may be charging you 2 to 3 percent per year in fees. That translates to annual fees on a $10,000 investment of $200 to $300 per year. That's $200 to $300 on which you'll never earn a dime in the future.

While mutual funds have been dropping "load" fees, management and administrative fees are increasing despite record dollar amounts under management. Logic says that a larger amount of money in a fund would create economies of scale in managing and administering funds, causing fee expense ratios to decline. However, the opposite has occurred. Why? Because fund investors, by and large, have no idea how much they pay in annual fees, thus allowing funds to raise these "hidden" fees aggressively.

Yes, you will avoid a sales fee when investing in no-load mutual funds. But don't believe for a second that investing in no-load mutual funds is truly "no-cost" investing.

From an NLS Perspective.   *How do the costs of investing in no-load stocks compare to the costs of no-load mutual funds? The clear winners are no-load stocks. Not only do you avoid any sales fees on the initial purchase of no-load stocks, but your annual costs to maintain your account are usually zero. All of your money works for you each and every year, making no-load stocks the only "no-cost" investing vehicle available to equity investors. Investors should also keep in mind that the cost advantage of no-load stocks versus funds means that a typical no-load mutual fund must outperform a portfolio of no-load stocks by at least 2 percent every year in order to generate the same "after-fee" returns. That gives no-load stocks a big edge in terms of long-term performance.*

Myth 5: My Portfolio of Mutual Funds Is Properly Diversified

One undeniable advantage mutual funds have over stocks is the ability to diversify with relatively small amounts of money. However, combining different types of mutual funds in a portfolio does not necessarily enhance diversification. Research has shown that fund investments are likely to overlap any time you chase the most popular funds. These funds may be concentrated in similar stock sectors that are relatively "hot" at a particular time. However, when these stocks turn down, it's possible that your portfolio of funds will turn down in unison, which is exactly what you don't want to happen when you diversify.

Another problem with diversification is that investors and fund managers take diversification to extremes. For example, an individual with a large number of general equity mutual funds, whether he or she realizes it, probably is close to "owning the market"—in other words, the portfolio is so diversified and so large that it replicates the entire stock market. At this point, diversification is only costing you money. You'd be better off owning a market-index fund and saving hundreds or even thousands of dollars each year in management fees. The same analysis goes for one stock fund that may own 300 or more individual stocks. At that point, the fund probably is close to being representative of the entire market (or market segment if it's a fund that specializes in, say, small capitalization stocks), and you'd be better off buying an index fund for that particular market sector and lowering your annual management expenses.

From an NLS Perspective.   *Diversification with no-load stocks is not as complete as diversifying with mutual funds. Still, investors can achieve a reasonable level of diversification with a portfolio of no-load stocks, especially when combined with bonds, money-market instruments, and other investments.*

Myth 6: My Fund Manager Is an Expert Who Trades Stocks Based Solely on Perceptions of Value and Appreciation Potential

Assuming any level of expertise about your fund manager may be dangerous to your wealth. Based on the underwhelming performance of most mutual funds, most fund managers do not add value to the investment process. And with talent continually being watered down by the creation of more mutual funds, the "expertise" of fund managers should be questioned even more.

One indication that your fund manager may not be an "expert," at least in investing during bear markets, is the fact that, according to Morningstar, Inc., the mutual-fund research firm, the typical equity fund manager has been running his or her portfolio for roughly five years. Of the more than 2,500 funds examined by Morningstar, fewer than 100 funds have had the same fund manager for at least 15 years. Given that the equity markets have been trending higher since 1982 without a protracted bear market occurring, very few fund managers have invested during both bear and bull markets. Thus, the jury is still out on how fund managers will perform during the next extended bear market, which ought to be of major concern to mutual-fund investors.

What's particularly interesting about the perception among fund investors that their fund managers are experts is the fact that very few fund investors even know who manages their funds. That's no accident.

Some mutual funds do their best to conceal the names of their fund managers. Since July 1, 1993, mutual funds have had to disclose the names of managers in their prospectuses. When a change in managers occurs, investors are to be notified immediately. However, the rule states that funds run by a committee do not have to list a fund manager. What has happened is that more and more funds are claiming that they are run by teams—30 percent of the funds tracked by Morningstar versus just 15 percent in 1989. Why may a fund be reluctant to say who manages the fund? Because if the manager becomes too closely associated with the fund and then leaves, an exodus of fund holders could occur. By saying that a fund is run by a committee, investors may not know who really is responsible for a fund's performance and therefore are less apt to jump ship should the key individual part ways with the fund group.

Regarding buy-and-sell decisions, fund managers presumably buy and sell stocks based on their perceptions of future returns. However, to say that fund managers sell stocks only when they turn negative on their potential may not always be correct. In some cases, fund managers may be forced to sell stock, even though they'd rather not. In fact, a fund manager may know that it's the worst possible time to sell a stock but may have little choice but to do so. Such scenarios usually unfold during sharp market downturns. Keep in mind that most mutual funds are fully or nearly fully invested in securities and hold very small amounts of cash, often 5 percent or less of total fund assets. This cash cushion is used as a source of funds to pay fund holders who redeem shares as well as to pay the fund's operating expenses, such as brokerage costs.

Let's say that a big market drop fuels substantial amounts of liquidations on the part of the fund's investors. The redemptions may exceed the fund's cash cushion. In this instance, the fund manager must raise cash by selling securities. Since large redemptions usually occur during declining markets, fund managers are forced to sell into an environment of falling prices. It's conceivable, indeed likely, that the fund manager would not normally choose to sell the stock at that time. However, the need to raise cash overrides the fund manager's valuation models. In fact, with the stock falling in price, the appropriate investment decision may be to buy more of the stock at its depressed price rather than to sell into the weakness. However, the fund manager's hands are tied because of the need to raise money to pay out to investors who are redeeming shares.

Another reason a mutual-fund manager may sell against his or her better judgment is to get rid of losers to save face with fund holders. Such "window dressing" usually occurs around the end of each quarter, before the quarterly statement is compiled. Let's say IBM undergoes a huge price drop during the quarter, and the fund manager is holding the stock. Even though the stock may be worth holding at its depressed level, the fund manager might sell the shares so he or she doesn't have to include the stock in the fund holders' quarterly report and risk the appearance of looking like a sap.

From an NLS Perspective.   *When investing in no-load stocks, you know exactly who the fund manager is (you) and the level of his or her expertise. Furthermore, you have complete freedom in buying and selling stocks. You'll never be forced to sell stocks at potentially the worst possible time in order to raise cash to redeem fund holders.*

Myth 7: I Know Exactly What Securities My Fund Holds

Knowing what a mutual fund has in its portfolio, if you go solely by the name of the fund, is extremely difficult. A mutual fund can use a certain name if, under normal market conditions, at least 65 percent of its assets are invested in that category. However, that also means that 35 percent of the fund's assets may be invested in totally different instruments carrying perhaps more risk.

But what about the quarterly reports in which the fund lists its holdings? Isn't this a useful source to find out what a fund holds? Perhaps, although this information is often out-of-date and fairly meaningless. Indeed, in funds with high portfolio turnover, what was reported as a substantial holding in a fund two months ago may not even be in the portfolio today.

Well, can't I call the fund manager to find out the fund's top holdings at any given time? The fact is that you'll probably get the runaround if you call your fund to find out its biggest holdings. Most mutual funds are very closemouthed about the securities they hold. Fund managers don't want others, especially big, institutional investors, to know what they are buying or selling because that information may affect prices.

Finally, even if you know what's in the portfolio, it may not help you to assess the real risk of the fund. Financial derivatives are a popular investment for funds. Derivatives are hybrid securities designed by Wall Street rocket scientists. Many fixed-income funds have been employing derivatives in their portfolios in order to boost returns. The problem is that these newfangled investments have tended to be extremely risky and volatile in the wrong hands. Therefore, even though the overall maturity of your bond fund may be very short—which would make it less susceptible to interest-rate movements—the inclusion of certain financial derivatives may actually make it riskier than you think.

The risks of financial derivatives were evident in 1994 when several money-market mutual funds registered losses due to derivatives. In a number of cases, the mutual funds, fearing a major backlash from investors who don't expect to see losses in "safe" money-market funds, kicked money into the funds to cover the losses. But investors shouldn't expect fund groups to always be this benevolent.

From an NLS Perspective.   *You never have to guess what securities are held in your portfolio of no-load stocks. And you can reach the "fund manager" any time you want.*

Myth 8: Picking No-Load Mutual Funds Is Easier Than Picking Stocks

One of the major selling points of mutual funds is that it's a lot easier to pick a winning fund than a winning stock. All you need to do is look at track records and stick with the top funds. Sounds easy, right?

The reality is that picking mutual funds has become a lot like picking stocks. First, the sheer number of funds presents problems. Sorting through the thousands of mutual funds to find winners is no different than sifting through thousands of stocks to find winners. In fact, it may be more difficult. At least with stocks, you can examine balance sheets and income statements, assess growth prospects of the industry, analyze new products, and so forth. With funds, the only pieces of information to go by are the fund manager—presuming you can even tell who the fund manager is—and the fund's track record. That's it. That's why so much emphasis in picking funds is placed on historical performance.

Muddying the waters are the aggressive promotional campaigns being waged by mutual-fund companies. These ads all focus on fund performance. However, a fund that advertises its impressive 10-year performance may be a fund that has turned in horrible results in the preceding 3-year period. Furthermore, the fund's excellent 10-year track record may have been compiled by a fund manager who is no longer in charge of the fund.

Even if the firm's track record has been impressive, there's no assurance that future results will match past performance. In fact, there's a pretty good chance that this year's top fund will be next year's laggard. John Bogle, the head of the Vanguard Fund group and someone with a vested interest in portraying mutual funds in a positive light, states, "The record is crystal clear that past performance success is rarely the precursor of future success." Bogle shows in his book, *Bogle on Mutual Funds* (Irwin Professional Publishing), that a top-20 fund's performance in one year has no systematic relationship to its ranking in the subsequent year. Bogle refers to this as *regressing to the mean,* the powerful tendency for returns on financial assets to regress toward the average following periods of abnormal performance. Bottom line: Picking funds based on historical performance may be no more effective than randomly selecting funds.

So if picking funds based on historical performance is not a surefire way to riches, how is one supposed to pick funds? Mutual-fund companies are spending big bucks on advertising, hoping that you'll pick the fund that fills your mailbox with the most stuff.

In the advertising game, the fund group with the most fund choices usually has the best chance to advertise top performance. That's because the more funds the group has, the more likely one or two of them will be among the top performers. How reliable is mutual-fund advertising in picking future winners? Not very. Still, it's likely that separating the "haves" from the "have nots" in the mutual-fund industry of the future will be which funds have the deepest pockets for advertising or make it easiest to buy their funds.

And your fund choices will only become more difficult with affinity groups, your local bank, your utility company (Dominion Resources, a Virginia-based power company, has marketed a utility fund to its utility customers), and even airlines (American Airlines peddles mutual funds via its in-flight reading material) getting into the fund business.

Another factor that will complicate fund selection is the merger activity that will likely heat up dramatically among mutual funds over the next several years. Low barriers to entry coupled with a slowdown in asset growth will increase competition and lower profit margins in the fund industry. Smaller fund groups will find it difficult to survive and will be acquired, while larger fund groups without a discernible advantage will likely be swallowed up as well. Already several prominent fund groups, most notably Dreyfus, have been acquired. When your fund company is acquired, how will performance of your funds be affected? Should you switch out of the fund? Are new fees being implemented? These issues increase the difficulty of investing in the best mutual funds.

From an NLS Perspective.   *Picking top-performing no-load stocks, like no-load mutual funds, is certainly no picnic. However, investors who do their home-*

work have much more information at their disposal to evaluate a no-load stock versus the limited quantitative tools available to analyze mutual funds.

Myth 9: It's Easy to Get out of Mutual Funds at a Moment's Notice

For the most part, mutual funds offer a high degree of liquidity. Investors usually can get in and out of funds relatively quickly and easily. However, that liquidity comes at a price. For example, the ability for investors to redeem shares with a phone call means that funds must maintain at least some cash holdings to cover redemptions. However, such cash may be a drag on results during an up market.

Furthermore, generous selling privileges make trading in and out of funds especially easy. The threat of redemptions may cause a fund manager to invest in the most liquid investments as opposed to investments that may have better long-term potential but may be more difficult to liquidate. Frequent trading of funds also generates potentially huge tax liabilities for fund holders, which affect portfolio returns.

And selling mutual funds, under certain circumstances, may not be as instantaneous as you think. Anyone who tried to sell funds during the October 1987 crash knows the potential problems that may occur during dramatic sell-offs. Some of the big mutual-fund families have tested emergency systems in the case of huge redemptions. But no one knows for certain how such emergency systems will hold up during a prolonged market meltdown.

From an NLS Perspective.   *Selling no-load stocks has its own problems in terms of delays. Furthermore, plenty of stock investors couldn't get in touch with their brokers to sell stocks during the October 1987 crash. What is encouraging is that several no-load stocks are improving the ability to sell stocks more quickly and cheaply. Also, investors who request shares that accumulate in a no-load stock program in the form of certificates have the ability to sell quickly by taking certificates to the broker of their choice.*

Myth 10: I Can Depend on the Fund's Directors to Protect My Interests

Corporate governance in mutual funds is similar to corporate governance issues with corporations. Just as equity shareholders are owners of the company, fund holders are the owners of the fund. And, just as equity shareholders have a corporate board of directors whose charge it is to protect the interests of stockholders, mutual funds have a board of directors whose job it is to protect fund holders. However, equity investors know all too well that directors are often just a rubber stamp for management, and the same can be said for directors of many mutual funds.

It's the fiduciary responsibility of the directors or trustees to make sure the fund earns acceptable returns while keeping fees reasonable. In addition, directors must satisfy themselves that portfolio managers have the expertise to employ such risky and complicated investments as financial derivatives. Directors are also responsible for making sure that fund management fulfills its responsibility as an active shareholder in terms of corporate governance questions.

How well do directors fulfill their responsibilities? "If you think the boards of ordinary corporations have been lax in doing their job, you should look at the behavior of the boards [of mutual funds]," Warren Buffet was quoted in *Money* magazine. "Almost without exception, they acquiesce in whatever . . . the sponsors of the funds ask them to do." The lack of accountability is due to a variety of factors:

- Fully 60 percent of a mutual fund's directors are permitted by law to be affiliated with the fund company. That means only 40 percent of a fund's directors are independent directors, and these directors are usually chosen by fund management. Often, these directors are buddies and/or business associates of the fund operators. It's unlikely that fund operators will pick independent directors who are truly independent, instead opting for directors who won't rock the boat.

- Many fund directors pick up nice cash for what amounts to a part-time job. *Money* magazine uncovered several trustees who serve on boards of a number of funds at one fund family collecting cumulative salaries of well over $100,000 annually. *Money* also found one fund trustee who, by the magazine's estimates, collects roughly $363,000 per year in director's fees. If you were pulling down six figures for a fairly cushy part-time job, would you raise a stink? Probably not.

- Many independent directors have no experience in the mutual-fund field and get their education via fund managers. Thus, their perspectives may be skewed by the agendas of fund management.

How successful have directors been in keeping watch over what should be perhaps the single biggest concern for fund holders—fees? According to Lipper Analytical Services, the average mutual-fund expense ratio rose roughly 20 percent in the last 10 years. And that's during a time when fees should have *fallen* because of increased economies of scale as a result of huge amounts of money under management.

Moral of the story: Don't expect fund directors to watch your back. More likely, they're in bed with fund management.

From an NLS Perspective. *Because you call the shots when investing in no-load stocks, you don't have outside fund directors consuming profits in the form of bloated salaries.*

Myth 11: Record Keeping Is Easier with Mutual Funds Than with Individual Stocks

I'm often surprised to hear investors talk about the drudgery of keeping track of their stock investments. This record-keeping issue comes up most often when investors sell stock and have to determine their cost basis of the shares sold for tax purposes.

You also have to keep track each time you buy and sell mutual-fund shares. Yet, for some reason, investors think this is much easier. Some fund families provide assistance in determining the average cost of your fund holdings, which comes in handy at tax time. Still, an investor without record-keeping disciplines will have a difficult time keeping track of fund investments. The record-keeping hassle is compounded with funds if you reinvest dividends and are involved in the fund's automatic monthly investment program. By reinvesting dividends and making monthly investments, you increase the number of purchases dramatically, which increases your potential tax headaches when you sell.

From an NLS Perspective. *Record keeping is not necessarily a snap with no-load stocks. As discussed in Chapter 2, frequent purchases of stock through direct-purchase programs make it imperative that you keep regular statements that are sent by the companies. My feeling with record keeping is that, for a disciplined investor, it's no problem. Develop some simple manual or even computer record-keeping system. There are a variety of software packages available to assist you in tracking your stocks. The biggest item to record is the cost basis every time you purchase stocks. If you have gaps in your investment history, you might get help by consulting with the company's transfer agent who should have a record of your purchase history.*

Myth 12: Mutual Funds Treat All Shareholders— Both Large and Small— Equally. On the Other Hand, Institutional Investors in Stocks Have Much Lower Commissions and Greater Accessibility to Company Management Than Small Equity Investors

People who think that all mutual funds treat fund holders equally have probably never heard of "hub-and-spoke" funds. Some banks, as well as a few mutual-fund families, offer "hub-and-spoke" funds for different types of clients. A "hub" is a single portfolio used by the "spoke" funds. Even though each "spoke" is invested in the same "hub" fund—and, therefore, is the exact same portfolio—the spokes may have different fee structures for different groups of investors. For example, one "spoke" may charge investors a 2 percent load fee and 1.5 percent in annual management fees while another spoke may have no load fee and lower annual management expenses. "Hub-and-spoke" funds discriminate against certain classes of investors who pay more in fees than other investors in the same fund.

And what about those instances when the same fund manager oversees two separate funds, each having the same investment objective but different fee structures? A May 10, 1994, issue of *FW* magazine reported that more than 100 mutual-fund managers handle funds for more than one mutual-fund group. What is particularly significant is that more than 40 manage funds with the same objectives for more than one company. For example, *FW* points out that John Marshall manages Harbor Growth and Nicholas-Applegate Core Growth Equity A. Both are growth funds. However, while the Harbor Growth carries no load fee and an expense ratio of 0.90 percent, the Nicholas-Applegate Core Growth Equity A has a 5¼ percent load fee and an expense ratio of 1.60 percent. Same fund manager. Same investment objective. Different fee structures.

Another way a number of funds treat fund holders differently is by offering various perks to large investors. For example, with a minimum balance of $250,000, the T. Rowe Price fund family provides a variety of premium services, such as a personal representative to handle your account. By calling your account representative, you'll probably get more timely answers to your questions than by going through the customer service personnel. Even more importantly, your representative has a direct pipeline to the fund manager with your questions. Other special services offered to big hitters—usually balances of $100,000 or more—include free advice on fund selection and portfolio allocation.

From an NLS Perspective.   *One of the biggest advantages an institutional stock investor has over a small investor—commission costs as a percentage of total investment—is negated when investing in no-load stocks. In nearly every instance, there are no commission costs with no-load stocks. In fact, unless a big, institutional investor is willing to have the shares registered in his or her own name as opposed to "street" name, he or she can't even participate in no-load stock programs. Clearly, no-load stocks are one of the very few investment vehicles where small investors are on equal footing with big investors in terms of invest-ment fees and availability.*

Myth 13: Investing in Mutual Funds Poses No Particular Tax Considerations That Are Not Common in Any Other Investment

Perhaps the biggest downside to investing in mutual funds is that, in many cases, buying a mutual fund means buying a tax liability. Investors in funds, especially those with high portfolio turnover, are likely to incur a tax liability at some point in the year. This occurs when the fund man-ager sells issues that have appreciated, thus turning an "unrealized" gain into a "realized" gain. Since funds with high turnover do a lot of selling, these funds generate a lot of realized gains each year, and these realized gains are distributed to fund holders. When this occurs, current share-holders of the fund incur a tax liability. The bad part is that *all* fund hold-ers must pay the tax on realized gains that are distributed to them each year. That means that even if you bought the fund in the last month of the year and weren't holding the fund when the big gains were achieved, you still must pay a capital gains tax on the realized gains if you received them. In fact, even if the value of the fund has dropped since your invest-ment—in other words, you're holding a paper loss in the fund—you still have to pay taxes on realized gains distributed to you.

Even funds with low portfolio turnover cannot escape the tax issue. Mutual funds with low turnover have large unrealized capital gains. While a fund that has huge unrealized gains is an indication of a fund that has been successful in picking winners, it also poses potential bombshells for new investors in the fund. At some point, the fund will sell these stocks and distribute the "realized" gains to current fund holders. Thus, buying a fund with low turnover may mean that you are also buying a fund with potentially huge "hidden" tax liabilities.

Keep in mind this tax burden is aside from the usual taxes you have to pay on dividend distributions the fund makes during the year as well as taxes you must pay when selling fund shares at a profit.

The tax issue concerning mutual funds is especially significant at this time given that the markets have been strong for so many years, and a plethora of funds have large unrealized gains. Should fund managers sour on the market and begin selling stock, the size of the distributions of realized gains—and therefore the size of your tax headache—could grow.

What if you invest in a tax-exempt mutual fund? This is one way to dodge the tax liability. But even this strategy may not be bulletproof when it comes to taxes. For example, a tax-exempt fund that has realized capital gains on its bond holdings that aren't offset by losses may pay out those realized profits in the form of taxable dividends. This scenario would be most likely to occur following a strong advance in the bond market and in a fund with high turnover. Some tax-exempt mutual funds handed their fund holders taxable distributions in 1993, which came as a big surprise to many investors who thought that tax-exempt funds were just that—tax-exempt.

Frequent switching among mutual funds within the same fund family and liberal check-writing privileges for some bond funds also present potential tax problems. Being able to switch from one fund to another with just a phone call is a major advertising point of the big fund families. Worried about the stock market? No problem. Just switch your funds from an equity fund to the fund family's money-market fund. Want more exposure to international markets? Simply take some of your money out of that bond fund and invest in the fund family's Pacific rim fund. The problem, from a tax standpoint, is that every time you switch funds, you incur a tax liability. Indeed, switching money from one fund to another is the same as selling shares in the fund and buying shares in the new fund. If you have a gain on the shares in the fund from which you are switching, you'll have to account for the gain at tax time. Thus, switching privileges are a double-edged sword for investors—more flexibility, but more tax headaches.

And those bond funds that have liberal check-writing features present another taxing problem. Investors who write checks against their holdings in a bond fund—not a money-market fund, mind you, but a bond fund—are, in effect, selling fund shares. Anytime you sell an investment that is held outside an IRA or other retirement-type account, you incur a potential tax liability. To illustrate the problem, I once knew an investor who was writing checks against his bond fund for everything—groceries, gifts, you name it. You can imagine his shock when he learned that each time he wrote a check against his bond fund, he had to account for the transaction to the IRS.

From an NLS Perspective.   *Fund investors are at the mercy of fund managers when it comes to incurring an unwanted tax liability. The fund managers decide when and how much realized gains to distribute. Fund managers also determine what types of stocks to purchase—high-dividend-paying stocks, which create additional tax liabilities for fund holders, or low-dividend-paying stocks. The fact is that fund managers don't necessarily manage the fund based on tax considerations. That's because mutual funds don't pay taxes—you do. Furthermore, the generous switching and check-writing features have tax consequences as well. However, with no-load stocks, you control your tax destiny. You decide when to realize capital gains. You decide if you want to invest in high-dividend-paying stocks—and incur the tax liability for dividend income—or low-paying or no-paying dividend stocks. You decide when to offset capital gains by taking losses. In short, no-load stock investors control when and how much to pay in taxes on their investments. This control, which is not available in mutual funds, can have huge implications in terms of after-tax investment returns over time.*

Myth 14: The Mutual-Fund Manager Is Investing in My Best Interests

I've already discussed a few ways that managers may be forced into acting in a way that is contrary to the fund holders' best interests. If fund holders begin redeeming shares *en masse,* the fund manager may have to sell stocks that he or she would not otherwise sell—stocks whose performance could help fund holders make money—in order to raise money to cash out fleeing investors. In addition, with many managers' compensations based on performance, a manager whose fund is having a good year may have an incentive to protect the fund's gains—and his or her bonus—by moving to cash. However, this move to cash could be detrimental to the best interests of fund holders. Or a fund manager who has underperformed for the year may have an incentive to invest in riskier investments toward the end of the year to try to salvage the fund's performance and his or her bonus.

There are other potential conflicts of interest that arise between fund managers and fund holders:

- *Unethical trading practices.*   Mutual-fund managers, especially those of large funds, have incredible power in that their buy-and-sell decisions can potentially move stocks, at least on a short-term basis. Furthermore, many fund groups encourage their fund managers to trade stocks in order to keep them close to the markets. Being in command of literally billions of dollars and having their own money at risk in the market present the opportunity to trade fund assets to benefit personal accounts. How can this occur? One way is through "front-running." *Front-running* is the practice whereby a fund manager buys or sells stocks in his or her personal account prior to making the same trades for the mutual fund. For example, the manager of the XYZ fund—a fund with $2 billion in assets—knows that if he buys a lot of a certain small capitalization, thinly traded stock for the mutual fund, his buying will drive the shares up in price in the short term. Before he buys for the fund, he buys for his own account and is positioned to benefit as the stock rises when he buys for the fund. Front-running has been a concern in the brokerage community for years. However, it is only recently that front-running became an issue in the mutual-fund industry.

Another way a fund manager could personally benefit at the expense of fund holders is by accepting money or favors from stock promoters or corporations themselves to purchase or hold a stock in the fund. For example, it's not unusual for fund managers to also be directors of small companies. Through the course of exploring companies, many fund managers become familiar with corporate management. In many cases, the fund managers-directors receive stock options in the companies as payment for being a director.

By itself, a fund manager who is also a director of a corporation doesn't necessarily imply a conflict of interest. However, what if the fund manager-director buys the company's stock for the fund, knowing the transaction will drive the price up and make his stock options more valuable? May he be less likely to sell the shares from the portfolio while he's on the board? Wouldn't his selling potentially hurt the value of the stock and, therefore, the value of his stock options? And what about insider-trading issues? As a director of the company, the fund manager might be privy to insider knowledge. What if it's bad news? Does he hold the company's stock in the portfolio or sell and break insider-trading rules?

It's also not unusual for fund managers to get a piece of private placements for their own accounts. Private placements of stock often occur before a firm goes public. While there is nothing inherently wrong with a fund manager owning private placement stock, the opportunity for unethical trading develops once the shares go public. At that point, the fund manager knows that, if he or she buys the stock in large quantities for the fund, it will likely increase the value of the shares he or she purchased during the earlier private placement.

Initial public offerings (IPO) are another area in which potential abuses may occur. Say a fund manager wants a piece of a hot IPO for his personal account. It probably won't hurt his chances of getting some of the offering as long as he agrees to buy some shares of another, not-so-attractive IPO for his mutual fund.

Do mutual-fund groups do anything to prevent abuses from occurring? Most mutual funds have compliance and reporting requirements on the books for their fund managers. In addition, the Investment Company Institute, a fund industry group, has proposed a variety of guidelines for fund managers to follow. How well fund families monitor and enforce these trading restrictions is another story. One can't help but wonder just how vigorously a fund family, especially a small one in which one fund manager oversees most of the fund family's assets, would enforce trading restrictions broken by its star manager.

- *Cross-trading between funds within the same fund family.* Cross-trading occurs when a money manager shifts securities from one mutual fund to another. Such trades must be reported to fund directors quarterly. In addition, the SEC monitors cross-trading that involves illiquid securities to ensure that swaps between funds are made at reasonable prices. When would cross-trading abuse occur? Say your fund manager also invests money for institutional investors outside the fund. The fund manager might have an incentive to shift poor-performing investments from favored institutional accounts to the fund, leaving fund holders holding the bag.

- *Soft dollars.* *Soft dollars* is the practice whereby fund managers run certain trades through brokerage firms in return for certain freebies or premiums. Many brokerage firms provide a variety of computerized research tools for fund managers if they throw enough commissions to the broker. I suppose one could argue that research tools obtained via "soft-dollar" deals improve the fund manager's ability to pick winners. However, are the soft-dollar "gifts" coming from a brokerage firm whose commission rates may be higher than someone else's? Also, what's stopping the fund manager from personally benefiting from the soft-dollar arrangement by using the premium for his or her own purposes?

From an NLS Perspective.   *With no-load stocks, you never have to worry in whose best interests the "manager" is acting.*

Myth 15: I Can Track the Value of My Mutual Fund Daily in the Newspaper

Given the popularity of mutual funds, most newspapers carry daily net asset values of the funds, but these reported values may be a far cry from the true value of the fund. One reason is that a mutual fund that holds relatively illiquid securities must estimate the value of these securities for net asset value computations. What if the fund's estimates are too high? The value in the newspaper may overstate the fund's true value.

Another problem with daily fund quotes is that there are limited checks and balances to catch most inaccuracies. During one day in 1994, fund giant Fidelity Investments admitted that it had knowingly reported day-old numbers for about 150 funds. *The Wall Street Journal* has reported that some 30 or 40 funds a day confess to the National Association of Securities Dealers (NASD) that they sent in wrong share prices the prior day. An additional 20 or 25 funds simply don't transmit any price at all.

Much of the problem is that, because of the huge number of funds and the growing difficulty of pricing diverse fund investments on a daily basis, mutual-fund companies are finding it difficult to meet the NASD's pricing deadline each day. And the problem is likely to get worse before it gets better because of the continued growth in the number of mutual funds and the increasing complexity of fund investments.

From an NLS Perspective. *Stocks don't suffer from the pricing problems found with mutual funds. Therefore, it's easier for no-load stock investors to track the true value of their holdings on a daily basis.*

Conclusion

This chapter discusses what I believe are common misconceptions about mutual funds versus individual stocks, especially no-load stocks. Do I believe that all mutual-fund managers are guilty of trading for their own accounts at the expense of their fund holders? Of course not. Nor do I believe that all fund directors are spineless. Nor that all mutual-fund families care only about asset accumulation at the expense of performance. Nor that all fund managers use certain brokerage firms because they provide the neatest computer toys. Nevertheless, history shows that abuses go where the money is, and there's plenty of money in mutual funds—more than $2 trillion by last count. Compounding the possibility of abuse is the fact that the regulatory cops who oversee mutual funds are stretched incredibly thin.

Do mutual funds have a place in a portfolio? Certainly. Mutual funds provide excellent ways to gain representation in foreign markets, for example. Funds are also good choices for diversifying fixed-income investments, such as bonds and government securities. However, to assume that no-load mutual funds are the only game in town is to overlook the many positive benefits of individual stock ownership, especially ownership of no-load stocks.

4

Why More No-Load Stocks Are on the Way

An axiom of business is that if demand for a product exists, supply will follow. What the customer wants, the customer eventually gets—if not from one vendor, then from someone else.

This relationship between demand and supply applies to financial products as well. If investors show an interest in new issues, the supply of new issues swells. When investors indicate their interest in tax-exempt and mortgage-backed securities, markets in these instruments explode with offerings. And when investors showed they wanted mutual funds, they got mutual funds—over 5,000 of them and still counting.

So what's with no-load stocks? Why, when it seems that demand for these investments is huge, hasn't supply followed?

No-load stocks are a different breed of financial instruments. Strong demand for the product isn't enough. Indeed, for no-load stocks to exist, different constituencies—investors, issuers, transfer agents, regulators, and, to some extent, brokers—all with different agendas must have a meeting of the minds. Building consensus when five distinct factions exist is no easy task, which is why there are only about 50 no-load stocks rather than 500.

Fortunately, several developments that will cause the number of no-load stocks to jump dramatically in the months and years ahead are under way.

This chapter examines the changing dynamics between investors, issuers, regulators, transfer agents, and brokers and how these changes are positively impacting the growth of no-load stocks.

Demand Side: Individual Investors

One thing is clear—individual investors like no-load stocks. The evidence is overwhelming:

- In the first month of Exxon's no-load stock program, the firm took 50,000 phone calls and opened 25,000 new accounts. In the program's first year, Exxon opened 187,000 new accounts.

- DQE, which is the holding company for Duquesne Light, opened more than 4,000 new accounts in the first year of its no-load stock program. More significantly, 70 percent of those individuals requesting information and an application sent in money.

- Philadelphia Suburban, a relatively small water company, added 3,400 new shareholders in 1992 through its no-load stock program. What's especially impressive about this statistic is that it represents more than one-third of the total shareholder base. The substantial growth in the shareholder base was achieved despite the fact that the firm's no-load stock program was open only to water utility customers.

- Procter & Gamble discontinued its no-load stock program in 1993. It wasn't from a lack of interest, however. Indeed, more than 120,000 investors participated in the program. The participation was so great that it became too much for Procter & Gamble to handle.

- Atmos Energy is another company that eliminated its no-load stock program because of too much, rather than too little, participation. The company, a natural-gas utility, stated that the no-load stock program "exceeded all expectations." The problem was that the firm was raising too much equity capital through the program. Utilities that raise too much equity run the risk of having their rates of return trimmed by regulators. Thus, the firm decided to suspend its no-load stock program.

- In a Harris poll commissioned by the National Association of Investors Corporation, 77 percent of individual investors said that they would be "very or somewhat interested" in buying stocks through programs that would allow them to buy stocks directly from corporations.

- One final piece of evidence indicating investors' attraction to no-load stocks is the success of my first book on direct-purchase plans, *Buying Stocks Without A Broker* (McGraw-Hill). There are over 150,000 copies in print since the book was published at the end of 1991, and demand remains strong.

Clearly, investor demand is not an issue with no-load stocks. Investors, particularly small investors, like no-load stocks and support no-load stock programs when available.

Supply Side: Corporate Issuers

Corporations hold the key to the supply side, for only corporations can decide to implement no-load stock programs.

What potential benefits can a corporation reap from offering a no-load stock? And what are the costs?

Raising Equity Capital

One of the biggest benefits a no-load stock program provides is a source of cheap equity capital. Firms raise capital in a variety of ways, e.g., bank loans, bond offerings, and stock offerings. When a company issues new debt or equity, the usual practice is to hire an investment bank to underwrite the offering. The investment bank establishes a syndicate of other investment banks and brokerage houses to help sell the securities to investors. For their work, investment banks receive a cut of the proceeds, usually 3 percent but sometimes up to 7 percent of the deal. For an offering of $50 million, that means the investment bankers' take could be as much as $3 million.

The beauty of a no-load stock program is that the company can bypass the investment banker and go directly to investors to sell stock. Companies have the option of either issuing new shares in their no-load stock program or going into the open market to purchase shares for participants. When firms buy shares on the open market, no new equity capital is created; the firm merely acts as a broker in buying shares for investors. The money that is sent to the company to purchase stock is not kept by the company but instead is used to purchase shares on the open market. When a firm chooses to issue new shares via a no-load stock program, the money sent to the company goes directly into its coffers. This capital can be used to buy equipment, reduce debt, make acquisitions, or fund research. Selling stock in this fashion is attractive to a company because equity can be raised much more cheaply via a no-load stock program than it can via an investment banker.

Philadelphia Suburban offers a good example of a firm's ability to raise funds cheaply through a no-load stock program. Philadelphia Suburban started its no-load stock program for water customers because it needed money for acquisitions and to reduce debt. In 1992 alone, the firm raised more than $24 million through its customer stock purchase plan. The firm estimated its costs to raise these funds at well under 1 percent of the total amount raised—much lower than if the firm had gone through an investment banker.

An indication that no-load stocks are effective tools for raising equity is the large number of electric, water, and natural gas utilities that offer such programs. Utilities are heavy users of capital in order to operate their businesses. The fact that so many have implemented no-load stock programs indicates the attractiveness of these plans as capital-raising vehicles. The Edison Electric Institute, an electric utility industry group, estimates that from 1982 through 1991, utility customer stock purchase plans (no-load stock programs offered to utility customers) raised more than $533 million.

Following is a listing, grouped by shareholder eligibility, of the various utilities that offer no-load stock programs:

Utilities whose no-load stock programs are open to all investors:
Atlantic Energy

DQE

Houston Industries

SCANA

Utilities whose no-load stock programs are available to residents in several states:
Central Vermont Public Service (available to investors in over 20 states)

Central & South West (available to residents in Arkansas, Louisiana, Oklahoma, and Texas)

Duke Power (available to residents in North Carolina and South Carolina)

Northern States Power (available to residents of Minnesota, Michigan, North Dakota, South Dakota, and Wisconsin)

NUI, Inc. (available to residents in Florida, New Jersey, North Carolina, and Pennsylvania)

Utilities whose no-load stock programs are available to residents of the state in which the company operates:
Central Maine Power

Florida Progress

Hawaiian Electric Industries

Puget Sound Power & Light (Washington)

Wicor (Wisconsin)

Utilities whose no-load stock programs are available to their utility customers:
American Water Works

Carolina Power & Light

Cascade Natural Gas

Centerior Energy (Ohio)

Central Hudson Gas & Electric

Connecticut Energy

Dominion Resources (Virginia)

Idaho Power

Interstate Power

Minnesota Power & Light

Montana Power

National Fuel Gas Co.

Nevada Power

New Jersey Resources

Oklahoma Gas & Electric

Philadelphia Suburban

Pinnacle West Capital

San Diego Gas & Electric

Southwest Gas

Union Electric

United Water Resources

Western Resources

Wisconsin Energy

For further information about these firms, see their reviews in Chapter 5.

Mitigates Negative Effects of Stock Issuance

Another attraction of raising equity through no-load stocks is that the negative price effects associated with secondary stock offerings appear to be mitigated.

Studies show that a company's stock price experiences an abnormal negative response to the announcement of new equity offerings. Academics attribute part of this negative response to the existence of what is called *asymmetric* information. When one party with specific information is attempting to transact with another party, to whom that information is not available, the concept of asymmetric information arises. When a company decides to issue new stock in a secondary offering, investors believe that the company has private information and is inclined to overprice the equity offering. Perhaps investors believe that the firm is taking advantage of an overvalued stock or is raising money because its financial situation needs help. Whatever the case, investors, because they are not privy to the information being held by the corporation, may believe the company is issuing stock based on its own best interests, which may cause investors to react negatively to the offering.

On the other hand, in a no-load stock program, stock is raised continuously, not in big chunks as is the case in secondary offerings. Since the company is not choosing a specific time to issue stock but is instead offering stock on a continuous basis, the issue of asymmetric information—in effect, investors' concerns over the company's motives for offering stock—is mitigated. Anecdotal evidence seems to bear out the notion that raising money via no-load stock programs does not have a detrimental effect on the company's stock price. Admittedly, more study needs to be done concerning no-load stocks and the impact of dilution and other negatives associated with stock offerings, but early indications are favorable.

No-Load Programs Save Capital

Not only are no-load stock programs effective for raising capital, but they're also good at saving capital. Most investors who participate in no-load stock programs also join the company's dividend reinvestment plan. In dividend reinvestment plans, participants have the company reinvest dividends to buy additional shares of stock. This means that instead of sending dividends to the shareholder, the dividends are kept by the company. These retained dividends are significant over time and can help to fund operations. The magnitude of dividends that are reinvested in just electric utilities is staggering. Indeed, the Edison Electric Institute estimates that from 1982 to 1991, more than $20 billion in dividends were reinvested in electric utilities.

Changing Capital-Raising Conditions Favor No-Load Stock Programs

With interest rates extremely low and the stock and bond markets doing well over the last decade, raising capital has been pretty easy for most of corporate America. This relative ease and low cost of raising money via conventional avenues is one reason more companies have not looked seriously at no-load stock programs as equity-raising tools. However, the environment is clearly changing. As I write, long-term bond rates have skyrocketed in recent months to well over 7.5 percent, and short-term rates have jumped as well. The bond market has been hit hard by the rise in rates, and stocks have not fared well either. In a climate of rising rates and weak financial markets, certain companies will find it much more difficult to raise capital at all, let alone in a cost-effective manner. In this type of environment, the appeal of no-load stock programs as capital-raising vehicles increases dramatically. That's why I believe that the ability of no-load stock programs to raise equity easily and cheaply—and without negatively affecting the stock price—will be one of the major drivers in the growth of these programs over the next decade.

Cementing Relationships

Another benefit corporations obtain by offering no-load stock programs is to cement relationships with shareholders. Being able to raise equity capital cheaply is not the only reason that the list of no-load stocks is flooded with utility issues. Utility executives understand that, in a regulated industry, it's crucial to have allies among your customers. That's why many utilities offer no-load stock programs to their utility customers. By turning a rate payer into a shareholder, the utility is hopefully turning a potential enemy into an ally, which may come into play when the firm seeks a rate hike.

Utilities also realize that they're in the service business. Service to utility customers takes many forms, e.g., making sure your lights stay on, responding promptly to your phone call concerning a leaky gas furnace, and even making it easy and convenient for interested customers to buy the utility's stock.

Utilities also have another reason for building goodwill with customers via no-load stock programs. As many of you are aware, the days of utilities being monopolies are numbered. The "C" word—competition—is coming to the industry. Already, California regulators have proposed opening the state's electric utility market to competition. Under the proposal, customers could buy electricity from their local utility, other utilities, or independent generators. Industrial customers could tap competitive power markets in January 1996, and all consumers would have such access by 2002. While California is usually at the vanguard of such regulatory changes, rest assured that increased competition will occur in practically every utility market over the next decade or so. In an environment where customers have a choice, it makes sense for utilities to be building allegiances now with customers in order to have a better chance to retain them when competitors enter the market. Making a current customer a shareholder is an interesting way of perhaps locking up a customer for the long term.

Another industry in which increased competition is only a matter time is telephone services. For example, SBC Communications (formerly Southwestern Bell), the regional Bell company, recently requested approval to offer telephone services in the market currently being served by another regional Bell, Bell Atlantic. SBC Communications has an extensive cable network in suburban Washington, DC, and is planning to spend more than $100 million to upgrade the network to deliver local phone service over cable lines. In regional markets where monopoly power is eroding, companies might have a better chance of keeping customers if they can convert customers into shareholders. It's no coincidence that U S West, a regional Bell company, implemented a no-load stock program in early 1994.

Another industry in which regional markets are being invaded by national competitors is banking. With relaxed interstate banking regulations and increased merger activity, regional banks will find it more difficult to keep customers. Converting these customers into shareholders by offering them no-load stock programs increases the banks' chances. That's probably why banks are well represented among the ranks of no-load stocks:

Arrow Financial

Bancorp Hawaii

Barnett Banks

Interchange Financial Services

Regions Financial

Companies realize that they not only must compete for retail customers, but they also must compete for retail investors. An executive of a natural gas company told me that his interest in direct-purchase programs increases every time he sees a competitor offer a no-load stock program. His point was why would an investor want to buy his company's stock through a broker and pay a hefty commission if he or she could buy a competitor's stock directly from the company and pay no brokerage fees. This need to compete for retail investors is one reason the current number of no-load stocks is concentrated in relatively few industries—oil, utilities, and banks. Indeed, among the oils, Exxon sees Texaco offering a no-load stock program and offers one of its own; Kerr-McGee sees Exxon's and Texaco's programs and launches its own; Mobil sees Kerr-McGee's, Exxon's, and Texaco's programs and starts its own no-load stock plan. As more companies from other industries offer no-load programs—and firms within those industries feel increased pressure to compete for retail investors—the number of no-load stock programs could explode.

Improving the corporate image with investors may be another reason to offer a no-load stock program. The evidence is overwhelming that small investors like no-load stock programs. A company that may be suffering from an image problem with investors—perhaps the firm has had a scandal related to executive improprieties or environmental issues—might offer a no-load stock program to repair its image with investors. Exxon started its no-load stock program in March 1992. It's probably no coincidence that the program came just a few years after the Exxon Valdez incident. Part of Exxon's motivation may have been to help improve its standing with small investors who were among the most vocal detractors of the company. Judging from the number of investors who jumped on the no-load stock program, Exxon's strategy seems to have worked.

Marketing and Competitive Advantage

No-load stocks can be effective marketing tools for companies. In the utility field, I've already discussed how a no-load stock program might be one way of securing long-term customer loyalty. Certainly in competitive markets, especially in consumer products, a company that turns a consumer into a shareholder has a better chance of having the shareholder buy the firm's products next time he or she goes to the store. **Dial**, the maker of *Dial* soap, *Lunch Bucket* microwaveable meals, and other consumer products, understands that every individual who becomes a Dial shareholder via its no-load stock program represents a potential customer of its soap and food products. **Exxon** realizes that the 187,000 new accounts opened in the first year of its no-load stock program represent 187,000 people more predisposed to buying Exxon gasoline and products rather than the competitors'. These 187,000 people also represent a targeted market for the company's credit card.

American Recreation Centers exemplifies a firm using a no-load stock program as a way to compete more effectively. The California-based company operates bowling alleys, primarily in Texas and California. The firm also has a majority stake in Right Start, a direct-mail marketer of high-quality products for infants and children. American Recreation understands the synergy between shareholder and consumer as well as anyone. Not only does the firm allow any investor to buy initial shares directly (minimum initial investment is only $100), but the company goes one step further. Those of you who've read my book, *Free Lunch on Wall Street* (McGraw-Hill, 1993), are familiar with American Recreation's shareholder perk program. Shareholders of 500 shares or more are entitled to five free games of bowling per day—10 if the individual is in a league—at any of the firm's bowling centers. Holders of fewer than 500 shares also receive free games. American Recreation Centers also gives shareholders a 20 percent discount on products in the company's Right Start children's catalog. Making it easy for a person to become a shareholder and then a customer is an excellent way for American Recreation Centers to build goodwill and increase customers in its bowling and catalog operations.

Shareholder Marketing Programs

A study conducted by Capital Analytics Inc. for Automatic Data Processing provides further insight into the potential benefits of shareholder marketing programs. The survey, conducted in March and April of 1993, was based on mail and telephone interviews with 111 investor relations officers and product and brand managers at major firms. Here are some of the more relevant findings of the survey:

- Companies that market to their shareholders as a distinct affinity group are in the minority. One in five of the firms interviewed has a shareholder marketing program. However, a substantial number of firms not running shareholder marketing programs say they are considering them.

- Awareness of shareholder marketing programs is limited. Only one in three companies said it knew of other firms running shareholder marketing programs.

- Companies that have shareholder marketing programs usually have a focus on retail markets, brand-name products, and a greater proportion of individual shareholders. These firms are also more likely to encourage participation in direct-stock purchase programs.

- Financial firms market to shareholders more actively than any other single industry group.

- Two-thirds of all respondents, irrespective of whether they run shareholder marketing programs, said individual shareholders are a high-priority constituency or have become more important to them over the last five years.

- Most shareholder marketing programs concentrate on providing shareholders with product information. Others offer price rebates, product samples, and customer privileges.

- The majority of shareholder marketing programs are implemented as adjuncts to standard shareholder communications rather than stand-alone marketing programs.

- Firms that run shareholder marketing programs largely consider them to be successful. Most also believe the programs are cost-effective, with unit costs the same or less than those on standard sales.

- Most companies that have considered shareholder marketing programs and rejected them did so because they seemed impractical.

Perhaps the most significant point to come out of the survey was that companies offering shareholder marketing programs felt they were successful in moving product at the same or lower unit costs than other marketing efforts. That's the type of information that usually wakes up marketing and brand managers and could cause companies to take a second look at using a no-load stock program in tandem with a shareholder marketing program.

Diversify Shareholder Base

A common complaint from corporate America is the myopic investment vision of institutional investors. If a company fails to meet or exceed earnings estimates each and every quarter, look out. An example of the fierce selling that can hit a stock that disappoints institutional investors occurred in April 1994. At that time, Morton International, the maker of airbags, salt, and specialty chemicals, announced a 46 percent increase in per share profits in the March quarter. How did Wall Street reward the company for its stellar performance? Immediately following the news, the stock fell 10 points—shaving almost $500 million from the company's capitalization in a single day. It seems that the strong earnings were still below some expectations.

Individual investors, on the other hand, are more stable and long-term oriented. Some corporations like small investors because they help to stabilize the stock price. For companies that want greater representation of small investors, offering a no-load stock program is an excellent way to draw small investors to its shareholder ranks.

A related benefit is that small investors tend to be more loyal to company management, or at least silent on corporate governance issues. Institutional investors have been rather vociferous in recent years concerning certain corporate matters. Companies that are under siege from institutional shareholders might find more friendly faces by boosting the ranks of small investors via a no-load stock program.

Another reason that certain corporations might want to broaden representation among small investors is to help ward off an unwanted takeover attempt. A large number of small investors make it more difficult to win proxy battles for control in the case of hostile takeovers.

I'm sure there are some readers who think that there's no way that a small contingent of individual investors can take on a hostile suitor with support from institutional investors. Don't tell that to executives of Texaco. The big oil company came under the gun a few years ago when a corporate raider made a run at the company. Texaco's base of individual investors played a critical role in the takeover battle's outcome. This base of small investors helped to level the battle field and was instrumental in Texaco turning back the hostile takeover bid.

Now I'm not saying shareholders were better or worse off because the takeover attempt was put down. The point I'm making is that for corporate executives who believe that their companies are targets of hostile suitors, expanding the number of small investors on the shareholder rolls via no-load stock programs might be the difference between keeping or losing their jobs.

Continuous Buying Support

Another potential benefit of no-load stock and dividend reinvestment programs is that they facilitate continuous buying activity in the company's stock. Of course, just because a company offers a no-load stock program with wide participation doesn't mean that the buying activity in the program will be enough to keep the stock afloat during a bear market. However, there is something to be said for a stock that has a steady level of buying. Such buying should provide some price support to the shares and contribute to more stable price action.

Getting Revenge on Wall Street

The relationship between corporate America and Wall Street is like a thirsty man in a desert who stumbles upon a can of warm Tab; he drinks the Tab in order to survive, but he sure wishes something else—anything else—was available.

Corporations and Wall Street have a classic love-hate relationship. Companies rely on investment banks and other Wall Street institutions to assist them in raising capital, hedging financial risk, and assisting in takeovers and acquisitions. While companies acknowledge their dependence on Wall Street institutions, it doesn't mean they are always happy with the relationship. Indeed, much resentment toward Wall Street exists in corporate America. Corporations, especially those among the hunted, resented the merger and acquisition mania of the 1980s—activity largely driven by Wall Street investment banks. Company CEOs resent having to listen to 20- and 30-year-old Wall Street pretty boys who've never run anything in their lives telling them how to manage their companies or face the possibility of fending off an unwanted suitor. Companies resent first being told by Wall Street bankers that diversifying via acquisitions was a good idea only to hear the same bankers say only a few years later that restructuring, "deconglomeritizing," was the optimal approach. Companies resent having financial derivatives sold to them by Wall Street pinheads in the name of risk management only to see these investments blow up into red ink when interest rates rise. Company executives resent having to manage their firms from quarter to quarter because not meeting Wall Street's quarterly earnings expectations gets the stock creamed.

Companies also resent the way brokerage firms service "street-name" shareholders. All correspondence between companies and individuals who hold shares in "street" name goes through the broker. Quarterly and annual reports, dividend checks, and proxy statements are all disseminated to "street" name accounts via the broker, and brokers charge companies to disseminate this material. The problem is that companies are never sure whether the material ever makes it to street-name accounts. Corporate shareholder services executives have a number of horror stories concerning paying brokers to disseminate quarterly and annual reports or tabulate proxy material only to find out later that the broker overcharged them. One oil executive told me that his firm was charged by a brokerage firm in connection with tabulating proxies. The broker billed on the basis of a 100 percent response by street-name holders to the proxy. However, when the executive reviewed the proxy voting, he saw responses that totaled well below the 100 percent participation for which he was billed. When he balked at paying the bill submitted by the brokerage firm, the broker lowered the bill to reflect the lower participation rate.

For companies seeking revenge on Wall Street institutions, no-load stock programs offer an interesting weapon. With no-load stock programs, companies can raise equity capital without an investment bank while giving small investors the opportunity to buy stock without a broker.

Costs of No-Load Programs

With all of the benefits of no-load stock programs, why aren't more companies offering them? One reason is that no-load stock programs cost money to operate. The ability to invest directly with companies is a big draw for individual investors. The problem is that the company must service these registered investors by preparing and sending them corporate quarterly and annual reports, maintaining their investment records, sending statements and 1099 tax forms, answering phone calls, and providing a host of other service programs to shareholders. To give you an idea of the magnitude of these costs, health-care giant Johnson & Johnson reported that merely by shrinking 18 pages from its 1993 annual report and mailing it third class, the firm saved $400,000.

Shareholder Communications Corp., a shareholder relations consulting firm, surveyed 115 companies on various issues related to the cost of servicing individual investors. The survey indicated that the average cost to service a registered shareholder is nearly $18 per year. The cost breakdown was as follows:

Account maintenance	$3.74
Dividend distribution	1.90
1099-related costs	0.34
Annual reports (print & mail)	5.99

Quarterly reports (per year)	1.75
Proxy solicitation	1.82
Other	2.30

Total: $17.84 per registered investor

I think it's important to note that one of Shareholder Communications' businesses is to operate odd-lot buyback programs for companies. Thus, it's in Shareholder Communications' best interests to have a survey showing a big cost for servicing investors because this makes their services that help companies to reduce the number of odd-lot holders of their stock more attractive. Still, companies pay a price for having a large contingent of registered investors in their shareholder ranks. For some companies, the potential cost of servicing the increased number of individual investors as a result of a no-load stock program outweighs the potential benefits.

With that said, there are ways to lower the cost of a no-load stock program. First, with the cost of computing power continuing to fall, administering a no-load stock program in-house may not be as expensive as companies think. Furthermore, securities transfer agents, which provide various shareholder record-keeping services for companies, have been aggressively discounting prices in recent years. Therefore, the cost to outsource the administration of a no-load stock program has declined.

Another way companies can defray costs is by charging investors fees to participate in no-load stock programs. A company that wants a no-load stock program but is afraid of the costs could charge a modest per transaction fee, perhaps $5. This fee would still be well below the cost of buying stock through a broker. An alternative approach would be to set up a fee structure akin to the mutual-fund industry. Each year, investors could be charged what would amount to a yearly "management" fee of, say, $5 or $10 to participate in the plan. Again, this fee would be much lower than annual fees associated with other forms of investing, such as mutual funds.

Admittedly, investors have not been happy with the trend in dividend reinvestment plans toward fees, and I'm sure most of you reading this don't want fees in no-load stocks. However, if charging a small fee is the difference between a company offering or not offering a plan, I think most investors would agree that paying a fee for the convenience of dealing directly with the company is still far better than paying the high commissions of a broker.

Another way companies can limit the costs of operating no-load stock programs is by providing certain filters to ensure that only committed investors participate. One filter is to keep the minimum initial investment low enough for small investors but high enough to keep out investors who buy only a couple of shares but then never expand their position. Three of the oil issues in the no-load stock group—**Exxon**, **Mobil**, and **Texaco**—require a minimum initial investment of $250; **U S West**, one of the "baby Bells," requires $300. These amounts seem adequately high to discourage "tire kickers" while low enough to permit most small investors to participate. Companies that want a still higher minimum could follow the lead of **Kerr-McGee**, which requires $750 to enroll in the program.

Finally, companies concerned that they'll be stuck with a large number of very small holders who have no intention of increasing their equity holdings could reserve the right to close out accounts where holdings are below some cutoff point—perhaps 5 or 10 shares—or where accounts have been dormant for more than one or two years. In this way, the firm won't be stuck with the cost of servicing very small accounts indefinitely.

Regulatory Hurdles

Overcoming regulatory hurdles is another reason companies are gun-shy about implementing no-load stock programs. Historically, getting a no-load stock program through the regulatory process has been time-consuming. Tom Ross, who runs shareholder relations for DQE, told me it took approximately eight months to get his company's program approved—and that was one of the quicker approval processes. Fortunately, there have been some key developments recently that should speed and simplify the regulatory process dramatically. More on the SEC and its role in the growth of no-load stock programs is discussed later in this chapter.

Other Factors to Consider

A company must consider a number of other factors before implementing a no-load stock program:

- *Does the company need the equity capital?* One of the biggest benefits of a program is to raise equity capital. However, not every company needs additional equity capital. True, a firm can have a no-load stock program that does not issue new shares. **Exxon**, for example, does not raise new equity with its no-load stock program. Rather, the company goes into the open market to buy shares for participants. A firm that does not want to raise money could still have a no-load stock program. Still, a company that doesn't need the capital has one less reason to offer a program.

- *Is the company worried that a no-load stock program would erode a control position in the voting stock?* Let's say that 55 percent of a company's voting stock is controlled by a single person or voting block. The controlling shareholders might not want to implement a no-load stock program since their controlling interest could be endangered because of dilution from the issuance of new shares in the program.

- *Can the company exploit the shareholder-consumer relationship?* A consumer products company, such as **Dial**, has an incentive to expand the number of shareholders via a no-load stock program because shareholders represent potential consumers of the company's products. A maker of heavy construction equipment does not. That's why the list of no-load stocks is dominated by utilities and consumer-related companies.

- *What are my competitors doing?* If my competitor offers a no-load stock program, I might have to offer one in order to compete effectively for retail investors.

- *What value do I place on my relationship with Wall Street?* I've had companies tell me that they are reluctant to start no-load stock programs because they are concerned about jeopardizing the relationship with their current investment banker. This might be a consideration for some companies, especially those that raise large amounts of money via secondary offerings and could not duplicate such large-scale capital raising via a no-load stock program.

Cost-Benefit Analysis

When it's all said and done, a company will offer a no-load stock program only if the benefits outweigh the costs. For many companies, the programs don't make sense. But keep in mind that there are over 10,000 publicly traded companies in the United States. If only 5 percent of those firms initiate no-load stock programs, that's 500 no-load programs. Companies that are naturals to start no-load stock programs because of their businesses and capital needs are highlighted at the end of this chapter.

Facilitators: Securities Transfer Agents

Securities transfer agents are another key player in the emergence of no-load stock programs. Transfer agents are hired by corporations to handle bookkeeping activities for securities transactions, including dividend reinvestment plans, stock transfers, and other shareholder record-keeping operations. In short, transfer agents make their money servicing a company's registered shareholders.

The securities transfer industry has consolidated over the last decade as a number of firms have sold their transfer operations. Big players are First Chicago Trust of New York, Harris Trust & Savings, American Stock

Transfer, Bank of New York, Bank of Boston, Chemical-Mellon Shareholder Services, First Interstate Bank, Norwest Bank, Society National Bank, and Boatmen's Trust.

The securities transfer business is facing a variety of challenges. First, the business is fairly labor and data processing intensive. Second, clients tend to have limited loyalty and can be extremely price sensitive. Indeed, a survey of corporations done by *SmartMoney* magazine showed that some firms changed transfer agents three times in a single year. Third, with computing power growing increasingly cheap and software costs declining, many firms have opted to handle transfer operations in-house, which provides further pressure on transfer agents.

The upshot is that the securities transfer business is a tough way to make a buck. Competition is keen, profit margins are narrow, and the ability for a corporation to do transfer work in-house is increasing.

Shortened Trade Settlement Period

And as if things weren't tough enough, the SEC has added to the transfer agent's woes with its mandate of a "T+3" settlement period. Beginning in June 1995, security transactions must be settled three days after the trade date. The current settlement period is T+5—trades are settled within five days after the trade date. The reason that the SEC wants to shorten the settlement time is that, in a nutshell, time is risk in the financial markets. Here's a simple example: Let's say you want to buy 1,000 shares of XYZ Corp. at $30 per share. You phone your broker, who executes your trade—1,000 shares of XYZ Corp. for $30. At this point, you haven't actually paid for the shares (there may be some cases when a broker will require prepayment; however, for established customers, payment occurs after the trade is completed). Now, you have five days to pay the broker $30,000 plus commissions. On the second day after the trade is made, XYZ Corp. reports bad earnings and the stock drops eight points. You've just lost $8,000. But you still haven't sent your check to the broker. At this point, you decide to "walk away" from the trade. In other words, you stiff your broker. Now the broker is holding 1,000 shares of XYZ Corp. with an $8,000 loss.

Admittedly, while brokers are concerned about individual investors stiffing them, a bigger worry is institutional investors who might leave brokers holding the bag on losses of, not $8,000, but $800,000 or $8 million. An even bigger concern is financial institutions that, perhaps because of a market crash, become insolvent and can't meet their settlement obligations. That's why many market watchers believe that the T+3 mandate is just a stopgap measure on the way to a T+1 settlement period.

You might be wondering what T+3 has to do with securities transfer agents and no-load stocks. The fact is that, as mentioned, transfer agents make their living by servicing registered stockholders. A T+3 settlement period, for reasons I'll soon discuss, could reduce the number of registered shareholders dramatically. Therefore, it's in the best interest of transfer agents to promote no-load programs and other direct-purchase programs because these programs increase the number of registered shareholders. It's probably not an overstatement to say that while individual investors want no-load stocks, transfer agents *need* them.

Higher Fees for Investors under T+3

As discussed in Chapter 1, when investors buy stock, the shares are registered either in "street" name—the name of the brokerage firm—or in their own name. Investors who register shares in their own name go directly onto the company's books as a shareholder of record. Transfer agents are usually paid by companies on a per registered shareholder basis. The more registered shareholders on a company's books, the more money the transfer agent charges for its services. Securities transfer agents like no-load stock programs because an investor must have the stock registered in his or her name to enroll in these programs. Conversely, securities transfer agents don't like anything that increases the probability that investors will hold stock in "street" name.

T+3 is providing plenty of fodder for brokerage firms to push "street" name ownership, and that has transfer agents nervous. The more investors who hold shares in street name, the fewer registered shareholders there are on a company's books, and transfer agents need registered shareholders in order to survive.

The brokerage industry has big bucks to advertise why "street" name ownership is the only way to go in order to ensure on-time settlement. Already, individual brokerage firms, as well as the industry trade group, the Securities Industry Association (SIA), have been advertising the merits of "street" name ownership. But what if an individual wants to be a registered shareholder? More than likely, he or she will pay dearly for the privilege. Some brokers already charge investors $15 or more to have stock registered in the investor's name and to mail the certificates.

Investor Registration Option

Securities transfer agents, seeing the possibility of having their market of registered investors decimated by T+3 and an aggressive advertising program by brokers pushing "street" name ownership, have come up with a plan of their own—Investor Registration Option (IRO).

IRO is a statement-based form of ownership for all registered investors. The major change is that, under IRO, certificates are not issued automatically to registered shareholders, as they are today. Rather, under IRO, when an individual investor purchases shares and requests to be registered directly, the shares are registered in book-entry form on the books of the company and held in custody by the issuer. Once the shares are registered in book-entry form, a statement is produced by the issuer and sent to the investor. Physical certificates are always available to the investor upon request.

Investor Registration Option offers many advantages for individual investors:

- Investors have total portability of shares under IRO. Thus, an investor may sell stock through whichever broker he or she prefers.
- Registered investors would not have the cost and risk of holding certificates but still have the ability to have physical certificates issued to them if they desire.
- Since shareholders are on the books of the company, quarterly and annual reports as well as dividend checks would be sent directly from the company to shareholders.

From an investor standpoint, IRO may not seem like much of a change. The only difference is that, instead of receiving stock certificates when becoming a registered shareholder, investors would receive a statement showing ownership of a certain number of shares. However, from the standpoint of securities transfer agents, IRO is significant because it provides investors with an extremely competitive alternative to "street" name ownership that can accommodate a T+3 standard.

IRO may be great for transfer agents, but what does it have to do with no-load stocks? It's true that no-load stock programs exist already without IRO, and growth of these programs will continue whether or not IRO is approved by the SEC. Still, because a major aspect of IRO is the ability for investors to buy and sell stock directly through corporations, transfer agents are confident that if IRO becomes a reality, no-load stock programs would proliferate.

"Model" No-Load Programs

One potentially encouraging development on the regulatory front is the expected approval of First Chicago Trust Co. of New York's "model" no-load stock program (it's quite possible that the program has already been approved by the time you read these pages). First Chicago Trust requested approval from the SEC for a no-load stock program that could be used by First Chicago Trust's corporate customers.

At this point, it is important to make the distinction between issuer no-load stock plans—plans that are brought by individual companies to the SEC for approval and are specific only to those firms—and no-load stock programs offered by transfer agents to their clients. At the time of this writing, the only no-load stock programs in existence are issuer programs. Because there is no true standard or "model" no-load stock program, any company wishing to implement a program must dance through various regulatory hoops to do so, which slows the approval process dramatically. However, the approval of First Chicago's plan would be significant because it would provide a "model" that could be readily adopted by clients. Say AT&T, which is one of First Chicago Trust Co. of New York's clients, wanted to offer a no-load stock program. The firm could try to get its own program through the SEC, which could take several months, or the firm could adopt First Chicago Trust's program and slide through the regulatory process much more quickly. Also significant is that First Chicago Trust is expected to allow other transfer agents to use its approved plan, which will help these agents offer no-load stock programs to their clients.

Approval of First Chicago Trust's "model" no-load stock plan would have huge implications for the growth of no-load stocks. With the regulatory approval process much less onerous, more companies might come forward to offer programs. And should IRO eventually be approved by the SEC, the number of no-load stock programs could grow even more quickly.

Be Aware of Agendas

Keep in mind that securities transfer agents have a self-serving agenda in seeing that IRO and more no-load stock programs come into being. I'm sure that individuals within the securities transfer industry feel that it is important to give small investors an alternative to street-name ownership and an easier and cheaper way to buy stocks—items that are accomplished by IRO and no-load stock programs. But transfer agents also realize that IRO and more no-load stock programs mean more registered shareholders. Indeed, I'm sure transfer agents are looking at no-load stock programs as ways to increase their fee-based services.

But even if transfer agents stand to benefit from no-load stock programs, that still doesn't negate the benefits the programs hold for small investors. Fortunately, with transfer agents helping to promote the programs and with the regulatory process not as onerous once First Chicago

Trust's "model" no-load program has been approved, investors should soon have a greater selection of no-load stocks from which to choose.

The Opposition: Stock Brokers

An interesting player in the emergence of no-load stocks is the brokerage industry. Obviously, the brokerage community is not interested in seeing no-load stock programs become widely available. No-load stock programs, as well as IRO, forward the notion of direct ownership of stock. Brokers want investors to hold shares in street name so the broker, not the investor, has control over the shares.

Protecting Its Turf

The brokerage industry's opposition to the development of no-load stocks and IRO is all about protecting its turf. Brokers clearly felt the impact from direct investing in no-load mutual funds and certainly don't want a repeat of history. The unfortunate thing is that investors who are most likely to take advantage of no-load stock programs—by and large, the small investor—aren't the investors brokerage firms want. If brokers did want small investors, they wouldn't be "feeing" them out of the market with inactive account fees, administrative fees, fees for closing accounts, and fees for having certificates sent out.

But even though brokerage firms don't want small investors, they don't want anyone else, including companies and transfer agents, to service them either. In a letter sent to the Securities & Exchange Commission dated December 16, 1992, Securities Industry Association President Marc Lackritz asked the SEC, in effect, to postpone any action as it relates to IRO:

> The Securities Industry Association ("SIA") is writing you with respect to the submission (actual and/or potential) of what we understand to be no-action letter requests to the Divisions of Market Regulation and Corporate Finance by issuers of various securities in connection with the implementation of a proposed Investor Registration Option ("IRO") Plan and other shareholder products and services . . . The SIA requests the Securities and Exchange Commission postpone any response to such no-action requests and solicit public comment on the proposals.

In response to Mr. Lackritz' letter, Mr. James Volpe, vice president of First Chicago Trust Company of New York and the "father" of IRO, sent a letter, dated February 2, 1993, to the SEC:

IRO supports the notion of "streamlining the use of certificates" in the clearance and settlement process, in an investor-friendly, investor-controlled way. We believe there are significant advantages to the individual investor, the corporate issuer and the U.S. securities markets with IRO.

Since IRO is not yet a reality, it appears that the brokerage community has had the upper hand in its fight against IRO. However, transfer agents tell me they are optimistic that some form of IRO will be approved in 1995. Should that occur, the number of no-load stock programs could grow dramatically.

The Gatekeepers: The SEC and State Regulators

These words come from a March 10, 1994, speech by SEC chairman Arthur Levitt to the Consumer Federation of America.

In the '90s, more than ever before, the people you work so hard to represent—America's consumers—are the same people we work to protect—America's investors. They're the biggest holders—directly and indirectly—of American securities. Not the banks, not the insurance companies, not big businesses—but people.

We must never forget that. Despite all of the exotic financial products and often complex financial regulations, America's markets—and the SEC—are really here to serve the people—the families—individual investors—whether they own 10 shares or 10 million—who fuel economic opportunity from Manhattan to Modesto.

Read that last sentence again. Doesn't it say that the SEC exists to serve the people—"the families"—whether they own 10 shares or 10 million? Later in his speech, Mr. Levitt states that the SEC is taking a good, hard look at its operations, "to see how we can better meet the needs of retail investors."

Unfortunately, actions speak louder than words, and the fact that the SEC has taken so long in approving IRO as well as individual no-load stock programs makes one wonder who the SEC is really protecting.

Who Has Clout?

It's a question of clout. For all of its rhetoric, the SEC is, to some extent, a political institution, one influenced by lobbying groups and big money. Among the major players for and against no-load stocks and IRO, who has a lobby? Investors? Of course not. They're supposed to be represented by the SEC (read Mr. Levitt's words again). Transfer agents? Forget it.

Although associations such as the Securities Transfer Association, Corporate Transfer Agents Association, and various regional groups exist, these industry groups seem to carry limited weight with regulators in a lobbying sense. For one thing, these groups have very little money at their disposal to lobby aggressively. Second, their numbers are small.

So who has the real power? Like anything else in Washington, it's the group with the deepest pockets. In this case, that's the brokerage industry. Little wonder then that brokers have the ability to stall developments in the securities industry that they oppose. And little wonder that brokers, and for that matter the rich and powerful mutual-fund industry, can advertise virtually any product they want, but companies are greatly restricted on how they can promote their no-load stock programs.

Another roadblock is state "blue sky" laws. In order for an investment to be sold to investors in specific states, it must pass each state's "blue sky" laws. Thus, no-load stock programs must not only pass scrutiny by Federal regulators but must get the go-ahead from state regulators as well. Because of blue sky laws and the tighter restrictions some states have relative to others, some no-load stock programs are not available to residents in certain states.

Fortunately, there does seem to be a renewed focus on the small investor on the part of the SEC. The commission's "Market 2000" report, released in early 1994, carried several recommendations that forward the rights of small investors (more on Market 2000 is covered in the Epilogue).

The Next No-Load Stocks?

If more no-load stock programs are on the way, which companies are the most likely to offer new programs? The following firms represent excellent candidates for no-load stock programs.

- *Sprint.* Sprint is currently the third-largest provider of long-distance services. When you're in third place, you have to try harder. One way to quickly expand its potential pool of long-distance users is via a no-load stock program. To be sure, Sprint probably wouldn't achieve the success that Exxon did (187,000 new participants in the first year). However, even a more modest number would be a big plus. Sprint spends big bucks each year to market its long-distance services. If Sprint could add, say, 30,000 new investors via a no-load stock program and convert just 10 percent of those to new long-distance customers, the no-load stock program would quickly pay for itself. Also, turning existing long-distance and local telephone customers into shareholders means that a competitor might have a harder time winning the business. Another reason Sprint makes a good candidate is that it is beefing up its presence as a player in the "information highway." Expanding its local, long-distance, and telecommunications operations requires large amounts of money—money that could be raised via a no-load stock program. Sprint already has a dividend reinvestment plan. But the ability for investors to make their initial purchases directly could have a major impact on expanding the number of participants.

For pretty much the same reasons, **AT&T** and **MCI Communications** could benefit from a no-load stock program. AT&T has the added benefit of being able to market its credit card to participants of a no-load program.

- *SBC Communications.* SBC Communications, formerly Southwestern Bell, is one of the seven regional Bells. In addition to local telephone service, the firm has extensive cable and cellular operations. The regulatory climate is changing dramatically for SBC Communications. Not only will the firm likely compete in the long-distance market in the future, but the company can also expect increased competition in its local telephone markets. A shifting regulatory and competitive environment makes relationships with end users even more important. An increasingly competitive environment requires more money for increased marketing expenses and customer services. A no-load stock program could meet both of these needs by solidifying relationships and enhancing customer relations while raising capital in the process. **U S West**, another regional Bell company, has already implemented a no-load stock program. A similar program by SBC Communications and the other baby Bells would not be a surprise.

- *SCEcorp.* SCEcorp is the parent company of Southern California Edison, one of the country's largest electric utilities. After years of strong results, the firm has had its troubles recently. Mission Energy Group, the company's nonutility unit, had to cancel a project in Mexico that resulted in a write-off. California regulators have been tough as well in setting rates of return. The stock price is down considerably from its highs of years past. Another potential problem for the company is that California regulators have proposed a new plan by which open competition in the utility industry in that state will occur in some form, perhaps as early as 1996. Poor investor image, rising competition in its regional markets, and the need for large amounts of capital to fund its operations are items that could be addressed by offering a no-load stock program. With nearly 11 million people living in its service region, SCE could have a very successful no-load stock program even if it offered it to just residents in its service region. Such a program would not be costly to market—a statement in the customer's monthly utility bill might suffice—and would likely raise large amounts of money.

Another utility in a similar boat is **Orange & Rockland Utilities**. It's likely that within the next decade or so, increased competition will be coming to its markets in the Northeast. Orange & Rockland also has an image problem with investors stemming from a scandal at the company related to misuse of corporate funds by top executives. A no-load stock program, particularly one focused at its customer base, might be a way to repair its image while solidifying ties with consumers who will likely face additional choices for power in the not-too-distant future.

- *Philip Morris Companies.* Talk about a company with an image problem. Saddam Hussein gets better "PR" than Philip Morris Companies. And now for the first time, the firm is feeling heat from institutional shareholders who want the firm to split into separate food and tobacco companies. A no-load stock program would provide a variety of benefits. First, it would be a way to perhaps alter or at least tone down the negative image some small investors have toward the company. Exxon wasn't a crowd favorite after its Exxon Valdez incident, but plenty of small investors apparently changed their minds toward the company by taking advantage of its no-load stock program in 1992. Philip Morris is still a "name" stock and might see similar success with a no-load stock program. Furthermore, since cigarette companies are relegated pretty much to advertising on sunken ships now that other advertising outlets have been closed off, expanding the list of shareholders through a direct-purchase program for first-time buyers would provide a new market that could be reached via direct mail. And this market could be targeted for the company's nontobacco products as well. Finally, with big institutional investors grumbling, it may be time for Philip Morris executives to increase their allies in order to save their jobs. Individual investors tend to side with management: in a Harris poll of individual investors, 78 percent think that top management should have the most influence on corporate decision-making versus just 26 percent who believe institutional investors should have a major influence on the company. Allowing investors to make first-time purchases directly would be a way to put more small investors onto the shareholder ranks in order to build support for management's decisions.

  Another company with an image problem, dissatisfied institutional shareholders, and a strong presence with the consumer is **Kmart**. A no-load stock program—perhaps one supplemented by various shareholder perks in the form of discounts on products at the stores—makes sense for this laggard retailer.

- *H&R Block.* Block is the largest provider of tax services in the country. The firm's CompuServe unit is a major provider of on-line computer services with over two million subscribers. A no-load stock program would provide Block with several benefits. First, given its strong consumer presence, bringing in more shareholders who potentially could use the firm's tax and on-line services is a plus. What may be even more beneficial is how a no-load stock program and CompuServe might be combined to promote an on-line stock market down the road. I'll get into this subject in more depth in the Epilogue, but suffice it to say that Block has the perfect vehicle for not only getting the word out about a no-load stock program but also effecting transactions. Wouldn't it be convenient to purchase H&R Block directly from the company using its own CompuServe on-line service? Wouldn't it be great to be able to purchase other stocks that way? Isn't Block in an interesting position to prosper from such a service given that it's already touching two million people? Doesn't its international customer base provide some interesting possibilities as it relates to a global on-line stock market? A no-load stock program could be the first step in the development of a national and, indeed, global on-line stock market that could be used by individuals buying from one another and directly from companies both in the United States and around the world.

- *Lands' End.* A no-load stock program for Lands' End would be an excellent way for the company to build its mailing list. Catalog sellers, such as Lands' End, know the value of a name and would be able to exploit the marketing possibilities afforded by a no-load stock program. Other catalog and direct-mail companies that are in a similar position are **CML Group** and **Spiegel**.

- *Ben & Jerry's Homemade.* Ben & Jerry's has a different agenda than a lot of companies. Sure, the company wants to be profitable. But its community involvement and social agendas give it an interesting angle on which to exploit a no-load stock program. Of course, no-load stock participants would be natural targets for marketing and couponing efforts for the company's ice cream. But a no-load stock program would perhaps bring on more supporters of the firm's social agenda. Ben & Jerry's is no stranger to no-load stock programs—the first stock offering of the company was directed exclusively at residents of Vermont. Now that the company has grown nationally in scope, perhaps a no-load stock program available to individuals across the country is in order.

Companies in the competitive consumer products and services markets are good candidates for no-load stock programs because every new participant represents a potential lifetime customer. **PepsiCo** and **McDonald's** would make great no-load stocks, as would firms in the leisure and entertainment markets, such as **Carnival** cruise lines and gambling and hotel concerns **Promus** and **Circus Circus Enterprises**. **American Express** and **Dean Witter, Discover & Co.**, both in the extremely competitive charge and credit card business, could perhaps build their customer bases via no-load stock programs.

- *Cifra.* Mexican stocks, such as Cifra—a leading retailer in Mexico—could benefit from a no-load stock program in several ways. First, such a program would increase visibility in the United States, which is a plus given the North American Free Trade Agreement (NAFTA) and increased cross-border trading. Furthermore, as consumer income and spending levels increase in Mexico, Cifra and other Mexican companies will have to expand to meet the growing demand. Funds raised through a no-load stock program would come in quite handy.

- *First Chicago.* Banks always need money, and First Chicago would certainly generate funds via a direct-purchase program for first-time buyers. As the parent company of First Chicago Trust Co. of New York, the largest transfer agent, First Chicago has another reason to implement a no-load stock program. Having its own no-load program may make it easier to convince transfer clients to implement a no-load stock program, thus enhancing the fee potential for First Chicago's transfer operations. Ditto for other publicly traded banks with big transfer operations, such as **Mellon, Chemical Banking, Norwest,** and **Bank of Boston.**

Conclusion

The number of no-load stocks has grown sharply in the last two years. But that growth should be nothing compared to what could occur over the next three to five years. The rising cost of capital, an increasingly competitive marketplace, regulatory developments, and the SEC approvals of "model" no-load stock programs should fuel an increasing number of programs.

What's particularly exciting is that as no-load stock programs become more widespread, variations and extensions of these programs, encompassing different financial instruments and different ways to buy and sell investments, should develop. The Epilogue examines the possibilities of applying the concepts of no-load stocks to bonds, convertibles, preferreds, tax-exempts, and other investments.

5

Directory
of No-Load Stocks

This book has introduced a new and exciting investment opportunity—no-load stocks. The book has examined the birth of no-load stocks, investment strategies using no-load stocks, the pros and cons of no-load stocks versus mutual funds, and the reasons more no-load stocks are on the way. While I hope you found the information interesting and useful, you and I know that the main reason you bought the book is because you want to know what no-load stocks are available and which ones make the best investments. This chapter answers both of those questions.

About the Directory

Each no-load stock review is divided into seven sections:

- Company and Stock Information
- Performance Rating
- Performance History
- Plan Specifics
- Corporate Profile
- Statistical History
- Investment Advice

Company Information

This section is self-explanatory. Each listing features the stock exchange on which the issue trades (NYSE: New York Stock Exchange; ASE: American Stock Exchange; NASDAQ: Nasdaq National Market) and the stock symbol. Also, some listings have two phone numbers—the number of the corporation and the number of the firm's transfer agent who administers the plan. Obviously, if an "800" number is given, try that number first to request information and an enrollment packet.

Performance Rating

A performance rating has been assigned to every no-load stock. The highest rating is four stars (* * * *) with the lowest rating being one star (*). The ratings are based on a variety of criteria. Financial strength was one of the major determinants. A firm with solid finances has the ability to weather ups and downs in the economy and business cycle. Because no-load investing is investing for the long term, strong finances provide the necessary staying power.

Earnings and dividend records also affected the performance rating. A company with steadily rising profits and dividends usually is a company with a steadily rising stock price over time.

The stability and growth prospects of the company's industry were taken into account. I prefer companies in growth industries, and the ratings reflect this bias.

I realize that many of you may be novice investors, perhaps embarking on your first entrée into the stock market. I tried to take that into account when assigning ratings. Thus, if I err in a rating, my guess is that it will be on the conservative side. Indeed, I gave mostly two- and three-star ratings and very few four-star ratings.

Performance History

This section will probably be the most closely read—and the most misinterpreted. The performance histories, which are given for every stock on which data were available, show what a $1,000 investment at the end of 1983 would have become 10 years later. The returns include reinvested dividends. (I'd like to thank Standard & Poor's for the use of its total return data.)

For comparison purposes, the Standard & Poor 500 was up roughly 302 percent during the time period. Interestingly, over half of all no-load stocks outperformed the S&P 500 during the 10-year period.

Now, before all of you go out and buy a no-load stock that posted huge gains over the last decade, it's important to remember that past performance is no guarantee of future results. As already discussed in these pages, the best performers one year are not necessarily the best performers the next. Investors should also remember that many no-load stocks are utilities, and utilities had an especially strong run from the end of 1983 to the end of 1993. It's unlikely that utilities as a group will repeat this performance.

Finally, the returns of stocks in general were extremely atypical during the 10-year period. Such strong market returns are not likely to be duplicated in the next 10 years, which will have a dampening effect on most individual stock's performance.

I guess what I'm trying to say is that, while I think performance histories provide important information, they should not be used for divining the future nor relied on exclusively for stock selection.

Plan Specifics

The plan specifics provide in detail various features of the company's no-load stock and dividend reinvestment plan (DRIP). Remember that once you enroll in the no-load stock program you can take advantage of the various features of the company's dividend reinvestment plan, such as optional cash payments (OCP) and automatic investment services.

One feature to which readers should pay special attention is the eligibility requirement for each plan. In some cases, companies may place certain restrictions on who can participate in the no-load stock program. These restrictions, if any, are addressed in the plan specifics section. *Please read eligibility requirements carefully.*

Keep in mind that, even if you don't qualify for a firm's no-load stock program, you can still enroll in its dividend reinvestment plan once you have become a shareholder of record. For example, **Duke Power** is a four-star electric utility. Unfortunately, only residents of the states of North and South Carolina may make initial purchases directly. However, any other investor who acquires one share of stock and has the share registered in his or her name—not street name—is eligible to join the company's dividend reinvestment plan and make optional cash payments. If you see a company that interests you but you don't qualify to buy your initial shares directly, contact the company to see how many shares you need to own in order to join the DRIP (in most cases it will be just one share). Below are explanations of some common no-load stock and DRIP features:

- Some plans permit partial dividend reinvestment. This option allows participants to receive dividends on part of the shares held in the plan while reinvesting dividends on the remainder.
- *Optional cash payments* (OCP) are the voluntary payments that participants may make directly into the plans in order to purchase additional shares. For example, **Exxon** allows OCPs of a minimum of $50 to a maximum of $100,000 per year. Each listing indicates how frequently OCPs are invested by the company.
- In most cases, companies charge no fees for purchases made in the plans, although most charge a nominal fee when selling shares from the plans. Fees are addressed in the plan specifics.
- A few no-load stocks have IRA options in their plans. This option allows participants to make investments directly with the company, and

these investments are put into an IRA that is administered by the company. If a firm offers an IRA option, it will be listed in the plan specifics.

- Automatic investment services are becoming a popular feature of no-load stock and DRIP programs. These services provide a mechanism for investors to make optional cash payments automatically by having money taken each month from a checking or savings account. If a company offers automatic investment services, it will be listed in the plan specifics.

- A few no-load stocks provide a little something extra for investors by buying stock at a discount to the market price. This discount is usually applied only to shares purchased with reinvested dividends, but a few no-load stocks apply the discount to optional cash payments as well as reinvested dividends. Companies with discounts are earmarked in the plan specifics.

- If a company has an outside agent administering its plan, the agent's name and phone number are given.

- Dividend-payment dates are listed in plan specifics. One reason this information is valuable is that, by buying certain stocks, you can receive a dividend check every month. For example, **American Recreation Centers** pays dividends in the months of January, April, July, and October. **American Water Works** pays dividends in February, May, August, and November. **Exxon** pays dividends in March, June, September, and December. By owning these three stocks and choosing to receive dividends instead of reinvesting them, an investor would receive a dividend check every month of the year.

Corporate Profile

This section provides a snapshot of the company's business and operating environments.

Statistical History

It is often difficult to make intelligent investment decisions without examining the numbers. This section highlights what I believe are some important financial numbers.

The first table of this section gives the stock's trading history for the last five years. The stock prices are the high and low trading prices for each year.

The second table displays a variety of financial information for the last five years. **Revenues** are a company's total receipts for the year. **Net income**, also known as profits, shows how much money the firm has made. **Earnings per share** is net income divided by the number of outstanding shares. **Book value**, loosely speaking, is the theoretical value of a share of common stock if the company were liquidated. **Dividends** are what a company pays, usually once every three months, to shareholders who own the stock. For example, in 1993, **Exxon** paid dividends of $2.88

per share for the year. If you held 100 shares of Exxon for the entire year, you would have had $288 in dividends reinvested in additional common shares (or received $288 in dividends had you not enrolled in the DRIP). **Net profit margin** is found by dividing net income by revenues. This figure shows the percentage of profits squeezed out of every dollar of revenues. **Debt/Capital** is a ratio of a company's long-term debt to its total capital (long-term debt plus shareholders' equity). This figure gives some idea about the company's debt level. **Return on equity** is found by dividing net income by average shareholders' equity. This figure shows the amount of money that is being earned on shareholders' investment.

Investors should always look at financial data as part of a continuum. Trends are more important than absolute numbers. Ask yourself the following questions: Are revenues, earnings per share, book value, and dividends rising on an annual basis? More importantly, are they growing at accelerating rates? Has the company's debt level been rising? Debt ratios will be higher in some industries than others. However, rising debt ratios, especially if the firm is starting from a high level already, are a red flag. Are dividends per share higher than earnings per share? Since dividends are paid ultimately out of profits, a firm that persists in paying out more in dividends than it is earning in profits will eventually have to cut or eliminate the dividend. Finally, are net profit margins and return on equity shrinking? Companies whose costs are out of control or which are being hurt by increased competition and price wars usually have declining profit margins and return on equity.

Whenever possible, I used company quarterly and annual reports as my sources for financial information. When such information was not available or inadequate, I used research information prepared by *Value Line Investment Survey* and Standard & Poor's. Also, in instances when information was not meaningful, e.g., when a company reported a loss for a year and therefore had no net profit margin or return on equity, an "NM" was used.

Investment Advice

This section gives my specific opinion and advice on the stock. Am I always going to be right? Of course not. But at least I'm objective.

An Important Reminder

I said this at the beginning of the book, but it bears repeating. Companies frequently change features of their no-load stock and dividend reinvestment plans. Fortunately, all companies offering no-load stock and DRIP plans must prepare a prospectus explaining all of the details of the program. Always request a copy of a plan prospectus—and make sure you *read it* when you get it—before investing.

American Recreation Centers, Inc.
NASDAQ: AMRC
11171 Sun Center Dr., Suite 120
Rancho Cordova, CA 95670
916-852-8005

Performance Rating: * *

Performance History ─────────────────────────────

- $1,000 invested on 12/31/83 was worth $1,413 on 12/31/93—a 41 percent increase in 10 years.

Plan Specifics ─────────────────────────────

- Initial purchase is available to investors in all 50 states ($100 minimum initial investment).
- Partial dividend reinvestment is not available.
- No discount.
- OCP: $25 to $5,000 per month.
- OCP is invested monthly.
- There are no purchasing fees. Selling fees include brokerage commissions and other expenses.
- Plan administrator: First Interstate Bank 800-522-6645
- Dividends are paid January, April, July, and October.

Corporate Profile ─────────────────────────────

American Recreation Centers operates bowling alleys, predominantly in California and Texas. The firm also has alleys in Kentucky, Missouri, and Oklahoma. In addition to its bowling business, American Recreation holds a majority ownership stake in The Right Start, Inc., a leading direct marketer of high-quality products and clothing for infants and children. The firm mails some 10 million catalogs per year and has retail outlets as well.

American Recreation Centers has been expanding its operations over the last few years to the Midwest and South. The expansion has helped to lessen the dependence on California and take advantage of stronger economies in other areas of the country. The firm has made substantial investments in modernizing and improving bowling centers during the past five years. All of the company's alleys are equipped with computerized, automatic scoring equipment.

Profits have been rather erratic over the years. After peaking at $0.60 per share in fiscal 1992, per share profits were $0.38 in fiscal 1993 and 1994. Fortunately, expansion and strength from its Right Start business should help earnings growth improve over the next several years. Dividends have been raised annually for a quarter of a century, and improved profitability should help to keep this record intact.

The performance of ARC stock has been rather uneventful over the last decade. The stock has been mired in a trading range between $5 and $10 during most of the last ten years. It will likely take several quarters of sustained earnings improvement before Wall Street provides strong support to these shares.

Statistical History

Price range	1993	1992	1991	1990	1989
High	$7¾	8¼	9¼	7⅝	7½
Low	5½	5½	4¾	5¾	7

	1993	1992	1991	1990	1989
Revenues (mil)	$81.1	65.3	57.0	47.1	38.4
Net income (mil)	1.8	3.0	2.5	1.5	0.8
Earnings per share	0.38	0.60	0.52	0.31	0.17
Book value	5.56	5.36	4.82	4.68	4.52
Dividends	0.20	0.18	0.16	0.14	0.13
Net profit margin	2.3%	4.6	4.5	3.2	2.1
Debt/capital	42.4	40.1	43.6	42.4	38.5
Return on equity	6.9	11.9	10.9	6.7	3.8

Investment Advice

American Recreation Centers, at roughly $100 million in annual sales, is one of the smaller no-load stocks and certainly one of the more aggressive issues in the group. The stock's inability to sustain advances is a negative. However, the firm's bowling business should capitalize on an aging population and the increased emphasis on more leisure activities. Its Right Start business offers another growth avenue. I can't give the company more than two stars because of its spotty track record. However, this could be a surprise performer over the next three to five years. Enhancing appeal is the company's shareholder perk program, which includes free games at its bowling centers and discounts on purchases made through the Right Start catalog.

American Water Works Company, Inc.
NYSE: AWK
1025 Laurel Oak Rd.
PO Box 1770
Voorhees, NJ 08043
609-346-8200

> **Performance Rating: * * ***

Performance History

- $1,000 invested on 12/31/83 was worth $5,939 on 12/31/93—a 494 percent increase in 10 years.

Plan Specifics

- Initial purchase is available for customers of the utility ($100 minimum initial investment).
- Partial dividend reinvestment is available.
- 5 percent discount on reinvested dividends and optional cash payments.
- OCP: $100 to $5,000 per month.
- OCP is invested monthly.
- There are no purchasing fees. Selling fees include brokerage commission and an administrative fee (minimum $1, maximum $10).
- Plan administrator: First National Bank of Boston 800-442-2001
- There are approximately 25,000 participants enrolled in the plan.
- Dividends are paid February, May, August, and November.

Corporate Profile

American Water Works is the nation's leading water supply business, providing service to six million people in 21 states. The largest revenue contribution states are Pennsylvania (25 percent of 1993 sales), New Jersey (23 percent), Indiana (8 percent), and Illinois (7 percent).

American Water Works has a number of favorable attributes. Its spread across 21 states helps to limit adverse regulatory decisions in any one market. Geographic diversity also helps to lessen extreme weather conditions in any one area. This was especially telling in 1993 when several of the firm's operating areas in Illinois, Missouri, and Iowa were hit with flooding. The firm's finances are solid, which has allowed the company to be active on the acquisition front. In 1993 alone, the company purchased four water utilities, adding 350,000 new users. With the opportunities increasing for private companies to purchase or operate municipal water sources, American Water Works should have no shortage of acquisition opportunities. The modest payout ratio—per share dividends divided by per share earnings—means dividends have ample room to expand. Profits have been uneven through the years, although 1993 was a record year for the firm.

Statistical History

Price range	1993	1992	1991	1990	1989
High	$32¼	28½	26¾	19⅝	21½
Low	24⅝	20⅝	15½	12½	16¾

	1993	1992	1991	1990	1989
Revenues (mil)	$717.5	657.4	636.0	573.0	527.5
Net income (mil)	71.4	64.1	69.9	56.4	47.6
Earnings per share	2.29	2.07	2.27	1.85	1.56
Book value	20.97	19.64	18.47	17.04	16.00
Dividends	1.00	0.92	0.86	0.80	0.74
Net profit margin	9.9%	9.8	11.0	9.8	9.0
Debt/capital	61.0	56.8	58.4	58.4	59.1
Return on equity	11.3	10.9	12.8	11.2	10.0

Investment Advice

American Water Works offers an attractive issue among utilities. Geographic diversification is a plus, as are growth opportunities via acquisitions. Dividend growth should be well above average for utilities. The stock has shown steady gains through the years, and the upward trend in the stock price should continue. These shares are a suitable holding in any portfolio. The 5 percent discount the firm offers on shares purchased with reinvested dividends and optional cash investments is a nice kicker.

≡Arrow Financial Corporation

Arrow Financial Corp.
NASDAQ: AROW
250 Glen St., PO Box 2161
Glens Falls, NY 12801
518-745-1000

Performance Rating: * *

Performance History: Not available. ————————

Plan Specifics ————————————————————

- Initial purchase is available to investors in all 50 states ($300 minimum initial investment).
- Partial dividend reinvestment is not available.
- No discount.
- OCP: $50 to $10,000 per quarter.
- OCP is invested monthly.
- There are no purchasing fees. Selling fees include brokerage commission.
- There are approximately 1,300 participants enrolled in the plan.
- Dividends are paid March, June, September, and December.

Corporate Profile ————————————————————

Arrow Financial is a holding company for the following New York and Vermont banks: Glens Falls National Bank & Trust, Saratoga National Bank & Trust, and Green Mountain Bank. The company has posted erratic results over the years. However, 1993 was a decent year for the firm. Net income was $9.6 million, over 2½ times the amount earned in 1992. Earnings were positively affected by an increase in net interest income, a decrease in the provision for loan losses, and recognition of substantial income tax benefits. Results also benefited from a significant reduction in the cost of troubled assets. Return on equity increased to 21.0 percent, more than double the 10.1 percent return on equity for 1992. At the end of 1993, nonperforming assets totaled $20.1 million, down from $29.7 million in 1992. All three of the banks exceed the "well-capitalized" ratios standards, the highest classification established by regulators.

The stock benefited from the improved operating performance, rising more than 50 percent in 1993. The stock continued to do reasonably well in 1994 in line with the action of many regional banks.

Statistical History

Price range	1993	1992	1991	1990	1989
High	$13¾	8⅛	12	16⅞	18
Low	7⅞	4⅞	4⅛	9⅛	15½

	1993	1992	1991	1990	1989
Net interest income (mil)	$32.3	29.4	30.2	34.8	34.1
Net income (mil)	9.6	3.7	–33.4	7.0	9.4
Earnings per share	1.83	0.72	–6.63	1.38	1.86
Book value	9.45	7.64	6.93	13.71	12.94
Dividends	0.11	None	0.25	0.56	0.55
Debt/capital	9.6%	11.9	16.8	9.5	9.9
Return on equity	21.0	10.1	NM	10.3	15.4

Investment Advice

Arrow has gotten its house in order in recent years. Still, there are other banking stocks among the list of no-load stocks—Regions Financial comes to mind—that I think are superior. To be sure, these shares are not without some appeal, especially as takeover activity heats up in the banking group. Still, investors should not have a large exposure to the stock.

ATLANTIC ENERGY

Atlantic Energy, Inc.
NYSE: ATE
6801 Black Horse Pike
PO Box 1334
Pleasantville, NJ 08232
609-645-4506

Performance Rating: * *

Performance History

- $1,000 invested on 12/31/83 was worth $4,030 on 12/31/93—a 303 percent increase in 10 years.

Plan Specifics

- Initial purchase is available to investors in all 50 states ($250 minimum initial investment).
- Partial dividend reinvestment is not available.
- No discount.
- OCP: up to $100,000 per year.
- OCP is invested monthly.
- Purchasing and selling fees may include brokerage commissions.
- Automatic Investment Services are available.
- There are approximately 22,131 participants enrolled in the plan.
- Dividends are paid January, April, July, and October.

Corporate Profile

Atlantic Energy is the holding company for Atlantic City Electric, which supplies electricity in a 2,700-square mile area in southern New Jersey. Residential customers account for nearly 50 percent of sales, with commercial and industrial users accounting for the remainder. Coal and nuclear energy provide roughly two-thirds of the utility's energy. The firm is co-owner of three nuclear plants. Nonregulated activities include cogeneration projects and real estate.

After showing impressive gains for several years, Atlantic Energy, along with most utility stocks, had rough going for the latter part of 1993 and 1994. Rising interest rates, the prospects for increased competition, stringent regulatory bodies, and concerns over dividend cuts are plaguing utility stocks. Atlantic Energy has felt the sting of competition, especially from cogeneration companies. In an attempt to keep its customers, the firm has been trying to keep rates down by cutting costs. The firm is cutting capital outlays by relying more on purchased power. Refinancing of debt has helped to lower interest expense.

The dividend payout ratio has been increasing, which could limit growth in the dividend.

Statistical History

Price range	1993	1992	1991	1990	1989
High	$25⅜	24⅝	21	19¼	19⅞
Low	20⅜	19½	16	16	16¼

	1993	1992	1991	1990	1989
Revenues (mil)	$865.7	816.8	778.0	716.8	705.0
Net income (mil)	95.3	86.2	85.6	68.9	81.0
Earnings per share	1.80	1.67	1.75	1.51	1.87
Book value	15.62	15.17	14.84	14.36	14.27
Dividends	1.53	1.51	1.49	1.47	1.42
Net profit margin	11.0%	10.6	11.0	9.6	11.5
Debt/capital	44.0	40.0	38.5	43.5	45.8
Return on equity	11.7	11.1	12.1	10.6	13.6

Investment Advice

Utility stocks will come back eventually, and any rebound will be felt in Atlantic Energy stock. Nevertheless, I'm not enamored with the utility's dividend-growth prospects. In fact, a good argument could be made that, should earnings falter, a dividend cut is not out of the question. I think there are better opportunities elsewhere in the utility sector.

Bancorp Hawaii, Inc.

Bancorp Hawaii, Inc.
NYSE: BOH
130 Merchant St.
Honolulu, HI 96813
808-537-8239

Performance Rating: * * *

Performance History

- $1,000 invested on 12/31/83 was worth $5,910 on 12/31/93—a 491 percent increase in 10 years.

Plan Specifics

- Initial purchase is available to residents of the state of Hawaii ($250 minimum initial investment).
- Partial dividend reinvestment is available.
- No discount.
- OCP: $25 to $5,000 per quarter.
- OCP is invested monthly.
- There are no purchasing fees. Selling fees are brokerage commissions, a service fee, and any applicable taxes.
- Plan administrator: Bank of New York 800-524-4458
- There are approximately 4,000 participants enrolled in the plan.
- Dividends are paid March, June, September, and December.

Corporate Profile

Bancorp Hawaii is a bank holding company for Bank of Hawaii, the largest commercial bank in the state. The firm has offices in several South Pacific island areas plus locations in Tokyo, Seoul, Hong Kong, Singapore, and Nassau. Business loans and residential mortgages make up roughly 60 percent of loans.

Bancorp Hawaii has turned in steady gains in the bottom line for more than a decade. The commercial and business growth of Hawaii helped to fuel gains. However, growth has slowed recently. Japan's economic restructuring has had an impact on Hawaii since it was Japanese money to a major extent driving growth in the state. The weak California economic climate did not help matters either. However, indications are that Hawaii's economy is improving, which should help the bottom line. Over the long term, growth in the Pacific Rim has potentially big implications for Bancorp Hawaii given its presence in this market.

Statistical History

Price range	*1993*	*1992*	*1991*	*1990*	*1989*
High	$35⅞	34⅝	31⅞	24⅝	25¼
Low	26⅝	26⅞	18⅞	14	15½

	1993	*1992*	*1991*	*1990*	*1989*
Net interest income (mil)	$473.4	440.7	407.9	350.1	286.3
Net income (mil)	132.6	127.5	112.7	95.7	79.9
Earnings per share	3.09	3.00	2.69	2.45	2.19
Book value	22.00	19.68	17.45	15.38	12.98
Dividends	0.90	0.85	0.78	0.70	0.59
Debt/capital	27.6%	9.2	9.4	15.7	9.0
Return on equity	14.9	16.3	16.5	17.0	17.6

Investment Advice

Bancorp Hawaii has a leadership position in an economy that should do reasonably well going forward. Its operations in the South Pacific are a plus. Rising interest rates will adversely affect these shares, in particular the firm's construction markets. Nevertheless, the company's strong finances, healthy dividend growth, and favorable earnings prospects give these shares above-average total return potential. Although only Hawaii residents may make initial purchases directly, the stock would be a worthwhile holding for any investor.

Barnett Banks, Inc.
NYSE: BBI
Shareholder Services Dept.
PO Box 40789
Jacksonville, FL 32203-0789
904-791-7720

Performance Rating: * * *

Performance History

- $1,000 invested on 12/31/83 was worth $3,324 on 12/31/93—a 232 percent increase in 10 years.

Plan Specifics

- Initial purchase is available to investors in all 50 states ($250 minimum initial investment).
- Partial dividend reinvestment is available.
- No discount.
- OCP: $25 to $10,000 per month.
- OCP is invested twice per month.
- There are no purchasing fees. Selling fees include brokerage commissions.
- Plan administrator: First Chicago Trust 800-446-2617
- IRA option is available.
- Automatic Investment Services are available.
- There are approximately 19,347 participants enrolled in the plan.
- Dividends are paid January, April, July, and October.

Corporate Profile

Barnett Banks is Florida's largest bank holding company. The firm also has outlets in Georgia. The company focuses primarily on retail and small business banking services. Installment and credit card loans and credit lines were roughly one-third of total loans in 1993. Residential mortgages were 36 percent.

Barnett Banks has a number of positive factors affecting earnings. First, the company's location in the Southeast assures above-average population growth. In addition, its active acquisition program should spur growth. Keep in mind that much of the gains in recent years were due to falling interest rates and favorable interest-rate spreads. As rates rise and the firm's cost of money rises as well, margins could narrow. The firm is attempting to beef up its fee-based business. Barnett Banks will likely see increased competition in its markets because of the region's attractive growth opportunities and reduced restrictions on interstate banking. It's quite possible that the company could be acquired by a larger bank seeking quick access to these markets, although these shares have merit regardless of any takeover developments.

Statistical History

Price range	1993	1992	1991	1990	1989
High	$50⅜	43⅜	36⅜	37¼	40
Low	37⅜	31	15½	14⅛	32¼

	1993	1992	1991	1990	1989
Net interest income (bil)	$1.7	1.7	1.6	1.5	1.4
Net income (mil)	421.0	207.7	81.4	55.5	296.1
Earnings per share	4.10	1.97	0.80	0.65	3.46
Book value	28.34	25.40	24.19	24.16	24.69
Dividends	1.41	1.32	1.32	1.29	1.16
Debt/capital	19.2%	21.5	23.5	20.3	15.7
Return on equity	15.5	8.5	3.8	2.7	14.8

Investment Advice

Barnett Banks offers a worthwhile holding among banking stocks. Its location is a plus and should spur further growth. The firm's no-load stock program is especially attractive because of its various enhancements, such as an IRA option, twice monthly purchases with optional cash payments, and automatic investment services. Banking stocks may not show the gains that they've enjoyed in recent years, especially if interest rates rise. Still, for representation in the financial services sector, the stock is an acceptable investment.

Carolina Power & Light Co.
NYSE: CPL
411 Fayetteville St.
Raleigh, NC 27601-1748
919-546-6111

Performance Rating: * * *

Performance History

- $1,000 invested on 12/31/83 was worth $5,396 on 12/31/93—a 440 percent increase in 10 years.

Plan Specifics

- Initial purchase is available to utility customers living in North Carolina and South Carolina ($20 minimum initial investment).
- Partial dividend reinvestment is available.
- No discount.
- OCP: $20 to $2,000 per month.
- OCP is invested monthly.
- Purchasing and selling fees include brokerage commissions.
- Plan administrator: Wachovia Bank of NC 800-662-7232
- Automatic Investment Services are available.
- There are approximately 80,000 participants enrolled in the plan.
- Dividends are paid February, May, August, and November.

Corporate Profile

Carolina Power & Light provides electric power to more than one million customers in central, eastern, and western North Carolina and central South Carolina. The firm has 16 plants providing a mix of fossil, nuclear, and hydroelectric power. Major industries in the firm's service region include textiles, chemicals, metals, paper, automotive components, and electronic machinery and equipment.

Carolina Power has done a good job lately of retaining key customers. In 1993 the firm reached new long-term power agreements with several major wholesale customers. The company's service region is showing good growth. In fact, North Carolina has led the nation in new facilities and expansions in five of the last six years. *Fortune* magazine has recognized the Raleigh-Durham area of North Carolina as the best place in the United States to conduct business. Profits have been relatively flat in the last few years. However, dividends have managed to move higher. The firm should continue to show dividend increases on the order of 2 to 3 percent.

Statistical History

Price range	1993	1992	1991	1990	1989
High	$34⅝	28¼	27⅛	23¾	24
Low	27	24½	21⅝	19	17½

	1993	1992	1991	1990	1989
Revenues (bil)	$2.9	2.8	2.7	2.6	2.6
Net income (mil)	346.5	379.6	377.0	280.4	376.1
Earnings per share	2.10	2.36	2.27	1.58	2.10
Book value	17.75	17.27	16.52	15.80	15.59
Dividends	1.65	1.59	1.53	1.47	1.43
Net profit margin	12.0%	13.7	14.0	10.7	14.7
Debt/capital	48.2	50.0	50.7	50.2	47.7
Return on equity	13.0	15.4	15.7	12.0	14.6

Investment Advice

Carolina Power & Light has a number of things going for it, such as a strong service region and decent finances. The firm's nuclear exposure—nuclear energy accounts for nearly 30 percent of fuel mix—could scare some investors. However, the stock has reasonable total return potential.

**Cascade Natural Gas
Corporation**

Cascade Natural Gas Corp.
NYSE: CGC
222 Fairview Ave. North
Seattle, WA 98109
206-624-3900

> **Performance Rating: * ***

Performance History

- $1,000 invested on 12/31/83 was worth $5,545 on 12/31/93—a 455 percent increase in 10 years.

Plan Specifics

- Initial purchase is available to residential customers of the company in Washington and Oregon ($250 minimum initial investment).
- Partial dividend reinvestment is available.
- No discount.
- OCP: $50 to $20,000 per year.
- OCP is invested monthly.
- There are no purchasing fees. Participants must go through own broker to sell shares from the plan.
- Plan administrator: Bank of New York 800-524-4458
- Dividends are paid February, May, August, and November.

Corporate Profile

Cascade Natural Gas distributes natural gas in communities in Washington and Oregon. Residential and commercial customers account for one-half of total revenues. Major industries in the company's service region produce pulp, paper, plywood, and industrial chemicals.

Cascade's service region is both a blessing and a curse. On the positive side, its service region is experiencing nice growth. Indeed, the firm added more than 9,000 customers in 1993, a 7.5 percent growth rate. More than half of these new customers converted to natural gas from other energy sources. The firm added over 11,200 furnaces and other space heat appliances and over 6,600 water heaters to its systems in 1993. The downside to rapid growth, however, is the fact that the company must service growth via capacity additions, and that requires money. Capital outlays to fund this type of growth usually result in lower returns in the early years of the spending, which will likely impact earnings in the short term.

Statistical History

Price range	1993	1992	1991	1990	1989
High	$19½	17	16⅞	12⅝	13¾
Low	15½	13⅝	11⅛	10¼	9⅜

	1993	1992	1991	1990	1989
Revenues (mil)	$187.5	152.5	154.3	160.5	173.5
Net income (mil)	8.9	4.8	7.7	8.4	8.5
Earnings per share	1.05	0.64	1.14	1.26	1.29
Book value	10.00	9.09	8.63	8.37	7.96
Dividends	0.94	0.93	0.90	0.87	0.85
Net profit margin	4.7%	3.2	5.0	5.2	4.9
Debt/capital	48.3	49.2	46.6	51.5	52.4
Return on equity	11.0	6.7	13.4	15.4	16.6

Investment Advice

Natural gas utilities have held up a bit better than electric utilities, although natural gas stocks, including Cascade Natural Gas, are off their highs. The region's growth prospects are a long-term plus. Also, clean-burning natural gas has environmental advantages over other fuel sources, which should help profits as well. Still, I'm neutral on these shares going forward. Investors should not expect a duplication of the strong returns posted over the last decade.

Centerior Energy Corp.
NYSE: CX
PO Box 94661
Cleveland, OH 44101-4661
800-433-7794

> **Performance Rating: ***

Performance History

- $1,000 invested on 12/31/83 was worth $1,520 on 12/31/93—a 52 percent increase in 10 years.

Plan Specifics

- Initial purchase is available to customers of Cleveland Electric Illuminating and Toledo Edison ($10 minimum initial investment).
- Partial dividend reinvestment is available.
- No discount.
- OCP: $10 to $40,000 per year.
- OCP is invested monthly.
- Purchasing and selling fees include brokerage commissions and a service charge.
- IRA option is available.
- There are approximately 65,000 participants enrolled in the plan.
- Dividends are paid February, May, August, and November.

Corporate Profile

Centerior Energy was formed in 1986 upon the affiliation of the Cleveland Electric Illuminating Company and Toledo Edison. Centerior is one of the largest electric utility systems in the country. The firm serves 2.6 million people in a combined service area of 4,200 square miles. Commercial and industrial customers account for roughly 60 percent of revenues. Fuel sources are coal (67 percent) and nuclear (33 percent).

Centerior Energy has been a beleaguered utility in recent years. Earnings have been erratic, and the firm trimmed its dividend in 1994. A problem for the company is that its rates are among the highest in the region. These high rates, coupled with a large base of commercial and industrial users, put the firm in a poor position to compete against new players in its markets. The company is attempting to improve its cost position. The work force was reduced by 19 percent in 1993, largely through early retirement. The staff reduction should help the cost picture going forward.

Statistical History

Price range	1993	1992	1991	1990	1989
High	$20	20	19⅞	21⅛	20⅞
Low	12	15¾	15	16⅛	13⅜

	1993	1992	1991	1990	1989
Revenues (bil)	$2.5	2.4	2.6	2.4	2.3
Net income (mil)	−943.0	212.0	237.0	264.0	267.0
Earnings per share	−6.51	1.50	1.71	1.90	1.90
Book value	12.14	20.22	20.37	20.30	19.99
Dividends	1.60	1.60	1.60	1.60	1.60
Net profit margin	NM	8.7	9.3	11.2	11.6
Debt/capital	61.2%	50.6	51.5	51.8	50.2
Return on equity	NM	7.4	8.4	9.4	9.6

Investment Advice

Even when utilities were going strong, Centerior Energy lagged. With its high rates, the firm will find it difficult to compete in the utility markets of the future. The poor dividend record is yet another negative. The stock has some speculative appeal as a turnaround situation, especially if utilities improve in general. However, for most investors, the opportunities are better elsewhere.

Central and South West Corporation

Central & South West Corp.
NYSE: CSR
PO Box 660164
Dallas, TX 75266-0164
800-527-5797

Performance Rating: * * *

Performance History ───────────────────

- $1,000 invested on 12/31/83 was worth $5,882 on 12/31/93—a 488 percent increase in 10 years.

Plan Specifics ───────────────────

- Initial purchase is available to residents of the states of Arkansas, Louisiana, Oklahoma, and Texas ($100 minimum initial investment).
- Partial dividend reinvestment is available.
- No discount.
- OCP: $25 to $100,000 per year.
- OCP is invested semimonthly.
- Purchasing and selling fees may include brokerage commissions and other fees.
- Automatic Investment Services are available.
- There are approximately 34,000 participants enrolled in the plan.
- Dividends are paid February, May, August, and November.

Corporate Profile ───────────────────

Central & South West owns all of the common stock of four electric operating subsidiaries—Central Power & Light, Public Service Company of Oklahoma, Southwestern Electric Power, and West Texas Utilities. These companies provide electric service to more than 4 million people in an area covering 152,000 square miles—the second largest area served by any electric utility in the United States. The fuel mix is primarily natural gas and coal, with the remainder being nuclear. Residential and commercial customers account for roughly 65 percent of revenues. The firm also owns an intrastate natural gas transmission company, a developer of nonutility power projects, and a leasing business.

Central & South West is attempting to boost its operations via the acquisition of El Paso Electric. The deal, if completed, could cause earnings dilution in the near term. However, if the firm can maximize the economies of scale from the deal, the acquisition should be beneficial over the long term. The regulatory climate of Texas has been no picnic in recent years, which provides an element of uncertainty. On the plus side, the company has increased dividends annually for more than 40 years—one of only four companies on the New York Stock Exchange to have such an uninterrupted history of dividend increases.

Statistical History

Price range	1993	1992	1991	1990	1989
High	$34¼	30	27⅛	23	20⅛
Low	28¼	24¼	20¾	18¼	14⅞

	1993	1992	1991	1990	1989
Revenues (bil)	$3.7	3.3	3.0	2.7	2.5
Net income (mil)	327.0	404.0	401.0	386.0	337.0
Earnings per share	1.63	2.03	1.99	1.89	1.63
Book value	15.55	15.54	15.05	14.58	14.06
Dividends	1.62	1.54	1.46	1.38	1.30
Net profit margin	8.9%	12.3	13.2	14.1	13.2
Debt/capital	45.6	44.5	43.8	44.5	45.5
Return on equity	10.6	13.5	13.4	13.2	11.7

Investment Advice

Although I'm not a big fan of Texas utilities, in part because of the regulatory environment, Central & South West offers a reasonable choice in the utility field. Its solid dividend record enhances appeal. Finances are adequate. To be sure, it will be difficult for any utility, including Central & South West, to match its total return performance of the last decade. Still, the stock is a suitable holding for exposure to the utility group.

Central Hudson Gas & Electric Corp.
NYSE: CNH
284 South Ave.
Poughkeepsie, NY 12601-4879
914-452-2000

Performance Rating: * *

Performance History ─────────────────────────

- $1,000 invested on 12/31/83 was worth $3,105 on 12/31/93—a 211 percent increase in 10 years.

Plan Specifics ──────────────────────────

- Initial purchase is available to customers of the utility ($100 minimum initial investment).
- Partial dividend reinvestment is available.
- No discount.
- OCP: $25 to $10,000 per quarter.
- OCP is invested quarterly.
- There are no purchasing fees. Selling fees include brokerage commissions.
- Plan administrator: First Chicago Trust 800-428-9578
- Dividends are paid February, May, August, and November.

Corporate Profile ──────────────────────────

Central Hudson Gas & Electric supplies electricity to more than 250,000 customers in the Hudson River Valley of New York. Electric sales accounted for more than 80 percent of revenues in 1993. Residential and commercial customers accounted for 72 percent of revenues. Coal is the company's largest fuel source. IBM is a major customer, accounting for 14 percent of total electric revenues in 1993.

Central Hudson's exposure to IBM is a negative at this time given the downsizing going on at the computer giant. Economic conditions are improving in its service region, which should help profits to some extent. Finances have been improving over the last five years. Dividend growth has been decent, although future growth will likely be somewhat limited.

Statistical History

Price range	1993	1992	1991	1990	1989
High	$35¾	31¼	29	24⅞	24⅛
Low	28⅜	25⅞	22⅝	20	20⅜

	1993	1992	1991	1990	1989
Revenues (mil)	$517.4	523.6	494.7	503.6	470.0
Net income (mil)	50.4	47.7	42.9	41.0	39.1
Earnings per share	2.68	2.65	2.40	2.38	2.28
Book value	24.65	23.60	22.84	22.31	21.76
Dividends	2.03	1.96	1.88	1.80	1.76
Net profit margin	9.7%	9.1	8.7	8.1	8.3
Debt/capital	44.0	49.0	48.5	49.6	52.7
Return on equity	11.3	10.8	10.6	10.8	10.1

Investment Advice

Central Hudson has come a long way in the last five years. The payout ratio—the dividend divided by 12-month earnings per share—is at a reasonably comfortable level. Utilities could be swimming upstream in the near term, especially if interest rates continue to rise. The stock has some upside potential, but an uncertain regulatory environment limits appeal.

Central Maine Power

Central Maine Power Co.
NYSE: CTP
83 Edison Dr.
Augusta, ME 04336
207-623-3521
800-695-4267

Performance Rating: *

Performance History

- $1,000 invested on 12/31/83 was worth $2,500 on 12/31/93—a 150 percent increase in 10 years.

Plan Specifics

- Initial purchase is available to customers of the company residing in Maine ($25 minimum initial investment).
- Partial dividend reinvestment is available.
- No discount.
- OCP: $10 to $40,000 per year.
- OCP is invested monthly.
- There are no purchasing fees. Selling fees include brokerage commissions and transfer taxes.
- Automatic Investment Services are available.
- Approximately 24,426 shareholders in the plan.
- Dividends are paid January, April, July, and October.

Corporate Profile

Central Maine Power provides electricity in central and southern Maine to about 500,000 customers. Residential users account for roughly 40 percent of total revenues. The fuel mix is approximately 28 percent nuclear, 40 percent cogeneration or small power products, and 30 percent oil and hydro. Major industrial customers have businesses in pulp and paper, chemicals, processed food, and ship building.

Central Maine is a company that has been having problems in recent years. Regulatory decisions have hurt profits. Tough economic conditions in the state limited profits as well. The weak earnings fueled a dividend cut in 1994. The company is taking steps to restore profitability, including better cost controls. However, earnings growth is expected to be limited over the next year at least. Thus, investors shouldn't expect much in the way of dividend increases.

Statistical History

Price range	*1993*	*1992*	*1991*	*1990*	*1989*
High	$24½	23⅞	23	20⅝	20⅜
Low	14⅜	19⅞	16⅝	16⅛	16⅞

	1993	*1992*	*1991*	*1990*	*1989*
Revenues (mil)	$893.6	877.7	866.5	780.8	727.2
Net income (mil)	61.3	63.6	59.1	48.8	48.6
Earnings per share	1.65	1.85	1.82	1.68	1.92
Book value	17.09	16.71	16.32	16.02	16.05
Dividends	1.40	1.56	1.56	1.56	1.53
Net profit margin	6.9%	7.2	6.8	6.2	6.7
Debt/capital	45.4	42.6	47.7	47.7	48.2
Return on equity	9.8	11.3	11.3	10.3	11.8

Investment Advice

The relatively weak performance for Central Maine over the last decade versus the big gains by other utilities reflects the subpar quality of these shares. To be sure, a rebound in utilities in general would probably be felt by these shares. Still, with the likelihood of little or no dividend growth over the next few years and continued regulatory and costs concerns, these shares have below-average prospects.

Central Vermont Public Service Corporation

Central Vermont Public Service Corp.
NYSE: CV
77 Grove St.
Rutland, VT 05701
802-747-5406

Performance Rating: *

Performance History

- $1,000 invested on 12/31/83 was worth $4,217 on 12/31/93—a 322 percent increase in 10 years.

Plan Specifics

- Initial purchase is available to investors in more than 20 states ($50 minimum initial purchase).
- Partial dividend reinvestment is not available.
- No discount.
- OCP: $50 to $2,000 per month.
- OCP is invested monthly.
- There are no purchasing fees. Selling fees include brokerage commissions.
- There are approximately 9,000 participants enrolled in the plan.
- Dividends are paid February, May, August, and November.

Corporate Profile

Central Vermont Public Service supplies electricity to customers in nearly three-quarters of Vermont. Residential and commercial or industrial customers make up nearly 80 percent of total revenues. The paper and food industries account for nearly 27 percent of industrial energy sales. Sources of power are primarily nuclear (38 percent) and hydro (33 percent). The company's Catamount Energy unit invests in nonregulated energy-related projects. Per share profits have been flat over the last five years, and earnings could remain erratic in the near term.

Central Vermont Public Service has been attempting to improve its cost structure. The firm plans to reduce annual costs by $20 million by the end of 1995. Consolidations of several functions as well as reduction in staff will help to lower costs. An improvement in the local economy would be a plus as well.

Finances are not particularly noteworthy, nor is the company's dividend-growth prospects. In fact, dividends may remain flat in the near term.

Statistical History

Price range	1993	1992	1991	1990	1989
High	$25¾	25	22⅞	19⅝	19⅜
Low	20⅛	19½	17	14⅝	14¾

	1993	1992	1991	1990	1989
Revenues (mil)	$279.4	275.4	233.5	231.6	227.4
Net income (mil)	21.3	21.4	18.6	17.5	18.2
Earnings per share	1.64	1.71	1.65	1.62	1.73
Book value	15.03	14.21	14.03	13.68	13.32
Dividends	1.42	1.39	1.39	1.37	1.34
Net profit margin	7.6%	7.8	8.0	7.6	8.0
Debt/capital	37.9	37.8	42.3	46.5	45.0
Return on equity	11.0	11.8	11.8	12.0	13.0

Investment Advice

There's nothing particularly stellar about Central Vermont Public Service to warrant taking positions. Dividend growth prospects are unappealing, and the firm's service region will likely see only limited growth. With most utilities expected to be under pressure, there is no urgency to add this stock to a portfolio when there are other more attractive issues in the group.

Comsat Corp.
NYSE: CQ
6560 Rock Spring Dr.
Bethesda, MD 20817
301-214-3200

Performance Rating: * * *

Performance History

- $1,000 invested on 12/31/83 was worth $2,683 on 12/31/93—a 168 percent increase in 10 years.

Plan Specifics

- Initial purchase is available to investors in all 50 states ($250 minimum initial investment).
- Partial dividend reinvestment is not available.
- No discount.
- OCP: $50 to $10,000 per month.
- OCP is invested monthly.
- There are no purchasing fees. Selling fees include brokerage commissions and a $5 fee for each sale of shares.
- Plan administrator: Bank of New York 800-524-4458
- Dividends are paid March, June, September, and December.

Corporate Profile

Comsat furnishes international communication, information, and entertainment distribution services. It provides voice, video, and data services to customers worldwide by fixed and mobile technologies. The company is a major owner and user of the global INTELSAT and Inmarsat communications satellite networks. The firm offers on-demand entertainment information services to the hospitality industry.

The company also owns the Denver Nuggets of the National Basketball Association.

Comsat offers one of the more interesting no-load stocks. The firm's operations are situated in high-growth markets. However, these markets are also becoming increasingly competitive, which gives the firm's three to five year prospects some uncertainty. Comsat's video operations, which provide on-command video service to hotels, have been growing at a rapid rate and offer one avenue for long-term growth. Earnings have been a bit uneven over the years. Indeed, after showing per share profits of $1.68 in 1989, the firm's bottom line went into the red in 1990. However, results have been relatively strong of late. The company has been expanding its operations via acquisitions, including the 1994 purchase of Radiation Systems, a manufacturer of antenna turnkey systems for various telecommunications markets.

Statistical History

Price range	1993	1992	1991	1990	1989
High	$35¼	24½	19	19¼	20¼
Low	23¾	17⅛	11½	10¼	13

	1993	1992	1991	1990	1989
Revenues (mil)	$640.4	563.6	522.9	456.8	411.5
Net income (mil)	74.0	42.9	71.4	−16.3	62.5
Earnings per share	1.82	1.09	1.88	−0.44	1.68
Book value	16.34	15.80	15.36	14.84	15.93
Dividends	0.74	0.70	0.67	0.66	0.66
Net profit margin	11.6%	7.6	13.7	NM	15.2
Debt/capital	36.5	43.9	39.6	40.2	38.2
Return on equity	11.3	7.1	7.8	NM	10.9

Investment Advice

Comsat could be a big winner for investors over the next decade and beyond. Telecommunications markets are likely to be some of the fastest-growing sectors during that time. The wild card is increased competition and technological obsolescence. Comsat's stock has had a history of volatility, and such will likely be the case going forward. The stock would add some spice to a no-load stock portfolio, but only a limited exposure is suggested.

❥**CONNECTICUT ENERGY CORPORATION**

Connecticut Energy Corp.
NYSE: CNE
PO Box 1540
Bridgeport, CT 06601
203-382-8156

> **Performance Rating: * * ***

Performance History ──────────────────

- $1,000 invested on 12/31/83 was worth $5,933 on 12/31/93—a 493 percent increase in 10 years.

Plan Specifics ──────────────────────

- Initial purchase is available to residential customers of Southern Connecticut Gas Company ($250 minimum initial investment).
- Partial dividend reinvestment is available.
- No discount.
- OCP: $50 to $50,000 per year.
- OCP is invested monthly.
- There are no purchasing fees. Selling fees include brokerage fees and an administrative fee (minimum $1, maximum $5).
- Plan administrator: Bank of Boston 800-442-2001
- IRA option is available.
- Automatic Investment Services are available.
- There are approximately 6,000 participants enrolled in the plan.
- Dividends are paid March, June, September, and December.

Corporate Profile ────────────────────

Connecticut Energy is a holding company engaged in the retail distribution of natural gas through its principal subsidiary, Southern Connecticut Gas. Southern delivers natural gas to over 152,000 customers in 22 Connecticut communities. Residential customers account for nearly two-thirds of total revenues.

Connecticut Energy has done a good job at gaining market share of the local residential market. There is still room for the firm to expand its position in this market, which should help earnings growth going forward. The firm has put together three consecutive years of higher profits, which is rather impressive compared to other utilities. An improving economy in the Northeast is a plus for future results.

Finances are in good shape. The dividend has increased in 14 of the last 15 years. Connecticut Energy, through its predecessor companies, has paid cash dividends on its common stock since 1850, the longest consecutive dividend payment record of any utility or nonfinancial company listed on the New York Stock Exchange.

Statistical History

Price range	1993	1992	1991	1990	1989
High	$26½	24¾	20⅝	18	18⅞
Low	22½	18⅞	14¼	14½	14

	1993	1992	1991	1990	1989
Revenues (mil)	$212.8	203.0	179.2	174.1	171.2
Net income (mil)	11.1	10.2	9.0	6.9	7.8
Earnings per share	1.50	1.43	1.38	1.12	1.28
Book value	13.33	12.80	12.49	11.91	12.14
Dividends	1.28	1.26	1.24	1.23	1.20
Net profit margin	5.2%	5.0	5.0	4.0	4.6
Debt/capital	54.5	50.2	49.4	54.9	51.2
Return on equity	11.5	11.3	11.0	9.3	10.6

Investment Advice

Connecticut Energy offers a suitable holding in a portfolio. The company's dividend record is impressive, and the firm's focus on the residential market is a plus. Of course, should the weakness in utility stocks last, these shares will have trouble mounting much of a sustained upside advance. Still, for the income portion of a portfolio, these shares have merit. Enhancing appeal is the IRA option available in the dividend reinvestment plan.

The Dial Corp

The Dial Corp
NYSE: DL
Dial Tower
Phoenix, AZ 85077-1424
602-207-4000
800-453-2235

Performance Rating: * * *

Performance History

- $1,000 invested on 12/31/83 was worth $2,377 on 12/31/93—a 138 percent increase in 10 years.

Plan Specifics

- Initial purchase is available to investors in all 50 states ($100 minimum initial investment).
- Partial dividend reinvestment is available.
- No discount.
- OCP: $10 to $5,000 per month.
- OCP is invested monthly.
- No fees for buying or selling shares.
- Sells may be made via the telephone.
- Approximately 20 percent of shareholders are in the plan.
- Dividends are paid January, April, July, and October.

Corporate Profile

Dial is a leading consumer products company. Brand names include Purex, Dial, Tone, Renuzit, Brillo, Armour Star, and Lunch Bucket. Other businesses include Dobbs airline catering business, travel and leisure services—the firm operates Premier cruise lines—and convention services. The company is a leader or in second place in the majority of its businesses.

Dial has undergone a major restructuring over the last decade. Gone is the firm's financial services and bus operations. The changes are now allowing the firm to concentrate on its consumer products operations. This business has been showing good results. New products and acquisitions will help profits grow further. The airline catering business was expanded with the purchase of United Airlines' catering business.

Earnings have picked up nicely over the last year, and further gains are expected. While the bulk of restructuring is behind the company, Wall Street still speculates that the Premier cruise business could be sold for the right price. The improved profit outlook should help dividend growth over the next several years.

Statistical History

Price range	1993	1992	1991	1990	1989
High	$44½	50⅝	46⅛	32¼	37¾
Low	35⅞	33⅜	24⅝	19	28¾

	1993	1992	1991	1990	1989
Revenues (bil)	$3.0	2.9	2.8	2.9	2.7
Net income (mil)	110.3	74.3	25.8	75.4	41.0
Earnings per share	2.56	1.74	0.62	1.87	1.02
Book value	11.00	9.29	23.57	25.92	27.47
Dividends	1.12	1.19	1.40	1.36	1.32
Net profit margin	3.7%	2.6	0.9	2.6	1.5
Debt/capital	54.9	61.1	33.5	62.1	59.1
Return on equity	25.6	11.2	2.6	7.2	10.5

Investment Advice

With Dial now being able to focus on its most profitable businesses, look for Wall Street to return to these shares. Consumer products stocks run in and out of favor with Wall Street but have decent long-term prospects. Dial's no-load stock program is especially attractive in that it allows all investors to participate, has a low initial investment minimum ($100), and picks up all costs on the buy and sell sides. Furthermore, shares may be sold over the phone. This stock would fit nicely into any no-load stock portfolio.

Dominion Resources, Inc.
NYSE: D
PO Box 26532
Richmond, VA 23261
800-552-4034

> **Performance Rating: * * ***

Performance History

- $1,000 invested on 12/31/83 was worth $6,016 on 12/31/93—a 502 percent increase in 10 years.

Plan Specifics

- Initial purchase is available to customers of the utility ($20 minimum initial investment).
- Partial dividend reinvestment is available.
- No discount.
- OCP: up to $50,000 per quarter.
- OCP is invested monthly.
- There are no purchasing fees. Selling fees include brokerage commissions and any taxes.
- There are approximately 150,000 participants enrolled in the plan.
- Dividends are paid March, June, September, and December.

Corporate Profile

Dominion Resources is a holding company for Virginia Electric & Power, which provides electric service to parts of Virginia and, to a much lesser extent, North Carolina. The firm also operates Virginia Natural Gas. The region's economy includes government installations and technology companies. The company's nonutility businesses are involved in power projects and residential real-estate development. These operations accounted for nearly 10 percent of 1993 profits. Residential users account for approximately 45 percent of total revenues. Primary fuels are nuclear and coal.

Dominion Resources has been a decent utility through the years. Earnings growth should be reasonable over the next few years. Dividend growth of 2 to 3 percent annually is expected. The company's service region is showing good growth prospects, which is a plus for future profits. Finances are in good shape.

Statistical History

Price range	1993	1992	1991	1990	1989
High	$49½	41	38⅛	32⅝	32
Low	38¼	34⅛	29⅞	27⅞	27

	1993	1992	1991	1990	1989
Revenues (bil)	$4.4	3.8	3.8	3.5	3.7
Net income (mil)	558.7	474.6	511.4	478.5	470.3
Earnings per share	3.12	2.66	2.94	2.75	2.76
Book value	26.38	25.22	24.41	23.41	22.67
Dividends	2.48	2.40	2.31	2.23	2.15
Net profit margin	12.6%	12.5	13.5	13.5	12.7
Debt/capital	47.5	47.0	48.8	50.1	52.0
Return on equity	11.9	10.5	12.4	12.6	12.5

Investment Advice

Dominion Resources would be a worthwhile holding in a portfolio. Dividend growth should at least match the industry average. Finances are strong and should fund customer growth. While the stock will not likely match its impressive performance of the last 10 years, its total returns should be in the upper half of all utilities.

DQE ✱

DQE
NYSE: DQE
PO Box 68
Pittsburgh, PA 15230-0068
800-247-0400

Performance Rating: * * *

Performance History ─────────────────

- $1,000 invested on 12/31/83 was worth $5,537 on 12/31/93—a 454 percent increase in 10 years.

Plan Specifics ─────────────────────

- Initial purchase is available to investors in every state except Florida, Nebraska, North Carolina, North Dakota, Ohio, Oklahoma, and Vermont ($100 minimum initial investment plus a $5 one-time account setup fee). The firm is exploring the possibility of allowing investors from all 50 states to make initial purchases.
- Partial dividend reinvestment is available.
- No discount.
- OCP: $10 to $60,000 per year.
- OCP is invested monthly.
- Purchasing fees are approximately 4 cents per share. Selling fees are approximately 5 cents per share.
- Automatic Investment Services are available.
- Dividends are paid January, April, July, and October.

Corporate Profile ────────────────────

DQE is the holding company whose principal subsidiary is Duquesne Light. Its service territory of approximately 800 square miles in southwestern Pennsylvania has a population of 1.5 million. Nuclear power generates roughly 22 percent of electricity. Coal accounts for the remainder.

DQE has improved sharply over the last decade. Indeed, the mid-1980s were not kind to the company, and the firm was forced to cut its dividend. The decline of the steel industry, a major customer, hurt results. However, the situation has improved to the point where the firm was voted by *Electric Light & Power* magazine in 1992 as the electric utility of the year. Profit performance has been decent recently. Finances are relatively strong and should improve since no new major construction is expected. Consequently, annual dividend growth for the utility should be above average, perhaps in the 3 to 4 percent area.

Statistical History

Price range	*1993*	*1992*	*1991*	*1990*	*1989*
High	$37	32⅜	31	25¼	23⅞
Low	31⅜	26⅞	23⅝	20⅜	17⅜

	1993	*1992*	*1991*	*1990*	*1989*
Revenues (bil)	$1.2	1.2	1.2	1.1	1.1
Net income (mil)	141.0	141.5	133.6	121.7	113.0
Earnings per share	2.67	2.67	2.50	2.24	2.03
Book value	23.11	22.12	21.00	20.07	19.27
Dividends	1.62	1.54	1.46	1.38	1.30
Net profit margin	11.8%	11.9	11.1	10.8	10.1
Debt/capital	51.9	52.0	53.2	54.2	54.5
Return on equity	11.8	12.4	12.2	11.3	10.6

Investment Advice

DQE offers one of the better utilities among no-load stocks with open enrollment. Strong dividend-growth prospects and limited need for external financing point to steady total returns above the industry average. This stock is a suitable selection for a no-load stock portfolio.

Duke Power Co.
NYSE: DUK
Power Building
422 S. Church St.
Charlotte, NC 28242-0001
800-488-3853

> Performance Rating: * * * *

Performance History

- $1,000 invested on 12/31/83 was worth $5,961 on 12/31/93—a 496 percent increase in 10 years.

Plan Specifics

- Initial purchase is available to residents of North Carolina and South Carolina (minimum initial investment $25).
- Partial dividend reinvestment is available.
- No discount.
- OCP: $25 to $20,000 per quarter.
- OCP is invested monthly.
- There are no purchasing fees. Selling fees may include brokerage commissions.
- Automatic Investment Services are available.
- Dividends are paid March, June, September, and December.

Corporate Profile

Duke Power sells electric energy in the central portion of North Carolina and the western portion of South Carolina. The company's service area covers about 20,000 square miles and has an estimated population of roughly 5 million. The firm ranks sixth in the United States among investor-owned electric utilities in kilowatt-hour sales. Residential customers account for roughly one-third of total revenues; commercial and industrial, 52 percent. Power sources are primarily nuclear and coal.

Duke Power has a number of attractions. First, its service area should grow at an above-average rate. Second, the company's rates are on the low side, which puts it in good position to fend off increased competition down the road. Third, finances are solid, with high fixed-charge coverage and moderate debt as a percentage of capital. Strong finances, coupled with steady earnings gains and a relatively low payout ratio, should fuel above-average dividend growth.

Statistical History

Price range	1993	1992	1991	1990	1989
High	$44⅞	37½	35	32⅜	28¼
Low	35⅜	31⅜	26¾	25½	21⅜

	1993	1992	1991	1990	1989
Revenues (bil)	$4.3	4.0	3.8	3.7	3.7
Net income (mil)	626.4	508.1	583.6	538.2	571.6
Earnings per share	2.80	2.21	2.60	2.40	2.56
Book value	21.17	20.26	19.86	18.84	18.05
Dividends	1.84	1.76	1.68	1.60	1.52
Net profit margin	14.6%	12.8	15.3	14.6	15.7
Debt/capital	39.1	40.0	39.7	40.5	39.5
Return on equity	13.6	11.1	13.5	13.1	14.7

Investment Advice

Investors who live in North Carolina and South Carolina should take advantage of the firm's no-load stock program. Strong dividend-growth prospects, an attractive service region, and above-average appreciation prospects relative to the rest of the industry make this issue an excellent holding. Investors who cannot buy their initial shares directly should still consider joining the firm's DRIP after making initial purchases through a broker.

EX**X**ON CORPORATION

Exxon Corp.
NYSE: XON
PO Box 160369
Irving, TX 75016-0369
214-444-1900

Performance Rating: * * * *

Performance History

- $1,000 invested on 12/31/83 was worth $5,591 on 12/31/93—a 459 percent increase in 10 years.

Plan Specifics

- Initial purchase is available to investors in all 50 states ($250 minimum initial investment).
- Partial dividend reinvestment is available.
- No discount.
- OCP: $50 to $100,000 per year.
- OCP is invested weekly.
- There are no purchasing fees. Selling fees include an administrative charge of $5 and applicable brokerage commissions.
- Plan administrator: Bank of Boston 800-252-1800
- IRA option is available.
- Automatic Investment Services are available.
- Dividends are paid March, June, September, and December.

Corporate Profile

Exxon is a leading oil company. Foreign exploration, production, and refining operations account for about two-thirds of total profits. The firm has small operations in chemicals and coal.

Profits have generally trended higher. Future results will be impacted by judgments stemming from the Exxon *Valdez* incident. However, Exxon's financial position is strong enough to absorb setbacks on the litigation front. Exxon's exposure to production and exploration makes the firm sensitive to oil prices. Long term, higher oil prices should help profits. Cost controls should help the bottom line as well.

Statistical History

Price range	1993	1992	1991	1990	1989
High	$69	65½	61⅞	55⅛	51⅜
Low	57¾	53¾	49⅝	44⅞	40½

	1993	1992	1991	1990	1989
Revenues (bil)	$97.8	103.2	102.8	105.5	86.7
Net income (bil)	5.3	4.8	5.6	5.0	3.0
Earnings per share	4.21	3.82	4.45	3.96	2.32
Book value	28.05	27.20	28.12	26.54	24.19
Dividends	2.88	2.83	2.68	2.47	2.30
Net profit margin	5.4%	4.7	5.4	4.7	3.4
Debt/capital	20.0	20.4	19.7	18.9	23.5
Return on equity	15.6	14.0	16.5	15.8	9.6

Investment Advice

Despite the problems related to the *Valdez* incident and the possibility of periodic volatility, Exxon remains one of the top no-load stocks. Its "user-friendly" no-load program, with such options as IRA, weekly investments, and automatic investment services, enhances the appeal of these shares. Among no-load stocks in the oil group, Exxon is the most attractive. I'm a participant in the plan and recommend these shares for most investors.

**FLORIDA
PROGRESS**
CORPORATION

Florida Progress Corp.
NYSE: FPC
PO Box 33028
St. Petersburg, FL 33733-8028
800-352-1121

Performance Rating: * * *

Performance History

- $1,000 invested on 12/31/83 was worth $4,768 on 12/31/93—a 377 percent increase in 10 years.

Plan Specifics

- Initial purchase is available to residents of the state of Florida ($100 minimum initial investment).
- Partial dividend reinvestment is available.
- No discount.
- OCP: $10 to $100,000 per year.
- OCP is invested monthly.
- Fees for purchasing and selling may include brokerage commissions and other fees.
- There are approximately 29,728 participants enrolled in the plan.
- Dividends are paid March, June, September, and December.

Corporate Profile

Florida Progress owns Florida Power, which provides electric service to over 1.2 million customers. The firm also has operations in coal mining, transportation, financial services, and real-estate development. Residential customers account for roughly 47 percent of total revenues. The energy mix is approximately 20 percent oil, 18 percent nuclear, 45 percent coal, and 17 percent purchased and other.

Florida Progress, like most utilities, is trying to get its costs under control. The growth in the firm's service region is above average, which should help profits. Dividends have been raised annually for over 40 consecutive years, and growth in the payout of 2 to 3 percent should continue. Florida has generally been a reasonable regulatory state, which is a plus.

Statistical History

Price range	1993	1992	1991	1990	1989
High	$36⅜	33¼	31½	27	26¾
Low	31¼	27⅞	24½	22¼	22¼

	1993	1992	1991	1990	1989
Revenues (bil)	$2.5	2.1	2.1	2.0	2.1
Net income (mil)	212.6	192.4	191.3	196.6	199.4
Earnings per share	2.26	2.06	2.16	2.33	2.39
Book value	20.40	19.85	19.14	18.37	17.92
Dividends	1.95	1.90	1.84	1.77	1.72
Net profit margin	8.7%	9.2	9.2	9.8	9.4
Debt/capital	48.7	45.9	46.5	44.5	41.2
Return on equity	11.0	10.6	11.6	12.9	13.9

Investment Advice

While Florida Progress is a cut below other utilities, such as Duke Power, it nevertheless has worthwhile total return prospects. The stock was hit hard when utilities sold off, and it could take some time to repair this damage. However, Florida residents who desire to add to the income portion of a portfolio should consider these shares.

HEI
Hawaiian Electric Industries, Inc.

Hawaiian Electric Industries, Inc.
NYSE: HE
PO Box 730
Honolulu, HI 96808-0730
808-532-5841

Performance Rating: * *

Performance History

- $1,000 invested on 12/31/83 was worth $4,243 on 12/31/93—a 324 percent increase in 10 years.

Plan Specifics

- Initial purchase is available to residents of the state of Hawaii ($100 minimum initial investment).
- Partial dividend reinvestment is not available.
- No discount.
- OCP: $25 to $25,000 per quarter.
- OCP is invested monthly.
- There are no purchasing fees. Selling fees include brokerage commissions and a $10 service charge.
- Automatic Investment Services are available.
- Approximately 26,370 shareholders are in the plan.
- Dividends are paid March, June, September, and December.

Corporate Profile

Hawaiian Electric Industries is a public utility holding company providing electric service to nearly all of Hawaii's population. Residential customers account for roughly one-third of revenues. Approximately 10 percent of 1993 revenues were derived from federal government agencies. The primary fuel source is oil. A nonutility subsidiary is American Savings Bank, a major savings and loan based in Hawaii.

Hawaiian Electric Industries had traditionally been a good utility, although performance in the last few years has been sluggish. One factor limiting earnings was the firm's insurance subsidiary, which the company closed in 1992 because of heavy losses caused by Hurricane Iniki. With earnings being weak in recent years, the likelihood of above-average dividend growth has diminished.

Statistical History

Price range	1993	1992	1991	1990	1989
High	$38⅞	44⅝	37⅞	40	40¼
Low	31	34¾	29⅜	27¼	29⅜

	1993	1992	1991	1990	1989
Revenues (bil)	$1.1	1.0	1.1	1.0	0.9
Net income (mil)	68.2	68.4	61.7	50.7	68.7
Earnings per share	2.38	2.54	2.40	2.02	3.06
Book value	23.24	22.12	24.36	23.29	23.18
Dividends	2.29	2.25	2.21	2.17	2.07
Net profit margin	6.0%	6.6	5.7	5.0	7.8
Debt/capital	46.9	46.6	44.6	38.9	38.7
Return on equity	9.9	10.7	9.6	8.6	13.4

Investment Advice

The likelihood of modest dividend growth limits the appeal of these shares. The nonutility unit has been a plus in recent years but also lends some volatility to the earnings stream. Hawaiian Electric has performed well over the last decade, but performance going forward will likely be average at best.

⊞ Houston Industries Incorporated

Houston Industries, Inc.
NYSE: HOU
PO Box 4567
Houston, TX 77210
713-629-3000
800-231-6406

Performance Rating: * *

Performance History ─────────────────────

- $1,000 invested on 12/31/83 was worth $5,507 on 12/31/93—a 451 percent increase in 10 years.

Plan Specifics ──────────────────────────

- Initial purchase ($250 minimum) is available to investors in all 50 states. (Plan is pending.)
- Partial dividend reinvestment is available.
- No discount.
- OCP: $50 to $120,000 per year.
- OCP is invested monthly.
- There are no purchasing fees. Participants must go through own broker to sell shares from the plan.
- Dividends are paid March, June, September, and December.

Corporate Profile ────────────────────────

Houston Industries is a utility holding company with nonutility interests in the cable television field. The firm's Houston Lighting & Power Company is the nation's ninth-largest electric utility in terms of kilowatt-hour sales. The firm provides electric service to a 5,000-square mile area. The company's KBLCOM is the nation's 14th-largest cable television operator. KBLCOM owns a 50 percent interest in Paragon Communications, a cable television partnership. The firm's Houston Industries

Energy, formed in 1993, is involved in foreign utility privatizations and power generation projects. Commercial and industrial users account for more than 50 percent of total revenues. Power requirements are derived primarily from gas and coal. The company also has exposure to nuclear power through its South Texas Project nuclear facilities.

Houston Industries has had some problems with its nuclear exposure. The South Texas Project nuclear facilities were closed for over a year with repairs, which hurt results. The firm faces liability suits stemming from the outage. The cable unit was unprofitable in 1993. It would not be surprising to see the company sell part or all of this unit.

Statistical History

Price range	*1993*	*1992*	*1991*	*1990*	*1989*
High	\$49¾	46⅞	44⅜	37⅛	35⅞
Low	42½	40⅛	34⅝	30⅝	26¾

	1993	*1992*	*1991*	*1990*	*1989*
Revenues (bil)	\$4.3	4.1	3.9	3.7	3.3
Net income (mil)	416.0	341.0	417.0	343.0	413.0
Earnings per share	3.20	2.63	3.24	2.70	3.32
Book value	25.06	25.36	24.96	26.76	29.05
Dividends	3.00	2.98	2.96	2.96	2.96
Net profit margin	9.6%	8.4	10.7	9.3	12.6
Debt/capital	52.8	53.6	55.5	52.3	52.9
Return on equity	12.8	13.4	12.7	3.6	11.7

Investment Advice

Regulatory and legal uncertainties will continue to plague these shares. Dividend growth will likely be small or nonexistent over the next few years. Prior to 1994, these shares had posted good total returns. However, these shares have limited prospects over the next few years.

Idaho Power Co.
NYSE: IDA
PO Box 70
Boise, ID 83707
208-383-2200
800-635-5406

Performance Rating: * *

Performance History

- $1,000 invested on 12/31/83 was worth $3,601 on 12/31/93—a 260 percent increase in 10 years.

Plan Specifics

- Initial purchase is available to residential customers of the company ($10 minimum initial purchase).
- Partial dividend reinvestment is available.
- No discount.
- OCP: $10 to $15,000 per quarter.
- OCP is invested quarterly.
- Purchasing fees may include brokerage commissions.
- Must go through own broker to sell shares.
- There are approximately 14,000 participants enrolled in the plan.
- Dividends are paid February, May, August, and November.

Corporate Profile

Idaho Power, which began operating in 1916, supplies nearly 318,000 customers in a 20,000-square mile area encompassing parts of southern Idaho, eastern Oregon, and northern Nevada. The firm has 17 hydroelectric plants and part ownership in three coal-fired generating plants. The biggest contributors to revenues are commercial and industrial customers, together accounting for roughly 36 percent of total sales.

Idaho is one of the country's fastest-growing states in terms of percentage population growth. Indeed, analysts expect the state's population to grow nearly 50 percent during the next 20 years. Such growth should help boost profits over time, although Idaho Power will have to service this growth, which means additional capacity and external financing. Idaho's exposure to hydroelectricity has been a negative in recent years in that drought conditions hurt its hydroelectric system. The firm may have to increase its dependency on coal-fired power. On the plus side, the company is a low-cost producer, which should help to keep its current customer base as well as provide expansion opportunities.

Statistical History

Price range	1993	1992	1991	1990	1989
High	$33	28¾	28¾	29⅜	30
Low	27¼	24⅜	24¼	22¾	22

	1993	1992	1991	1990	1989
Revenues (mil)	$540.4	498.1	483.2	464.9	496.2
Net income (mil)	84.5	60.0	57.9	69.2	84.7
Earnings per share	2.14	1.55	1.56	1.91	2.37
Book value	17.86	17.28	17.07	17.40	17.35
Dividends	1.86	1.86	1.86	1.86	1.83
Net profit margin	15.6%	12.0	12.0	14.9	17.1
Debt/capital	46.6	48.9	47.8	46.4	45.6
Return on equity	13.1	10.0	9.9	11.7	14.6

Investment Advice

Idaho Power has a few things going for it, such as a fast-growing service region and a position as a low-cost power producer in the Northwest. However, the need for external financing to service its growing region could put a strain on finances. The company already pays out nearly all of its earnings in dividends, so there isn't much room for the dividend to rise. On balance, the stock is unattractive relative to other no-load utility stocks.

Interchange
Financial Services
Corporation

Interchange Financial Services Corp.
ASE: ISB
Park 80 West/Plaza Two
Saddle Brook, NJ 07662
201-703-2265

> **Performance Rating: * ***

Performance History: Not available. ─────────

Plan Specifics ──────────────────────

- Initial purchase is available to investors in all 50 states ($100 minimum initial investment). Investors should note that the company is considering dropping the plan.
- Partial dividend reinvestment is not available.
- No discount.
- OCP: $25 to no maximum (must be in multiples of $10).
- OCP is invested monthly.
- Purchasing and selling fees include brokerage commissions.
- Plan administrator: Continental Stock Transfer & Trust Co. 212-509-4000 Ext. 209
- There are approximately 400 participants enrolled in the plan.
- Dividends are paid January, April, July, and October.

Corporate Profile ─────────────────────

   Interchange Financial Services operates full-service banks in Bergen and Passaic counties of New Jersey. Residential real estate is the firm's biggest source of loans. Profits have picked up nicely in the last few years. The total number of shares outstanding is less than 3 million, with corporate insiders owning more than 20 percent of the stock.

Interchange Financial has risen nicely since bottoming at less than $6 in 1990. The interest-rate spread as a result of falling rates helped profits. However, earnings will likely be impacted by higher interest rates.

Statistical History

Price range	1993	1992	1991	1990	1989
High	$18	15¼	12	12	15½
Low	13	10	6½	5⅝	10¾

	1993	1992	1991	1990	1989
Net interest income (mil)	$19.0	16.9	13.9	12.0	11.4
Net income (mil)	4.8	3.7	2.6	2.1	3.1
Earnings per share	1.80	1.79	1.26	0.99	1.54
Book value	11.47	10.45	8.70	8.07	7.73
Dividends	0.70	0.70	0.70	0.70	0.63
Debt/capital	Nil	Nil	Nil	3.0	6.1
Return on equity	15.6%	16.3	13.3	11.3	17.2

Investment Advice

Interchange has done well over the last few years. However, investors should not expect the banking group to continue to post such strong gains. Interchange's relatively small size makes these shares a logical takeover candidate. While I prefer Regions Financial among no-load regional banks, these shares have reasonable upside potential.

Interstate Power Co.
NYSE: IPW
1000 Main St.
PO Box 769
Dubuque, IA 52004-0769
319-557-2230

> **Performance Rating: * ***

Performance History

- $1,000 invested on 12/31/83 was worth $3,685 on 12/31/93—a 269 percent increase in 10 years.

Plan Specifics

- Initial purchase is available to utility customers (minimum initial investment $50).
- Partial dividend reinvestment is available.
- No discount.
- OCP: $25 to $2,000 per month.
- Company purchases stock once a month with OCPs.
- There are no purchasing fees. Selling fees are approximately 10 cents per share.
- Dividends are paid March, June, September, and December.

Corporate Profile

Interstate Power provides utility services to customers in Iowa, Minnesota, and Illinois. The service area, which covers about 10,000 square miles, is primarily rural, although the firm does have a sizable exposure to industrial and commercial users. Electricity services generate more than 80 percent of total revenues, with natural gas services accounting for the remainder. Coal is the primary fuel source to generate electricity.

Interstate Power has been having problems in recent years. The firm's per share profits did not cover the dividend in 1992 and 1993. Thus, dividend growth has been nonexistent, and further earnings sluggishness could adversely impact the current payout. Without dividend growth, the total return of these shares is apt to be below the industry average.

Statistical History

Price range	1993	1992	1991	1990	1989
High	$34⅛	35¼	34¼	26¾	25¾
Low	29	28⅜	24⅞	22⅞	21¼

	1993	1992	1991	1990	1989
Revenues (mil)	$309.5	285.3	291.8	273.6	275.6
Net income (mil)	19.0	19.2	29.5	27.0	28.6
Earnings per share	1.73	1.74	2.84	2.56	2.73
Book value	20.21	20.47	20.80	20.00	19.43
Dividends	2.08	2.08	2.04	2.00	2.00
Net profit margin	6.1%	6.7	10.1	9.9	10.4
Debt/capital	47.5	46.2	47.1	44.8	46.5
Return on equity	8.5	8.4	13.9	13.1	14.4

Investment Advice

There is nothing particularly noteworthy about Interstate to warrant investment. The current yield is on the high side but reflects the lack of dividend growth expected in these shares. The stock is suited only for more aggressive utility investors.

520 1

Johnson Controls, Inc.
NYSE: JCI
Shareholder Services, X-32
PO Box 591
Milwaukee, WI 53201-0591
414-228-2363

Performance Rating: * * *

Performance History

- $1,000 invested on 12/31/83 was worth $3,070 on 12/31/93—a 207 percent increase in 10 years.

Plan Specifics

- Initial purchase is available to investors in all 50 states ($50 minimum initial investment).
- Partial dividend reinvestment is available.
- No discount.
- OCP: $50 to $15,000 per quarter.
- OCP is invested monthly.
- There are no purchasing fees. Selling fees include brokerage commissions. There is a $5 service charge for termination.
- Approximately 17,000 shareholders are in the plan.
- Plan administrator: Firstar Trust Co. 800-828-1489
- Dividends are paid March, June, September, and December.

Corporate Profile

Johnson Controls has operations in four primary markets. The biggest division in terms of revenues and profits is automotive. This unit manufactures seats and seating components. The controls segment, accounting for one-third of sales and nearly 30 percent of profits, manufactures, installs, and services control systems for nonresidential buildings. These systems control temperature and energy use. The plastics and batteries units comprise the remainder of sales and profits. Plastics operations include the production of plastic soft drink bottles. The battery segment makes lead-acid batteries for the automotive replacement market.

Johnson Controls has put together three years of higher per share profits. The improving economy has helped results. Also, strength in the auto sector boosted profits in recent periods. The stock enjoyed strong gains from 1991 to 1993 before tailing off in 1994. Profits will be impacted by the 1994 loss of the battery business of Sears, Roebuck. Dividends, which have been paid since 1901, have trended higher over the last decade.

Statistical History

Price range	1993	1992	1991	1990	1989
High	$59⅛	46⅛	36⅝	32¼	46¾
Low	43	34⅝	21⅞	17⅛	27⅞

	1993	1992	1991	1990	1989
Revenues (bil)	$6.2	5.2	4.6	4.5	3.7
Net income (mil)	137.9	123.0	95.1	92.4	97.5
Earnings per share	3.16	2.86	2.19	2.13	2.55
Book value	26.54	29.47	26.64	26.12	24.73
Dividends	1.36	1.28	1.24	1.20	1.16
Net profit margin	2.2%	2.4	2.1	2.1	2.6
Debt/capital	31.7	29.6	31.6	31.8	31.3
Return on equity	12.1	10.9	9.1	9.2	10.7

Investment Advice

Johnson Controls is a quality company with strong market positions in its primary markets. The cyclical bent to its business could cause earnings to be erratic on a quarterly basis. Nevertheless, profits should trend higher over the long term, which should aid the stock price. The stock is one of the better no-load stock programs with open enrollment and may be purchased by most investors.

Kellwood Co.
NYSE: KWD
600 Kellwood Parkway
St. Louis County, MO 63017
314-576-3100

Performance Rating: * * *

Performance History

- $1,000 invested on 12/31/83 was worth $5,925 on 12/31/93—a 493 percent increase in 10 years.

Plan Specifics

- Initial purchase is available to investors in all 50 states ($100 minimum initial investment).
- Partial dividend reinvestment is available.
- No discount.
- OCP: $25 to $3,000 per month.
- OCP is invested monthly.
- There are no purchasing fees. Selling fees include brokerage commissions. There is a discontinuation fee of $5.
- Plan administrator: Society National Bank 800-321-1355
- Dividends are paid March, June, September, and December.

Corporate Profile

Kellwood is a leading marketer, merchandiser, and manufacturer of apparel, home fashions, and camping equipment. The company's products are sold in more than 25,000 stores in the United States, Mexico, and Canada. The biggest business is apparel. The firm's products are targeted for the moderately priced category. Sears has traditionally been a big customer, although sales to Sears now account for only 15 percent of total revenues, down from 50 percent in fiscal 1985. Kellwood has grown rapidly through acquisitions, and further moves on this front are expected.

Kellwood has improved its competitive position considerably in recent years, and the bottom line reflects the improvement. The firm's merchandising strategy, which includes focusing on branded products, has been successful in boosting profits and margins. Global sourcing has enabled the firm to keep its manufacturing costs down. The firm has used the consolidations and shakeouts in the retailing industry to expand market share. Dividends, after showing no growth from 1990 to 1993, are moving higher.

Statistical History

Price range	*1993*	*1992*	*1991*	*1990*	*1989*
High	$27⅛	22⅛	17⅞	15¼	23⅝
Low	15⅞	14¼	6¼	3½	13⅝

	1993	*1992*	*1991*	*1990*	*1989*
Revenues (mil)	$1,203.1	1,077.7	914.9	808.0	779.9
Net income (mil)	35.6	28.7	22.8	12.5	14.0
Earnings per share	1.71	1.39	1.26	0.71	0.80
Book value	14.64	13.51	12.66	11.31	11.17
Dividends	0.55	0.53	0.53	0.53	0.53
Net profit margin	3.0%	2.7	2.5	1.5	1.8
Debt/capital	33.3	26.9	29.8	37.5	39.3
Return on equity	12.1	10.6	9.9	6.3	7.2

Investment Advice

Kellwood is carving out a growing niche in the retail apparel sector. Strong earnings momentum should help these shares continue to move higher. Retailers tend to run hot and cold on Wall Street, and investors may have to accept some volatility with these shares. However, the stock ranks as one of the better holdings among no-load stocks.

**KERR-McGEE
CORPORATION**

Kerr-McGee Corp.
NYSE: KMG
PO Box 25861
Kerr-McGee Center
Oklahoma City, OK 73125
405-270-1313

Performance Rating: * * *

Performance History ―――――――――――――――――――――

- $1,000 invested on 12/31/83 was worth $2,046 on 12/31/93—a 105 percent increase in 10 years.

Plan Specifics ――――――――――――――――――――――――

- Initial purchase is available to investors in all 50 states ($750 minimum initial investment).
- Partial dividend reinvestment is not available.
- No discount.
- OCP: $10 to $3,000 per quarter.
- OCP is invested monthly.
- No fees for purchasing or selling shares.
- Plan administrator: Liberty Bank & Trust Co. of Oklahoma City 800-786-2556
- There are approximately 3,500 participants enrolled in the plan.
- Dividends are paid January, April, July, and October.

Corporate Profile ――――――――――――――――――――――――

Kerr-McGee is involved in a variety of natural resources markets. The firm's exploration and production unit conducts oil and natural gas activities in the Gulf of Mexico, Louisiana, Texas, Wyoming, Alberta Canada, and the North Sea. The company operates the nation's third-largest coal mine, located in Wyoming. Most of the coal production is sold to U.S. utilities. Chemical operations include inorganic industrial and specialty chemicals and treated forest products. The firm is attempting to sell or merge its refining operation.

Given the firm's exposure to the natural resources markets, it's not surprising that profits have been volatile over the years. However, earnings should firm due to improved prospects at its oil and gas production and exploration unit and continued demand for the company's low sulfur coal, which is highly desired by utilities as a way to hold down emissions. Dividends, which have been paid since 1941, have been relatively flat in recent years, reflecting the sluggish earnings performance.

Statistical History

Price range	*1993*	*1992*	*1991*	*1990*	*1989*
High	$56	46⅜	46⅞	53⅝	52
Low	41¾	35⅝	35⅛	42⅜	37⅜

	1993	*1992*	*1991*	*1990*	*1989*
Revenues (bil)	$3.3	3.4	3.3	3.7	3.0
Net income (mil)	77.0	–26.0	102.0	113.0	134.0
Earnings per share	1.57	–0.53	2.10	2.26	2.75
Book value	29.24	27.93	31.43	30.70	29.31
Dividends	1.52	1.52	1.50	1.41	1.27
Net profit margin	2.3%	NM	3.1	3.1	4.5
Debt/capital	28.1	37.0	37.9	35.1	36.8
Return on equity	5.4	NM	6.8	7.6	9.2

Investment Advice

Kerr-McGee provides a way to play a variety of natural resources markets. To be sure, the firm's track record is not exactly stellar. Still, restructuring of its business portfolio and better prospects for its production and exploration activities should help these shares post decent returns. The stock is a suitable selection for more aggressive investors.

**MINNESOTA POWER
&
LIGHT COMPANY**

Minnesota Power & Light Co.
NYSE: MPL
30 W. Superior St.
Duluth, MN 55802-2093
218-723-3974
800-535-3056

Performance Rating: * *

Performance History

- $1,000 invested on 12/31/83 was worth $4,780 on 12/31/93—a 378 percent increase in 10 years.

Plan Specifics

- Initial purchase is available to utility customers in Minnesota and Wisconsin ($10 minimum investment).
- Partial dividend reinvestment is available.
- No discount.
- OCP: $10 to $10,000 per quarter.
- OCP is invested monthly.
- There are no purchasing fees. Selling fees include brokerage commissions, taxes, and any other expenses (company will sell up to 25 shares).
- There are approximately 30,000 participants enrolled in the plan.
- Dividends are paid March, June, September, and December.

Corporate Profile

Minnesota Power provides utility and utility-related services in six states. The firm is the second-largest electric utility in Minnesota. More than half of its electricity is sold to large industrial users. Low-sulfur coal is the major power source. The company's Southern States Utilities subsidiary is the largest independent supplier of water and wastewater treatment service in Florida. Heater Utilities provides water and waste-water services in parts of North and South Carolina. Minnesota Power also has operations in coal mining, paper, and truck-mounted lifting equipment. The firm also owns real estate in southwest Florida.

Minnesota Power has traditionally been a good utility. Profits and dividend growth have been reasonable over the years. More recently, however, profits have slowed, which has lifted the dividend payout ratio. The firm has a big exposure to industrial customers, which makes it somewhat vulnerable to increased competition in its markets. However, its low rates should help the firm maintain its competitive position.

Statistical History

Price range	1993	1992	1991	1990	1989
High	$36½	35	32½	27¾	27⅝
Low	30	29⅝	26	22¼	22⅞

	1993	1992	1991	1990	1989
Revenues (mil)	$505.5	489.4	484.1	477.5	463.9
Net income (mil)	62.6	68.5	75.5	74.6	88.8
Earnings per share	2.20	2.31	2.46	2.37	2.90
Book value	18.06	16.58	16.02	16.36	17.46
Dividends	1.98	1.94	1.90	1.86	1.78
Net profit margin	12.4%	14.0	15.6	15.6	19.1
Debt/capital	49.4	50.2	50.4	47.3	47.7
Return on equity	11.5	15.3	15.4	13.6	16.9

Investment Advice

Minnesota Power is an average utility holding. The firm's large non-utility business is both a potential positive and negative in that it enhances growth prospects but increases the stock's risk level. The company's low rates should help to keep competitors from snaring its large industrial user base. Dividend growth will probably be only moderate over the next few years.

Mobil

Mobil Corp.
NYSE: MOB
3225 Gallows Rd.
Fairfax, VA 22037-0001
703-846-3000

Performance Rating: * * *

Performance History

- $1,000 invested on 12/31/83 was worth $4,670 on 12/31/93—a 367 percent increase in 10 years.

Plan Specifics

- Initial purchase is available to investors in all 50 states ($250 minimum initial purchase).
- Partial dividend reinvestment is not available.
- No discount.
- OCP: $10 to $7,500 per month.
- OCP is invested twice per month.
- There are no purchasing fees. Selling fees include brokerage commissions (approximately $0.10 per share). There is a $5 administrative charge to process a withdrawal.
- Plan administrator: Mellon Securities 800-648-9291
- IRA option is available.
- Approximately 48,000 shareholders in the plan.
- Dividends are paid March, June, September, and December.

Corporate Profile

Mobil is a major integrated oil company. The firm also has a presence in the chemicals industry. The firm has nearly 20,000 retail gasoline outlets. Foreign exploration, production, and refining account for nearly 80 percent of sales and profits. The firm has a strong presence in the Pacific Rim.

Despite the volatility of oil markets in general, Mobil has traditionally been a profitable oil company. The firm's heavy foreign exposure has helped to shield it from pricing volatility in this country. Dividends have been rising in recent years, and the firm's healthy cash flow should ensure continued gains in the dividend. The performance of the stock has been steady over the last five years, with these shares showing a nice upward trend. With oil prices expected to rebound, look for profit growth to accelerate for the firm.

Statistical History

Price range	1993	1992	1991	1990	1989
High	$84¾	69¾	73⅛	69½	63¼
Low	59½	57⅞	55⅛	55⅞	45¼

	1993	1992	1991	1990	1989
Revenues (bil)	$56.6	56.9	56.0	57.8	50.2
Net income (bil)	2.1	1.3	1.9	1.9	1.8
Earnings per share	5.07	3.13	4.65	4.60	4.40
Book value	42.74	41.06	43.74	42.44	39.84
Dividends	3.25	3.20	3.13	2.83	2.55
Net profit margin	3.7%	2.3	3.4	3.3	3.6
Debt/capital	20.1	20.4	18.2	16.9	20.9
Return on equity	12.3	7.8	11.1	11.6	11.3

Investment Advice

Mobil offers solid representation in the oil sector. Diversified operations, strong cash flow, and good dividend-growth prospects enhance the potential of these shares. The company's no-load stock program, which includes an IRA option, is attractive as well. The stock may be bought.

Montana Power Company
NYSE: MTP
40 E. Broadway
Butte, MT 59701-9394
800-325-6767
800-245-6767

Performance Rating: * * *

Performance History

- $1,000 invested on 12/31/83 was worth $3,600 on 12/31/93—a 260 percent increase in 10 years.

Plan Specifics

- Initial purchase is available for customers of the utility ($10 minimum initial investment).
- Partial dividend reinvestment is available.
- No discount.
- OCP: $10 to $15,000 per quarter.
- OCP is invested monthly.
- There are no purchasing fees. Selling fees include brokerage commissions.
- Automatic Investment Services are available.
- Approximately 21,776 shareholders in the plan.
- Dividends are paid January, April, July, and October.

Corporate Profile

Montana Power is a holding company for three business units. The firm's utility unit operates electric and natural gas systems serving 262,000 electric and 126,000 gas customers. Coal, hydro, and purchased power account for the firm's fuel mix. The company's Entech unit has operations in such nonutility markets as coal mining, oil and natural gas, and telecommunications. Entech is one of the nation's largest coal producers. The independent power group markets wholesale electricity and owns and operates nonutility electric generation facilities.

Montana Power's nonutility businesses have helped to boost profits over the years. The utility business is in reasonably good shape. The firm's rates are extremely competitive, which means new entrants will have a tough time winning the firm's customers. The company's goal is to attain a dividend payout ratio of 70 percent, which is lower than its current level. Thus, investors should not expect big dividend increases over the next few years.

Statistical History

Price range	1993	1992	1991	1990	1989
High	$28¼	28⅜	28⅜	22	21⅛
Low	24½	23⅝	18⅞	17⅞	17

	1993	1992	1991	1990	1989
Revenues (mil)	$1,075.6	988.4	920.1	823.4	775.2
Net income (mil)	107.2	107.1	105.7	95.0	74.4
Earnings per share	1.98	2.02	2.03	1.84	1.45
Book value	17.35	16.82	16.40	15.78	16.12
Dividends	1.58	1.54	1.48	1.42	1.38
Net profit margin	10.0%	10.8	11.5	11.5	9.6
Debt/capital	36.1	38.7	40.2	41.7	39.9
Return on equity	11.6	12.2	12.7	11.6	9.1

Investment Advice

Montana Power is a worthwhile selection for investors who can take advantage of the firm's no-load stock program. The company has a good competitive position, reasonably healthy nonutility businesses, and above-average growth prospects for the industry. The stock should at least match the industry performance.

National Fuel Gas
Company

National Fuel Gas Company
NYSE: NFG
10 Lafayette Square
Buffalo, NY 14203
716-857-7548

Performance Rating: * * *

Performance History

- $1,000 invested on 12/31/83 was worth $7,289 on 12/31/93—a 629 percent increase in 10 years.

Plan Specifics

- Initial purchase is available to customers of the company ($200 minimum initial investment).
- Partial dividend reinvestment is not available.
- No discount.
- OCP: $25 to $5,000 per month.
- OCP is invested monthly.
- There are no purchasing fees. Selling fees include brokerage commissions, any transfer tax, and a $15 bank service fee.
- Plan administrator: Chemical Bank 800-648-8166
- There are approximately 4,000 participants enrolled in the plan.
- Dividends are paid January, April, July, and October.

Corporate Profile

National Fuel Gas is an integrated natural gas company. The firm has three primary operations. Its pipeline and storage unit transports and stores natural gas for the firm's local user market as well as markets in northeastern United States. The company owns and operates 27 underground natural gas storage fields. Its Penn-York Energy unit operates three underground natural gas storage fields. The company's utility operations transport natural gas to over 724,000 customers in western New York and northwestern Pennsylvania. The company's nonregulated activities include oil and gas exploration, a sawmill and kiln business, and a collection service. Utility services account for more than half of total sales and the majority of profits.

National Fuel Gas has broad exposure to the natural-gas field. Thus, as this fuel grows in popularity due, in part, to its environmental advantages, these shares should do well. Dividends have increased annually for more than two decades, and further growth is expected.

Statistical History

Price range	1993	1992	1991	1990	1989
High	$36⅞	30½	25¼	27⅜	27⅛
Low	28¾	23¼	22⅛	21⅝	17⅞

	1993	1992	1991	1990	1989
Revenues (mil)	$1,020.4	920.5	865.1	892.0	855.8
Net income (mil)	75.2	60.3	49.0	52.0	52.4
Earnings per share	2.15	1.94	1.63	1.83	1.93
Book value	20.08	18.68	17.53	16.97	16.44
Dividends	1.51	1.47	1.43	1.36	1.28
Net profit margin	7.4%	6.6	5.7	5.8	6.1
Debt/capital	39.4	43.1	44.9	45.1	45.3
Return on equity	11.0	10.3	9.5	11.0	12.0

Investment Advice

National Fuel Gas has a good track record and favorable total return prospects. The stock is not likely to match its strong performance of the decade ending in 1993. Still, these shares should provide decent returns for patient investors.

Nevada Power Co.
NYSE: NVP
PO Box 98669
Las Vegas, NV 89193-8669
800-344-9239

| Performance Rating: * * |

Performance History ───────────────────────────

- $1,000 invested on 12/31/83 was worth $3,562 on 12/31/93—a 256 percent increase in 10 years.

Plan Specifics ──────────────────────────────

- Initial purchase is available to customers of the company ($25 minimum initial investment).
- Partial dividend reinvestment is available.
- No discount.
- OCP: $25 to $25,000 per quarter.
- OCP is invested monthly.
- There are no purchasing fees. Selling fees include brokerage commissions and transfer taxes.
- Automatic Investment Services are available.
- There are approximately 30,000 participants enrolled in the plan.
- Dividends are paid February, May, August, and November.

Corporate Profile ─────────────────────────────

Nevada Power provides electricity services to more than 400,000 customers in the Las Vegas area and southeastern Nevada. Residential customers comprise more than 40 percent of total revenue. The hotel-gaming industry is the largest customer at roughly 13 percent of total sales. Coal accounts for more than 90 percent of power generation.

Nevada Power's profits have been relatively uninspiring in recent years. The sluggish profit performance has put pressure on the company's dividend. Indeed, the payout ratio is at relatively high levels. Thus, little or no dividend growth is likely over the next few years. One positive is the attractive growth potential of the service region. However, a dependence on the gaming industry does leave the company a bit vulnerable to a downturn in this sector.

Statistical History

Price range	1993	1992	1991	1990	1989
High	$26¾	24	22½	25¾	25⅞
Low	22½	17⅞	16⅝	20	19¼

	1993	1992	1991	1990	1989
Revenues (mil)	$651.8	600.9	546.4	492.3	422.9
Net income (mil)	73.5	56.8	35.2	25.0	51.5
Earnings per share	1.76	1.47	1.05	0.78	1.81
Book value	15.56	14.34	13.96	14.05	14.27
Dividends	1.60	1.60	1.60	1.58	1.54
Net profit margin	11.3%	9.5	6.4	5.1	12.2
Debt/capital	51.0	55.4	53.5	53.7	51.9
Return on equity	12.5	11.4	8.1	6.3	12.8

Investment Advice

While Nevada Power's growth prospects are a plus, the company's overall investment merit is limited. Poor dividend prospects and a potentially more stringent regulatory environment will likely hinder returns.

*Ø*NJRESOURCES

New Jersey Resources Corp.
NYSE: NJR
1415 Wyckoff Rd.
PO Box 1468
Wall, NJ 07719
908-938-1230

> **Performance Rating: * ***

Performance History

- $1,000 invested on 12/31/83 was worth $4,307 on 12/31/93—a 331 percent increase in 10 years.

Plan Specifics

- Initial purchase is available to customers of the utility ($25 minimum initial investment).
- Partial dividend reinvestment is not available.
- No discount.
- OCP: $25 to $30,000 per year.
- OCP is invested twice per month.
- There are no purchasing fees. Selling fees include brokerage commissions.
- Plan administrator: Bank of Boston 800-442-2001
- There are approximately 20,000 participants enrolled in the plan.
- Dividends are paid January, April, July, and October.

Corporate Profile

New Jersey Resources is a holding company engaged in natural gas distribution, oil and gas production and exploration, commercial real estate, and independent power generation. The firm serves more than 330,000 customers in Monmouth and Ocean counties and parts of Morris and Middlesex counties. This service region has shown good growth in recent years.

New Jersey Resources has put together decent earnings growth in recent years. The firm's natural gas utility has performed admirably and should continue to experience customer gains. The firm carries a fairly high level of debt, which adds some risk to the financial position. Dividends have been relatively flat in recent years, and only modest growth is likely.

Statistical History

Price range	1993	1992	1991	1990	1989
High	$29½	25⅛	21⅛	20⅞	21½
Low	24	18¼	17	17⅛	17⅜

	1993	1992	1991	1990	1989
Revenues (mil)	$454.7	400.7	335.6	324.8	329.9
Net income (mil)	28.5	23.5	11.3	13.0	16.4
Earnings per share	1.72	1.64	0.83	0.97	1.45
Book value	14.72	14.16	12.85	13.27	13.54
Dividends	1.52	1.52	1.50	1.44	1.36
Net profit margin	6.3%	5.9	3.4	4.0	5.0
Debt/capital	53.5	48.9	55.3	54.2	52.1
Return on equity	11.9	11.4	6.3	7.2	10.5

Investment Advice

New Jersey Resources is an average holding. Little or no dividend growth offset the above-average growth prospects for the company's service region. The stock has some appeal as an income investment. However, there are probably better opportunities elsewhere.

**NORTHERN STATES
POWER COMPANY**

Northern States Power Co.
NYSE: NSP
414 Nicollet Mall
Minneapolis, MN 55401
612-330-5560
800-527-4677

Performance Rating: * * * *

Performance History

- $1,000 invested on 12/31/83 was worth $4,114 on 12/31/93—a 311 percent increase in 10 years.

Plan Specifics

- Initial purchase is available to residents of Minnesota, North Dakota, South Dakota, Wisconsin, and Michigan ($10 minimum initial investment).
- Partial dividend reinvestment is available.
- No discount.
- OCP: $10 to $10,000 per quarter.
- OCP is invested monthly.
- There are no purchasing or selling fees. Participants may sell up to 25 shares through the plan.
- There are approximately 38,000 participants enrolled in the plan.
- Dividends are paid January, April, July, and October.

Corporate Profile

Northern States Power serves customers in Minnesota, Wisconsin, North Dakota, South Dakota, and Michigan. The company distributes electricity to about 1.4 million customers and distributes natural gas to more than 390,000 customers. Coal, nuclear, and purchased power are the primary fuel sources.

The firm's Prairie Island nuclear plant has one of the best performance records of any nuclear power plant in the country. The company has a fairly sizable exposure to industrial customers. However, its relatively low rates should help to limit customer defections as competition increases. Finances are strong and highlighted by ample fixed-charge coverage and healthy equity levels. Because the firm invested early in pollution-control equipment, no additional major investments to comply with federal environmental regulations are anticipated. Dividends have increased annually for two decades.

Statistical History ⎯⎯⎯⎯⎯⎯⎯⎯⎯⎯⎯⎯⎯⎯⎯⎯⎯⎯⎯⎯⎯⎯⎯

Price range	1993	1992	1991	1990	1989
High	$47⅞	45⅜	44	40½	40
Low	40⅛	38½	31¾	28⅜	30¼

	1993	1992	1991	1990	1989
Revenues (bil)	$2.4	2.2	2.2	2.1	2.0
Net income (mil)	211.7	160.9	207.0	193.0	219.2
Earnings per share	3.02	2.31	3.02	2.79	3.20
Book value	27.32	25.91	25.21	24.42	23.76
Dividends	2.57	2.50	2.40	2.30	2.20
Net profit margin	8.8%	7.5	9.4	9.3	11.1
Debt/capital	38.5	40.7	39.7	40.4	41.4
Return on equity	11.4	9.1	12.2	11.6	13.7

Investment Advice ⎯⎯⎯⎯⎯⎯⎯⎯⎯⎯⎯⎯⎯⎯⎯⎯⎯⎯⎯⎯⎯⎯⎯

Investors who have the opportunity to take advantage of the firm's no-load stock program should do so. Strong finances, dividend growth at least in line with the industry average, and competitive rates put the company in good position to outperform the industry over the long term.

NUI Corp.
NYSE: NUI
550 Route 202-206
PO Box 760
Bedminster, NJ 07921-0760
908-781-2026

Performance Rating: * *

Performance History

- $1,000 invested on 12/31/83 was worth $3,112 on 12/31/93—a 211 percent increase in 10 years.

Plan Specifics

- Initial purchase is available to residents of Florida, New Jersey, North Carolina, and Pennsylvania ($125 minimum initial investment).
- Partial dividend reinvestment is available.
- No discount.
- OCP: $25 to $60,000 per year.
- OCP is invested monthly.
- There are no purchasing fees. Selling fees include brokerage commissions, service charges, transfer tax, and an administrative fee charged by the agent.
- Plan administrator: Mellon Securities 800-526-0801
- Automatic Investment Services are available.
- Dividends are paid March, June, September, and December.

Corporate Profile

NUI is a geographically diversified provider of natural gas services. The firm provides services primarily in New Jersey and Florida. The company expanded its operations with the 1994 acquisition of Pennsylvania & Southern Gas. The bulk of the company's gas supplies comes from purchases with various producers and gas marketers.

Earnings have been uneven over the years. Dividends had been increasing, but the firm decided to cut its dividend in 1994 in preparation for increasing competition in its markets. One plus for the firm is its exposure to service regions showing decent growth rates.

Statistical History

Price range	1993	1992	1991	1990	1989
High	$29¾	25¼	20¼	19	19⅛
Low	23⅜	18⅛	13¾	13¼	16⅞

	1993	1992	1991	1990	1989
Revenues (mil)	$354.9	291.0	291.3	296.0	265.5
Net income (mil)	13.8	11.8	3.4	8.7	7.2
Earnings per share	1.70	1.68	0.55	1.42	1.39
Book value	14.93	14.55	13.43	14.39	14.44
Dividends	1.59	1.58	1.57	1.56	1.56
Net profit margin	3.9%	4.1	1.2	2.9	2.7
Debt/capital	55.8	55.4	58.7	56.0	52.3
Return on equity	11.5	11.7	4.0	9.9	9.3

Investment Advice

NUI has some appeal, especially as utility stocks strengthen. Still, poor dividend prospects limit total return potential. The stock will likely be only an average performer in its group.

Oklahoma Gas & Electric Co.
NYSE: OGE
101 N. Robinson
PO Box 321
Oklahoma City, OK 73101-0321
405-272-3000

Performance Rating: * *

Performance History

- $1,000 invested on 12/31/83 was worth $3,449 on 12/31/93—a 245 percent increase in 10 years.

Plan Specifics

- Initial purchase is available to residential customers of the company ($25 minimum investment).
- Partial dividend reinvestment is available.
- No discount.
- OCP: $10 to $5,000 per quarter.
- OCP is invested monthly.
- There are no purchasing fees. Selling fees include brokerage commissions.
- Plan administrator: Liberty Bank & Trust Co. 800-395-2662
- There are approximately 16,000 participants enrolled in the plan.
- Dividends are paid January, April, July, and October.

Corporate Profile

Oklahoma Gas & Electric provides electric service to over 658,000 customers in Oklahoma and western Arkansas. The firm has eight natural gas and coal-fired plants. The firm's natural gas activity is conducted through Enogex, a wholly owned gas transportation subsidiary. Residential customers account for roughly one-third of total revenues. Major industrial customers are the oil and gas industries.

Oklahoma Gas has been hurt by a tough regulatory climate in recent years. Per share profits peaked in 1990. The drop in profits has put pressure on the dividend, which was not covered by earnings in 1992 and only barely covered in 1993. Because of the high dividend-payout ratio, dividend growth is likely to be nonexistent. The company's industrial rates are fairly competitive, which should help the firm fend off increased competition in its markets.

Statistical History

Price range	1993	1992	1991	1990	1989
High	$38⅝	44	44	39¾	39
Low	32⅞	30⅛	36½	32⅞	32

	1993	1992	1991	1990	1989
Revenues (bil)	$1.4	1.3	1.3	1.2	1.1
Net income (mil)	114.3	99.7	133.9	139.2	129.4
Earnings per share	2.78	2.42	3.27	3.38	3.05
Book value	22.48	22.35	22.59	21.92	21.28
Dividends	2.66	2.66	2.58	2.48	2.38
Net profit margin	7.9%	7.6	10.2	11.3	11.3
Debt/capital	46.7	46.9	47.1	47.8	47.9
Return on equity	12.4	10.7	14.7	15.6	12.1

Investment Advice

Little or no dividend growth and a tough regulatory climate make these shares relatively unattractive. Investors should preference other utilities for the income portion of their no-load stock portfolio.

PHILADELPHIA
SUBURBAN
CORPORATION

Philadelphia Suburban Corp.
NYSE: PSC
762 Lancaster Ave.
Bryn Mawr, PA 19010-3489
610-527-8000

Performance Rating: * * *

Performance History

- $1,000 invested on 12/31/83 was worth $4,032 on 12/31/93—a 303 percent increase in 10 years.

Plan Specifics

- Initial purchase is periodically available to customers of the company ($250 minimum initial investment).
- Partial dividend reinvestment is available.
- 5 percent discount on reinvested dividends.
- OCP: $25 to $10,000 per year. Utility customers may invest up to $30,000 annually.
- OCP is invested three times a year (June, September, December).
- There are no purchasing fees. Selling fees include brokerage commission and taxes.
- Plan administrator: Mellon Securities, 800-756-3353.
- Dividends are paid March, June, September, and December.

Corporate Profile

Philadelphia Suburban is a water utility servicing more than 800,000 people in Chester, Delaware, and Montgomery counties in southeastern Pennsylvania. On an average day, the company treats and delivers 89 million gallons of water. The firm has built state-of-the-art treatment facilities that meet or exceed the latest regulations of the Federal and

State Safe Drinking Water acts. Residential customers account for
approximately two-thirds of total sales.

Philadelphia Suburban has been on a "back-to-basics" kick in recent
years. The firm has been focusing on expanding its water utility business
while divesting its non-water-related subsidiaries. This approach should
help profits return to a more stable environment. Attention to service has
paid off in the fact that the firm has had the lowest customer complaint
ratio of any utility in Pennsylvania for the last two years.

Statistical History

Price range	1993	1992	1991	1990	1989
High	$20¾	16⅝	16⅜	15	14½
Low	15⅝	13¾	11¾	10⅜	12¾

	1993	1992	1991	1990	1989
Revenues (mil)	$101.2	93.3	88.6	82.3	76.0
Net income (mil)	13.9	10.6	10.2	9.7	9.3
Earnings per share	1.27	1.23	1.29	1.27	1.25
Book value	11.89	10.88	10.66	10.95	11.39
Dividends	1.07	1.04	1.00	1.00	0.94
Net profit margin	13.7%	11.4	11.5	11.8	12.2
Debt/capital	49.9	56.8	63.7	67.3	65.5
Return on equity	11.4	11.0	11.9	11.4	11.0

Investment Advice

Philadelphia Suburban is a well-managed utility that would be an
acceptable holding in any no-load stock portfolio. Dividend growth
should be above average for its industry. The firm has ample opportunities to expand via acquisitions, and finances are adequate to fund further
deals. The stock should produce worthwhile returns over the next several years.

PINNACLE WEST
CAPITAL CORPORATION

Pinnacle West Capital Corp.
NYSE: PNW
PO Box 52133
Phoenix, AZ 85072-2133
800-457-2983
602-379-2500

> **Performance Rating: * ***

Performance History: Not available. ─────────

Plan Specifics ──────────────────────────────

- Initial purchase is available to customers of the company ($10 minimum initial purchase). The company is planning open enrollment in 1995.
- Partial dividend reinvestment is available.
- No discount.
- OCP: $10 to $5,000 per quarter.
- OCP is invested monthly.
- When purchasing on the open market, fees include brokerage commissions. Selling fees include brokerage commissions.
- There are about 45,000 participants enrolled in the plan.
- Dividends are paid March, June, September, and December.

Corporate Profile ──────────────────────────────

   Pinnacle West Capital is the holding company for Arizona Public Service, the state's largest electric utility servicing approximately 654,000 customers. Sources of generation include coal and nuclear, which make up approximately 90 percent of fuel sources. The largest industrial customer is the mining industry. The firm's other subsidiaries are involved in residential and commercial development projects and venture capital.
   Pinnacle West has had its problems over the last five years. The firm posted a loss of nearly $4 per share in 1991. Problems with a company-

owned savings and loan hurt results. The firm was forced to eliminate its dividend, although the dividend was reinstated at the end of 1993. The company seems to be getting back on track, as profits have improved recently. Given the modest dividend currently being paid, above-average growth in the payout is expected. The company's rates for industrial users are on the high side. Thus, the firm may be vulnerable to increased competition in the future.

Statistical History

Price range	*1993*	*1992*	*1991*	*1990*	*1989*
High	\$25¼	20½	17⅞	18⅝	16⅜
Low	19⅝	16¾	9⅝	9⅜	5

	1993	*1992*	*1991*	*1990*	*1989*
Revenues (bil)	\$1.7	1.7	1.5	1.5	1.4
Net income (mil)	170.0	150.4	–340.3	70.2	124.6
Earnings per share	1.95	1.73	–3.91	0.81	1.44
Book value	18.87	17.00	15.23	17.40	16.31
Dividends	0.20	none	none	none	1.20
Net profit margin	10.1%	9.0	NM	4.7	8.6
Debt/capital	56.3	59.6	63.5	63.2	65.7
Return on equity	10.9	10.7	NM	4.8	7.2

Investment Advice

Pinnacle West is a utility on the mend. Dividend growth should be decent in upcoming years. However, competition could be a problem for the company down the road, and finances are a cut below most utilities. Thus, while these shares have some speculative appeal, they are geared more for aggressive investors.

Puget Sound Power & Light Co.
NYSE: PSD
PO Box 96010
Bellevue, WA 98009-9610
206-462-3719

> Performance Rating: *

Performance History ───────────────────────

- $1,000 invested on 12/31/83 was worth $4,014 on 12/31/93—a 301 percent increase in 10 years.

Plan Specifics ────────────────────────────

- Initial purchase is available to residents of Washington ($25 minimum initial investment).
- Partial dividend reinvestment is available.
- No discount.
- OCP: $25 to $100,000 per year.
- OCP is invested twice per month.
- Purchasing and selling fees include brokerage commissions.
- There are more than 30,000 participants enrolled in the plan.
- Dividends are paid February, May, August, and November.

Corporate Profile ─────────────────────────

Puget Sound Power and Light is the largest investor-owned electric utility in Washington State. The firm's 4,500-square mile service territory serves a population base of nearly 2 million people. Hydroelectric, coal, and purchased power make up the primary fuel sources. Residential customers account for approximately 45 percent of total revenue. Largest industries are oil refining and aircraft.

Puget Sound has had rough going recently. Tough regulatory decisions have impaired the dividend. Earnings have gone virtually nowhere since 1985. The firm's service region has decent growth prospects. The company has added more than 115,000 customers over the past five years. The company's industrial rates should keep it fairly competitive should new players enter its markets. Still, earnings are likely to lag in the near term, which will impact the stock.

Statistical History

Price range	1993	1992	1991	1990	1989
High	$29¾	27⅞	26⅞	22½	22½
Low	23½	23⅞	19⅛	18⅝	18

	1993	1992	1991	1990	1989
Revenues (mil)	$1,112.9	1,025.0	956.8	935.3	887.8
Net income (mil)	138.3	135.7	132.8	132.3	117.7
Earnings per share	2.00	2.16	2.21	2.16	1.88
Book value	18.65	17.76	16.96	16.52	16.12
Dividends	1.83	1.79	1.76	1.76	1.76
Net profit margin	12.4%	13.2	13.9	14.2	13.3
Debt/capital	42.6	44.6	48.8	48.0	47.8
Return on equity	11.0	12.6	13.2	13.3	11.7

Investment Advice

With dividends being pressured by poor earnings and regulators taking a tough stance toward the company, total return prospects appear to be limited. The stock is a below-average holding in the industry.

Regions
Financial Corp.

Regions Financial Corp.
NASDAQ: RGBK
PO Box 5260
Montgomery, AL 36102-1448
800-638-6431   *222-3000*
205-832-8450

Performance Rating: * * * *

Performance History

- $1,000 invested on 12/31/83 was worth $5,743 on 12/31/93—a 474 percent increase in 10 years.

Plan Specifics

- Initial purchase is available to investors in all 50 states ($20 minimum initial investment).
- Partial dividend reinvestment is not available.
- No discount.
- OCP: $20 to $10,000 per month.
- OCP is invested monthly.
- There are no purchasing fees. Selling fees include brokerage costs. In addition, a $50 charge will be assessed if account is closed within six months of its opening.
- There are approximately 10,000 participants enrolled in the plan.
- Dividends are paid January, April, July, and October.

Corporate Profile

Regions Financial, formerly First Alabama Bancshares, operates banks in Alabama, Florida, Georgia, Louisiana, Tennessee, South Carolina, and Mississippi. The firm changed its name to reflect its increased penetration of the Southeast. The company has been extremely active on the acquisition front, and further takeovers are expected.

Regions Financial has an outstanding track record. Net income has risen each year since the bank's inception in 1971. Dividends have expanded rapidly, rising more than threefold since 1982. With the dividend payout ratio at a relatively low level and earnings expected to rise at a healthy rate, look for outstanding dividend growth to continue in upcoming years. The company's presence in a rapidly growing area of the country is a plus, as is its asset quality.

Statistical History

Price range	1993	1992	1991	1990	1989
High	$38⅜	33⅞	27⅛	16⅞	17⅝
Low	29⅝	23¾	15⅞	13¼	13¾

	1993	1992	1991	1990	1989
Net interest income (mil)	$342.1	312.7	264.8	222.2	203.7
Net income (mil)	112.0	95.0	78.3	68.9	62.6
Earnings per share	3.01	2.60	2.16	1.91	1.73
Book value	20.73	17.62	15.76	14.54	13.48
Dividends	1.04	0.91	0.87	0.84	0.76
Debt/capital	35.2%	17.3	3.2	3.6	8.5
Return on equity	14.9	15.5	14.3	13.6	13.2

Investment Advice

Regions Financial is a top no-load stock. Strong profit and dividend growth, solid finances, a growing geographic region, and favorable expansion prospects point to steady gains over the long term. The firm's no-load stock program, with its minimum initial investment of just $20 and open enrollment, is especially attractive. These shares represent an excellent foundation stock for a portfolio. I'm a shareholder in Regions Financial, and you should be too.

San Diego Gas & Electric Co.
NYSE: SDO
101 Ash St.
San Diego, CA 92101
619-696-2020
800-826-5942

> **Performance Rating: * ***

Performance History

- $1,000 invested on 12/31/83 was worth $4,924 on 12/31/93—a 392 percent increase in 10 years.

Plan Specifics

- Initial purchase is available to customers of the company ($25 minimum initial investment).
- Partial dividend reinvestment is available.
- No discount.
- OCP: $25 to $25,000 per quarter.
- OCP is invested monthly.
- There are no purchasing fees. Selling fees include $2.50 plus any brokerage commission and other costs. There is a charge of $2.50 for each withdrawal of full-share certificates from continuing plan accounts.
- Plan administrator: First Interstate Bank of CA 800-243-5454
- There are approximately 40,000 participants enrolled in the plan.
- Dividends are paid January, April, July, and October.

Corporate Profile

San Diego Gas & Electric provides electric service to more than 1.1 million customers in all of San Diego County and the southern portion of Orange County. Gas is provided to 690,000 customers in San Diego

County. Residential users are the company's largest customer base at more than 40 percent of total revenues. Natural gas and purchased power are the two biggest fuel sources. Nuclear energy accounts for nearly 20 percent of fuel generation.

California utilities have not had an easy time in recent years. The regulatory environment has been rather stringent. Furthermore, it appears that California will be at the forefront of allowing increased competition in its utility markets. San Diego Gas & Electric's industrial rates, though low for the state, are on the high side relative to utilities in other parts of the country. Thus, the firm may be vulnerable to increased competition.

Statistical History

Price range	1993	1992	1991	1990	1989
High	$27¾	25	23¼	23½	22⅞
Low	23¼	21⅛	18⅝	19½	18¼

	1993	1992	1991	1990	1989
Revenues (bil)	$2.0	1.9	1.8	1.8	1.7
Net income (mil)	218.7	210.7	208.1	207.8	179.4
Earnings per share	1.81	1.77	1.76	1.76	1.57
Book value	13.01	12.53	12.00	11.58	11.16
Dividends	1.48	1.44	1.39	1.35	1.35
Net profit margin	11.0%	11.3	11.6	11.7	10.7
Debt/capital	46.3	48.6	43.7	44.7	44.2
Return on equity	14.8	15.1	15.7	16.3	14.5

Investment Advice

San Diego Gas & Electric provides a relatively high yield and reasonable appreciation prospects. However, given the traditionally tough California regulatory markets, I would not want to have a large exposure to these shares.

SCANA Corp.
NYSE: SCG
1426 Main St.
Columbia, SC 29201
803-733-6817
800-763-5891

> **Performance Rating: * * ***

Performance History

- $1,000 invested on 12/31/83 was worth $5,500 on 12/31/93—a 450 percent increase in 10 years.

Plan Specifics

- Initial purchase is available to investors in all 50 states ($250 minimum initial investment).
- Partial dividend reinvestment is available.
- No discount.
- OCP: $25 to $36,000 per year.
- OCP is invested monthly.
- Purchasing fees include brokerage commissions when purchased in the open market. Selling fees include brokerage commissions and taxes.
- Approximately 21,500 shareholders are in the plan.
- Dividends are paid January, April, July, and October.

Corporate Profile

SCANA is a utility holding company. The firm's electric service area extends into 24 of South Carolina's 46 counties covering more than 15,000 square miles. The two largest metropolitan areas serviced by the company are Columbia, the state capital, and Charleston. The company services nearly 500,000 customers. The firm has five fossil-fired steam plants, five hydroelectric plants, one nuclear plant, one pumped-storage hydro plant, and 13 internal combustion turbines. Coal and nuclear comprise the bulk of generating fuel. Natural gas service is provided to nearly 240,000 customers. The firm also owns transit systems in metropolitan areas of Columbia and Charleston.

SCANA has appeal on several fronts. The firm's service region should show growth at least matching the national average. The company is a low-cost producer in its region, which should help it retain customers and even expand market share over time. The dividend payout ratio is on the low end of the industry average. Thus, dividend-growth prospects should be above average in upcoming years. The firm has been successful in meeting emission standards set forth in the Clean Air Act.

Statistical History

Price range	1993	1992	1991	1990	1989
High	$52¼	44¾	44¼	35⅞	35¾
Low	40⅛	38⅝	33½	30¼	29⅝

	1993	1992	1991	1990	1989
Revenues (bil)	$1.3	1.1	1.1	1.1	1.1
Net income (mil)	168.0	117.6	135.9	181.6	122.6
Earnings per share	3.72	2.84	3.37	4.44	3.04
Book value	28.59	26.46	25.23	24.56	22.79
Dividends	2.74	2.68	2.62	2.52	2.46
Net profit margin	13.3%	10.3	11.8	15.8	10.7
Debt/capital	50.2	49.2	50.2	46.2	49.8
Return on equity	13.5	10.7	13.4	18.9	13.5

Investment Advice

SCANA is one of the better utilities among those with no-load stock programs. Boosting appeal is the fact that the plan is open to investors in all 50 states. Strong dividend-growth prospects enhance total return potential. Of course, the stock's performance will correlate closely with the performance of utility stocks in general. Still, investors who want exposure to this group should give these shares high priority.

SOUTHWEST GAS CORPORATION

Southwest Gas Corp.
NYSE: SWX
PO Box 98511
Las Vegas, NV 89193-8511
702-876-7280

Performance Rating: * *

Performance History

- $1,000 invested on 12/31/83 was worth $2,579 on 12/31/93—a 158 percent increase in 10 years.

Plan Specifics

- Initial purchase is available to customers of the company ($100 minimum initial investment).
- Partial dividend reinvestment is not available.
- No discount.
- OCP: $25 to $25,000 per year.
- OCP is invested monthly.
- There are no purchasing fees. Selling fees include brokerage commissions and service fees.
- There are approximately 13,000 participants enrolled in the plan.
- Dividends are paid March, June, September, and December.

Corporate Profile

Southwest Gas provides natural gas service to nearly one million customers in most of Arizona and Nevada and parts of California. The company's Paiute Pipeline company provides transportation service of natural gas to Southwest as well as to other utilities. The firm also owns PriMerit Bank, a savings bank with branches in Nevada.

Southwest Gas is in one of the fastest-growing natural gas regions of the country. The firm added almost 35,000 customers during 1993.

Growth comes at a price, however, because the firm has had to meet this increased demand. Debt levels are on the high side. The poor earnings performance is one reason the firm cut its dividend in 1991. The bank operation provides an avenue for earnings growth but also enhances the volatility of the bottom line.

Statistical History

Price range	1993	1992	1991	1990	1989
High	$18½	15⅜	17½	18½	20⅜
Low	13⅜	10⅜	9	11¾	16⅝

	1993	1992	1991	1990	1989
Revenues (mil)	$689.8	718.5	794.8	867.7	846.7
Net income (mil)	12.4	17.7	−14.2	37.2	42.7
Earnings per share	0.56	0.81	−0.76	1.81	2.15
Book value	16.38	15.99	15.88	17.63	17.30
Dividends	0.74	0.70	1.05	1.40	1.37
Net profit margin	1.8%	2.5	NM	4.3	5.0
Debt/capital	66.3	65.5	65.8	68.7	69.5
Return on equity	4.4	5.1	NM	10.3	12.7

Investment Advice

Southwest Gas has come back a bit since its slump in 1991 to 1993. Dividends should resume an upward bias as earnings continue to recover. Finances are still a cut below other gas suppliers, however, making these shares only an average selection in the group.

TEXACO

Texaco, Inc.
NYSE: TX
Investor Services Plan
2000 Westchester Ave.
White Plains, NY 10650
800-283-9785

Performance Rating: * * *

Performance History

- $1,000 invested on 12/31/83 was worth $3,569 on 12/31/93—a 257 percent increase in 10 years.

Plan Specifics

- Initial purchase is available to investors in all 50 states ($250 minimum initial investment).
- Partial dividend reinvestment is not available.
- No discount.
- OCP: $50 to $120,000 per year.
- OCP is invested every 10 days.
- Purchasing fees include brokerage commissions. Selling fees include a $5 charge per sale transaction and brokerage commissions.
- Dividends are paid March, June, September, and December.

Corporate Profile

Texaco is a leading integrated oil company. The firm sold its chemical operation in early 1994. Operations are evenly divided between U.S. and international exploration and marketing.

Texaco has been making strides in improving its cost position. The firm has reduced total expenses by more than $400 million since 1991. The company has also been diligent in broadening its overseas exposure.

Texaco has made inroads into the potentially huge China market. The firm has also been active in entering the Russian market.

Per share profits have been erratic in the last few years. Of course, Texaco's bottom line is dependent on oil prices. Continued economic growth in this country and abroad should provide some support to energy prices.

Statistical History

Price range	1993	1992	1991	1990	1989
High	$69½	66⅞	70	68½	59
Low	57⅞	56⅛	55½	55	48½

	1993	1992	1991	1990	1989
Revenues (bil)	$34.1	36.5	37.2	40.5	34.2
Net income (bil)	1.3	1.0	1.3	1.4	2.1
Earnings per share	4.47	3.63	4.60	5.01	7.93
Book value	33.96	32.78	33.40	31.72	30.31
Dividends	3.20	3.20	3.20	3.05	3.00
Net profit margin	3.7%	2.8	3.5	3.5	6.2
Debt/capital	37.5	39.2	34.5	32.3	33.9
Return on equity	11.3	12.0	12.8	15.9	28.1

Investment Advice

I like the oil stocks going forward and expect Texaco to perform well over the next few years. The yield, combined with capital gains, should produce total returns at least in line with the market. While I prefer Exxon among no-load oil stocks, Texaco would be a worthwhile holding as well.

Union Electric Co.
NYSE: UEP
PO Box 149
St. Louis, MO 63166
800-255-2237

> **Performance Rating: * * ***

Performance History

- $1,000 invested on 12/31/83 was worth $6,199 on 12/31/93—a 520 percent increase in 10 years.

Plan Specifics

- Initial purchase is available to customers of the company (no minimum initial investment).
- Partial dividend reinvestment is available.
- No discount.
- OCP: up to $60,000 per year.
- OCP is invested monthly.
- There are no purchasing fees. Selling fees include brokerage commissions.
- Sells may be made via the telephone.
- Dividends are paid March, June, September, and December.

Corporate Profile

Union Electric is the largest electric utility in Missouri. The service area covers about 24,500 square miles. Residential customers account for more than 40 percent of total sales. Primary fuel sources are coal and nuclear.

Union Electric has cut costs by trimming employee count by 15 percent since 1987. The Midwest floods of 1993 hindered results a bit, but the

firm still managed to post a decent year. The company's nuclear operations have been given high marks by regulators. Dividends have been
raised annually for the last decade, and further gains are expected. The
firm's industrial rates are competitive and should help the company
retain its industrial user base over time.

Statistical History

Price range	1993	1992	1991	1990	1989
High	$44⅝	38¾	38⅝	30	28⅝
Low	35¾	31¼	28½	24⅝	23

	1993	1992	1991	1990	1989
Revenues (bil)	$2.1	2.0	2.1	2.0	2.0
Net income (mil)	297.2	302.7	321.5	294.2	285.6
Earnings per share	2.77	2.83	3.01	2.74	2.61
Book value	21.60	21.19	20.62	19.79	19.14
Dividends	2.33	2.26	2.18	2.10	2.02
Net profit margin	14.4%	15.0	15.3	14.5	14.2
Debt/capital	42.2	41.1	42.7	46.5	49.1
Return on equity	13.0	13.7	15.0	14.2	14.0

Investment Advice

Union Electric combines a good yield with worthwhile upside potential relative to most utilities. Dividend growth should at least match the
industry average. The stock is an acceptable portfolio holding.

United Water Resources, Inc.
NYSE: UWR
200 Old Hook Rd.
Harrington Park, NJ 07640
201-767-2811

> **Performance Rating: * * ***

Performance History ————————————

- $1,000 invested on 12/31/83 was worth $3,343 on 12/31/93—a 234 percent increase in 10 years.

Plan Specifics ———————————————

- Initial purchase is available to customers of certain company subsidiaries ($25 minimum investment).
- Partial dividend reinvestment is available.
- 5 percent discount on reinvested dividends and OCPs.
- OCP: $25 to $3,000 per quarter.
- OCP is invested monthly.
- There are no purchasing fees. Selling fees include brokerage commissions and taxes.
- Plan administrator: First Interstate Bank of CA 800-522-6645
- There are approximately 10,000 participants enrolled in the plan.
- Dividends are paid March, June, September, and December.

Corporate Profile ——————————————

United Water Resources owns Hackensack Water and Spring Valley Water companies. The 1994 purchase of GWC Corp. nearly doubled the size of the firm and makes it the second-largest water utility in the country. The company provides services to over 2 million customers in 14 states. The geographical diversification provides benefits in the way of reducing weather fluctuations and regulatory problems that can affect one service area.

The merger with GWC should be a long-term positive for United Water Resources, although short-term problems could result while UWR incorporates GWC into its operations. The takeover could limit dividend growth in the near future, especially as UWR spends to upgrade and improve acquired operations.

Statistical History

Price range	1993	1992	1991	1990	1989
High	$15⅞	16⅝	16⅝	16½	17⅝
Low	14	13	10⅞	9⅞	15¾

	1993	1992	1991	1990	1989
Revenues (mil)	$200.4	164.9	161.8	164.6	133.4
Net income (mil)	20.0	15.8	16.4	18.3	14.3
Earnings per share	1.03	0.87	0.96	1.10	0.86
Book value	10.00	9.55	9.33	9.10	8.84
Dividends	0.92	0.92	0.91	0.88	0.88
Net profit margin	10.0%	9.6	10.2	11.1	10.7
Debt/capital	54.1	58.0	62.4	59.2	60.3
Return on equity	10.5	9.2	10.4	12.3	9.7

Investment Advice

United Water Resources' prospects are better over the long term than they are in the short term. Limited dividend growth will hold back total returns over the next few years. However, the GWC acquisition should help earnings grow nicely over the long term. Patient investors could consider these shares for a no-load stock portfolio.

U S West, Inc.
NYSE: USW
7800 E. Orchard Rd.
Englewood, CO 80111
303-793-6500

Performance Rating: * * * *

Performance History: Not available. ─────────────

Plan Specifics ──────────────────────────────

- Initial purchase is available to investors in all 50 states ($300 minimum initial investment).
- Partial dividend reinvestment is available.
- No discount.
- OCP: $25 to $100,000 per year.
- OCP is invested weekly.
- Fees include a $1 charge per account per quarter. Selling fees include brokerage commissions.
- Plan administrator: State Street Bank & Trust Co. 800-537-0222
- Automatic Investment Services are available.
- There are about 240,000 participants enrolled in the plan.
- Dividends are paid February, May, August, and November.

Corporate Profile ──────────────────────────

U S West is one of the seven regional telephone companies resulting from the AT&T breakup. The firm provides local telephone service in Arizona, Colorado, Idaho, Iowa, Minnesota, Montana, Nebraska, New Mexico, North Dakota, Oregon, South Dakota, Utah, Washington, and Wyoming. The company has nearly 14 million access lines in service. U S

West also has rapidly growing cellular telephone operations as well as international operations in the cable television and telephone markets.

U S West has favorable long-term growth prospects due to its position in several attractive telecommunications markets. The firm should be a player in the "information highway" via its interactive networks that it is planning with Time Warner. Cable operations meld nicely with these interactive markets of the future. Further enhancing long-term prospects is the likelihood of the firm being able to compete in the long-distance market. To be sure, the company's own local telephone markets will likely be invaded by new competitors. But, on balance, a changing regulatory environment should favor the company. Dividends have risen every year since 1984, and further growth in the payout is expected in line with the company's growth in profits.

Statistical History

Price range	1993	1992	1991	1990	1989
High	$50¾	40	40¾	40½	40⅜
Low	37¼	32⅞	33¾	32⅜	28⅜

	1993	1992	1991	1990	1989
Revenues (bil)	$10.3	10.3	10.6	10.0	9.7
Net income (bil)	1.1	1.2	1.1	1.2	1.1
Earnings per share	2.72	2.86	2.85	3.11	3.01
Book value	13.29	19.95	23.39	23.48	21.58
Dividends	2.14	2.12	2.08	2.00	1.88
Net profit margin	11.1%	11.5	10.8	12.0	11.5
Debt/capital	48.1	44.9	44.3	43.7	47.3
Return on equity	19.5	14.3	11.9	13.0	13.8

Investment Advice

Every investor should have some exposure to the telecommunications markets. U S West provides such exposure for no-load stock investors. A good yield, favorable growth prospects, and steady dividend gains should result in solid total returns. The stock is a suitable holding in any portfolio.

Western Resources, Inc.
NYSE: WR
818 Kansas Ave.
PO Box 889
Topeka, KS 66601
913-575-6300

> **Performance Rating: * * ***

Performance History

- $1,000 invested on 12/31/83 was worth $4,572 on 12/31/93—a 357 percent increase in 10 years.

Plan Specifics

- Initial purchase is available to customers of the company ($20 minimum initial investment). Enrollment is offered once a year in the customer stock purchase plan.
- Partial dividend reinvestment is available.
- No discount.
- OCP: $20 to $60,000 per year.
- OCP is invested monthly.
- Fees for purchasing and selling may include brokerage commissions. There is also a $15 service fee when selling shares.
- Plan administrator: Chemical Bank 800-648-8165
- There are approximately 16,767 participants enrolled in the plan.
- Dividends are paid January, April, July, and October.

Corporate Profile

Western Resources provides utility services to customers in Kansas and Oklahoma. Retail electric services are provided to nearly 600,000 customers. The firm also has over 600,000 natural gas customers. The economy of the service area is primarily agriculture, mineral production, aircraft, and vehicle manufacturing. Residential customers provide approximately 35 percent of total revenues. The fuel mix is roughly 80 percent coal and the remainder nuclear and gas. Nonutility operations include natural gas marketing, natural gas compression services, and technology development.

Western Resources has done a good job at incorporating the 1992 acquisition of Kansas Gas & Electric. Finances were aided by the sale of the Missouri gas properties. Dividends should grow at about the industry average over the next few years. The company's rates are fairly competitive relative to industry averages.

Statistical History

Price range	*1993*	*1992*	*1991*	*1990*	*1989*
High	\$37¼	32⅝	28⅜	25⅛	25⅜
Low	30⅜	25⅜	20¾	19¾	21⅝

	1993	*1992*	*1991*	*1990*	*1989*
Revenues (bil)	\$1.9	1.6	1.2	1.2	1.1
Net income (mil)	177.4	127.9	72.3	79.6	72.8
Earnings per share	2.76	2.20	1.91	2.25	2.05
Book value	23.08	21.51	18.59	18.25	17.80
Dividends	1.94	1.90	2.04	1.80	1.76
Net profit margin	9.3%	8.2	6.2	6.9	6.5
Debt/capital	48.8	57.5	43.2	47.2	45.8
Return on equity	12.3	12.2	10.4	12.5	11.6

Investment Advice

Western Resources should at least match the performance of the utility industry overall. Dividend growth of at least 2 percent plus capital gains should help these shares produce decent total returns.

WICOR, Inc.
NYSE: WIC
626 E. Wisconsin Ave.
PO Box 334
Milwaukee, WI 53201
414-291-7026
800-236-3453

Performance Rating: * * *

Performance History

- $1,000 invested on 12/31/83 was worth $5,619 on 12/31/93—a 462 percent increase in 10 years.

Plan Specifics

- Initial purchase is available to residents of Wisconsin ($100 minimum initial investment).
- Partial dividend reinvestment is not available.
- No discount.
- OCP: $100 to $10,000 per month.
- OCP is invested monthly.
- There are no purchasing fees. Selling costs include a $10 fee and brokerage commissions.
- Plan administrator: Chemical Bank 800-621-9609
- Dividends are paid February, May, August, and November.

Corporate Profile

WICOR is a holding company for Wisconsin Gas, the state's largest natural gas utility. The firm serves more than 485,000 customers in 487 communities. The company also has nonutility operations under its Sta-Rite Industries and SHURflo Pump Manufacturing units. Sta-Rite makes pumps and water-processing equipment. This unit accounts for nearly 30 percent of WICOR's total revenues. SHURflo makes pumps and fluid-handling equipment for the beverage, marine, and water purification markets. The unit was acquired by WICOR in 1993 and accounts for approximately 5 percent of total sales.

WICOR's profits have been trending upward of late. The firm's strategy of building its nonutility operations seems to be working. Dividend growth has been steady over the last decade, and further increases in the payout are expected.

Statistical History

Price range	1993	1992	1991	1990	1989
High	$32⅞	27⅞	24¼	25¼	25¼
Low	25⅝	22⅞	18⅝	18¼	19⅜

	1993	1992	1991	1990	1989
Revenues (mil)	$849.5	747.4	716.8	696.0	741.2
Net income (mil)	29.3	14.8	23.0	16.7	33.9
Earnings per share	1.82	1.40	1.54	1.04	2.40
Book value	16.47	15.60	15.84	16.12	16.83
Dividends	1.54	1.50	1.46	1.42	1.37
Net profit margin	3.5%	2.0	3.2	2.4	4.6
Debt/capital	37.9	40.1	40.9	35.4	33.4
Return on equity	11.2	9.2	9.5	6.8	14.3

Investment Advice

WICOR is an attractive holding in the natural gas field. Growing nonutility businesses provide a kicker to this utility and should help earnings and dividend growth. Investors who are eligible to make initial purchases directly should take advantage of the firm's no-load stock program.

WISCONSIN ENERGY
CORPORATION

Wisconsin Energy Corp.
NYSE: WEC
231 W. Michigan St.
PO Box 2949
Milwaukee, WI 53201
800-558-9663

Performance Rating: * * * *

Performance History

- $1,000 invested on 12/31/83 was worth $5,135 on 12/31/93—a 414 percent increase in 10 years.

Plan Specifics

- Initial purchase is available to customers of Wisconsin Electric Power and Wisconsin Natural Gas ($25 minimum initial investment).
- Partial dividend reinvestment is not available.
- No discount.
- OCP: $25 to $8,000 per month.
- OCP is invested monthly.
- There are no purchasing fees. Selling fees include brokerage commissions and stock transfer taxes.
- Automatic Investment Services are available.
- There are approximately 90,000 participants enrolled in the plan.
- Dividends are paid March, June, September, and December.

Corporate Profile

Wisconsin Energy is a holding company with primary operations in the electric and natural gas businesses. The firm's service region encompasses 12,600 square miles in parts of Wisconsin and Michigan. The operating area includes Milwaukee. Commercial and industrial users account for nearly 60 percent of total revenues. Coal and nuclear energy are the primary fuel sources.

The company's utility rates are on the low end of the industry range, so the firm should have no problem retaining customers in an environment of increased competition. Dividends have been rising steadily, and growth should outpace the industry average. Wisconsin Energy's cost position should only get better as the company has embarked on a major cost-savings program. Finances are excellent, with fixed-charge coverage high and debt at reasonable levels.

Statistical History

Price range	1993	1992	1991	1990	1989
High	$29⅜	28½	26½	21⅝	21½
Low	24¾	23¾	20	17¼	16¼

	1993	1992	1991	1990	1989
Revenues (bil)	$1.6	1.6	1.5	1.4	1.5
Net income (mil)	188.5	169.7	189.3	186.7	194.0
Earnings per share	1.81	1.67	1.87	1.85	1.92
Book value	15.67	14.97	14.35	13.70	13.01
Dividends	1.34	1.28	1.22	1.15	1.09
Net profit margin	11.5%	10.9	12.3	12.9	13.0
Debt/capital	43.3	42.4	41.4	40.0	41.4
Return on equity	11.8	11.3	13.4	13.8	15.2

Investment Advice

Wisconsin Energy is one of the best utilities in the market. The regulatory climate of Wisconsin has traditionally been one of the better ones in the country. Dividend growth on the order of 2 to 3 percent should be the norm over the next few years. Of course, the performance of these shares will have a lot to do with how well Wall Street supports utility stocks in general. Nevertheless, this stock will likely outpace the industry average.

Epilogue

Beyond No-Load Stocks

While the focus of this book has been on buying stock directly from companies, the essence of no-load stocks—direct investing—does not have to stop at just stocks. Why can't investors buy bonds directly? Or preferred stock? Or convertibles? Or tax-preferenced investments? This chapter looks beyond no-load stocks to offer some ideas on how to expand the "no-load" concept to other investments. In addition, I'll explore the changing structure of stock markets and examine ways investors will interact with companies and each other in the future.

Follow the Mutual-Fund Lead

For ideas on how to expand the no-load stock concept, the mutual-fund industry, as usual, is an excellent source. No-load stocks have copied a number of the most attractive attributes of no-load mutual funds—IRAs, automatic investment programs, and telephone sales. Why not copy other aspects of the no-load mutual-fund industry?

- *Corporate bonds.* Billions of dollars are invested in no-load bond funds. Investors buy these funds in the same way as no-load stock funds—directly from the fund group, without a broker and without commissions. If a company can sell its stock directly to individual investors, why can't the firm sell bonds directly as well? The demand from investors certainly seems to be there. A Harris poll of individual investors found that 71 percent of respondents would be "very or somewhat interested" in buying corporate bonds directly from corporations. Another indication of demand for direct purchase of fixed-income investments is the success of the Treasury's and Bureau of the Public Debt's "Treasury Direct" plan. Individuals who want to buy treasury bills, bonds, and notes can do so without using a broker by buying treasury securities directly from Federal Reserve banks and the Bureau of the Public Debt. (For further information about this program write the Federal Reserve Bank of Richmond, Public Service Department, PO Box 27622, Richmond, VA 23261.) The Bureau of the Public Debt estimates that more than $1.5 trillion of treasury securities were issued in 1993 through its Treasury Direct program. If investors' appetite for buying treasury securities directly is great, it's not a stretch to think that similar demand exists for buying corporate bonds directly.

Firms have danced around the notion of direct bond investing for individual investors. **Brooklyn Union Gas** permits participants in its dividend reinvestment plan to reinvest bond interest to purchase additional common shares. However, no firm to my knowledge has yet to sell its corporate debt directly. Mechanically, it doesn't seem like it should be that difficult to sell bonds directly. Utilities, with their customer stock purchase plans, seem well suited to peddling debt through a customer bond purchase program. Since investors buy utilities primarily for income, selling bonds directly to customers makes sense.

I'm sure that one hang-up to selling bonds directly is the SEC. I've been told by company shareholder services representatives that they figure on spending at least $50,000 in various legal and administrative fees in order to get a no-load stock program approved by the SEC. And that's for a program that runs through the approval process rather smoothly. My guess is that no firm wants to be the "pioneer" in offering a no-load bond plan since legal fees alone to get a new plan through the SEC could be substantial. Nevertheless, all it takes is one firm—one firm that sees the value in offering a no-load bond program and whose top management is willing to make the sacrifices in time and money to get a program approved. Once one company demonstrates that such a program is possible and, indeed, successful, pressure is placed on other firms, especially those in the same industry, to follow suit.

- *Preferred stock.* The Vanguard fund family offers a no-load mutual fund that invests in preferred stock. The fund has assets of more than $350 million. Might some of the same investors in the Vanguard Preferred Stock fund want to invest directly in company preferred stocks?

  Individuals, especially those investing for income, should find preferreds attractive. One interesting angle on issuing preferred stock directly is the tax laws surrounding investments in preferred stock. Because 70 percent of dividend income from preferred stock is tax exempt to corporations, a no-load preferred stock program potentially could be targeted to corporations as well as individual investors.

As was the case with bonds, companies currently dance around the notion of issuing preferred stock directly. Several firms, including **Minnesota Power & Light** and **K N Energy**, allow participants in their dividend reinvestment plans to reinvest dividends on preferred stock to purchase additional common shares. The next step would be for, say, a utility to sell preferred stock directly to customers.

■ *Convertible bonds.* A *convertible bond* is a debt obligation that allows the owner to tender the bond to the corporation and convert it into a given number of shares of stock. Companies like convertibles because the bonds carry lower yields than straight corporate bonds. Investors like them because they pay decent yields while providing the ability to convert into common stock. An indication of their appeal is that a number of mutual-fund groups have funds devoted exclusively to convertible securities. Since demand exists for these funds, it stands to reason that there would be demand to purchase convertibles directly from companies.

■ *Tax-preferenced investments.* Tax-exempt mutual funds that invest in such tax-preferenced investments as municipal bonds garner billions of dollars a year. And with tax rates trending upward, demand for tax-preferenced funds is likely to rise. Clearly, investors, especially those in the top tax brackets, like to shield their income from taxes. I'm sure investors in the top tax brackets wouldn't mind saving commissions by buying tax-preferenced investments directly from the issuer.

Municipal bonds are sold by states, counties, cities and other political bodies. "Munis," as they are often called, come primarily in two flavors: (1) general obligations that are backed by the full faith and credit of the issuer and repaid from taxes received by the issuing body and (2) revenue obligations that are sold to finance a particular project and are repaid from income earned on the project. A third type of municipal bond is an *industrial development bond.* These are bonds sold to build plants that are then leased to privately owned corporations. These bonds help to attract new businesses to a community.

What makes buying municipal bonds directly from the issuing agents so interesting is that, like utilities and their customer stock purchase plans, municipalities maintain strong ties to their service users. Thus, it's relatively easy for a municipality to publicize a bond offering to its local market. What's in it for the municipality to sell bonds directly? The municipality pockets the fees it otherwise would pay a bond syndicate. Also, by owning bonds, local residents may take more of an interest and be more supportive of the project.

While most tax-preferenced investments are municipal bonds, there's one company whose stock purchase plan provides an interesting way to invest directly while deferring taxes on dividends. **Citizens Utilities** is a diversified utility company providing telecommunications, electric, gas, and water and wastewater services. The company has one of the most impressive growth records on the New York Exchange, with revenues, earnings, and dividends advancing for 49 consecutive years.

Citizens is distinguished not only by its impressive growth record but also by its unique capital structure. The company has two classes of stock—"A" and "B" shares. Each class of stock pays a stock dividend every quarter. However, holders of the "B" shares have the option of having the company sell the shares for a modest fee and remit the funds to the shareholder. The only other difference is that "A" shares are convertible into "B" shares, but "B" shares are not convertible into "A" shares.

The beauty of Citizens' dividend arrangement is that shareholders who take dividends in the form of stock defer taxes on the dividends until the shares are sold. For those who choose to have the company sell their stock dividends, they're taxed at the capital gains rate of 28 percent, which is lower than the 39.6 percent top tax rate some investors pay on cash dividends. To look at it a different way, Citizens has in place what amounts to a tax-deferred dividend reinvestment plan. Granted, the company does not have a formal dividend reinvestment plan in a traditional sense. However, the fact that its dividend policy gives shareholders the option of taking stock or cash serves the same purpose.

Enhancing this attractive program even more is that shareholders can join the firm's stock purchase plan. Under the plan, investors may buy stock with optional cash investments up to $25,000 per quarter. There is a $6 processing fee for each investment. In addition, for shares purchased on the open market, the firm will charge investors roughly $0.05 per share. (For further information about the plan, contact the plan administrator, Illinois Stock Transfer, at 223 West Jackson Blvd., Suite 1210, Chicago, IL 60606, 312-427-2953.)

To be sure, Citizens Utilities falls a bit short of our "no-load stock" concept since you must be a holder of stock before you can buy stock directly from the firm. Nevertheless, the financial creativity the firm has shown with its unique capital structure and "tax-preferenced" dividend plan indicates the possibilities that are available in structuring tax-preferenced "no-load" investments.

■ *International investments.* Investing in international mutual funds has been extremely popular in recent years. The benefits of international investing, such as enhanced diversification, have been trumpeted by the mutual-fund industry, with huge success. One reason mutual funds have become the vehicle of choice for investing overseas is that direct stock investment in foreign countries is still a bit cumbersome. The advent of *American Depositary Receipts* (ADRs)—securities that trade on the U.S. exchanges and represent ownership in shares of a foreign company—has lowered the barriers of investing in foreign-based companies. Still, while some ADRs, notably **Glaxo Holdings PLC** and **Hanson PLC**, offer dividend reinvestment plans for current shareholders, no ADR permits first-time purchases directly. However, with the continuing development of global economies and the furtherance of free trade with foreign partners via NAFTA, it makes sense that overseas firms would want to make their shares more readily available to U.S. retail investors. Permitting a foreign-based company to sell ADRs directly to individual investors may require its own set of regulatory maneuverings, but increasing the availability of a foreign company's stock to U.S. retail investors may be worth the hassle.

- *Government securities.* I've already discussed how an individual can put together his or her own mutual fund of treasury securities by buying directly from the Federal Reserve Board. What if other government and quasi-government arms offered direct purchase of their investments? What if you could buy a Ginnie Mae bond directly from the Government National Mortgage Association? Or a Sallie Mae bond from Student Loan Mortgage Association? It's not as strange as it sounds. Since many government agencies have their own electronic bulletin boards into which individuals can tap via a modem, finding out information about a pending offering—and even placing an order—would be rather simple.

"Decentralization" of the Stock Market

In the future, not only will there be new investments that individuals can buy directly, but there will also be significant changes in how these investments are purchased. No-load stocks are really nothing more than a decentralized stock market of sorts. Instead of an investor going to an exchange to conduct a transaction, the deal is done directly between the two parties, without an intermediary. While such stock trading may be revolutionary for individual investors, "off-exchange" trading for institutional investors has been around for years and is growing rapidly. By looking at how institutions have decentralized the stock market will provide clues on how individual investors can accomplish the same thing.

Many Different "Stock Exchanges"

When investors think of the stock exchanges, they usually mean the New York and American Stock Exchanges as well as the Nasdaq National Market. However, in reality, a plethora of "stock exchanges" that conduct trades for institutional investors exist.

Ever hear of the Arizona Stock Exchange? This privately owned exchange is what amounts to a computerized auction market. No specialists, no market makers, just a mainframe computer acting as the intermediary between buyers and sellers. The exchange is open for one hour each day, from 4 to 5 p.m., eastern standard time. Institutional investors can log onto the exchange's computer and track buy orders as they come into the exchange. When the exchange closes, the computer matches as many buy and sell orders as possible.

Ever hear of POSIT? *Portfolio System for Institutional Trades* is another "off-exchange" exchange that caters to big institutional investors. POSIT provides crossing systems for institutional investors and trades more than 3 million shares daily.

And then there is Instinet. This system, owned by Reuters, is the largest of the automated trading systems and is yet another avenue for institutional investors to avoid the traditional exchanges.

Overall, it's estimated that in the first half of 1993 alone, the total share volume on proprietary trading systems was 4.7 billion shares, almost equal to their entire volume in 1992.

The Fourth Market

Automated trading systems represent just one way institutional investors can trade away from the major exchanges. Another is what is called the *fourth market*. In a nutshell, the fourth market refers to the trading of shares directly between institutional investors, without a broker dealer. For example, a mutual-fund manager at Fidelity may buy or sell stock directly with another mutual-fund manager at Fidelity. Doing so keeps trading costs to a minimum while providing another source of liquidity for the fund—the latter an extremely important point given that some mutual funds may control 5 percent of a stock and may find limited opportunities on the exchanges to accommodate their buy and sell decisions. Fidelity has gotten so big that it operates its own electronic order routing system for trades called Investor Liquidity Network. The system is used by more than 400 brokerage and institutional clients. Fidelity claims that the network handles in excess of 5 percent of the volume on the New York Stock Exchange.

The attraction of the Arizona Stock Exchange, POSIT, Instinet, and the "fourth market" is that they provide increased liquidity for institutional investors at a low cost. For example, institutions can buy or sell a stock for an average of just 1 cent a share on the Arizona Stock Exchange versus maybe 6 cents or more on the New York Stock Exchange.

What About the Individual Investor?

By now, you're probably saying to yourself, "Where do I sign up?" Paying commissions of a penny a share is a small investor's dream come true. But before looking up the telephone number for Instinet, POSIT, or the other automated trading systems, be warned: the systems are available only to institutional investors.

Indeed, while the emergence of alternative trading arenas is certainly good news for big investors, it doesn't release the individual investor from the broker's shackles. But it doesn't have to be that way. Why shouldn't an individual investor be able to use an electronic trading system?

"On-Line" Stock Exchange

By now, I'm sure you've all heard of the vaunted "information highway" being developed in this country that will bring to your computer and television set any and every service known to mankind. Admittedly, I'm somewhat of a skeptic when it comes to technology and the supposedly revolutionary impact it will have on my life. I was probably the last person in the world to buy a VCR. And as for the sweeping changes computers will have on the home front, it seems to me that most home computers are still being used as nothing more than glorified typewriters.

Nevertheless, when I read of Prodigy, CompuServe, and other electronic on-line services having millions of users, it doesn't take a leap of logic to see just how on-line services, if policed properly, could quickly become the electronic stock exchanges of the future.

Take CompuServe, which has over two million subscribers. How hard would it be, aside from potential regulatory roadblocks, to establish a national "on-line" stock exchange on CompuServe? Such an exchange could work similarly to the automated trading systems for institutional investors, bringing a buyer and seller together via matching in a central computer. Sound farfetched? Don't tell Uniform Capital Access Network, Inc. The North Carolina firm is establishing a nationwide electronic stock market for nonrestricted exempt securities. The firm is taking advantage of regulatory changes in the issuance of small stock offerings by providing an on-line clearinghouse matching companies with venture capitalists and individual investors. Such a service would be a natural for one of the major on-line services, such as CompuServe. As discussed in Chapter 4, **H&R Block**, which owns CompuServe, could make available a prospectus and information on purchasing its own stock on CompuServe as a way to kick off the service and demonstrate to other corporations the effectiveness of reaching the individual investor in this way. The on-line services already provide conduits for investors who want to trade electronically with their brokers. Why not provide an avenue for investors to deal directly with companies and each other?

Do What the Funds Do

Mutual funds have already discovered that the "information highway" is an excellent way to disseminate prospectuses and application information. In 1994, the Internet network, used by some 20 million subscribers, began offering NETworth, a service designed for mutual-fund companies to deliver prospectuses and marketing data to potential shareholders electronically. The cost for mutual funds to use the network is $250 plus $100 per prospectus listed. From a mutual fund's standpoint, the program helps eliminate costly mailings and better qualifies a prospect. Of course, mutual funds are looking at this service as a stopgap until the time when direct fund purchases will be available over the network.

Another way mutual funds are using technology to simplify the investment process is via ATM machines. **Wells Fargo**, for example, currently sells mutual funds through its ATMs.

Wouldn't it be nice to receive information and purchase no-load stocks so easily? Imagine going to your local Wal-Mart and seeing, next to the photofinishing and optical departments, an ATM devoted exclusively to buying and selling Wal-Mart stock. All you have to do is pull out your Wal-Mart debit card, insert it into the machine, and punch in your stock purchase. The whole process takes less than 30 seconds. Now that's decentralized stock buying!

Uneven Playing Field

This last example gets down to what small investors really want—the ability to buy stock like they buy toothpaste or bug spray. Of course, the SEC probably cringes when it hears such talk. Certainly making it as easy to buy stock as it is to buy a comb increases the potential for fraud. Still, it doesn't make any sense to me why the SEC won't permit me to buy McDonald's stock at one of its restaurants, but I can call up a discount broker and buy any stock I want. Granted, the broker is supposed to "know the customer" and protect the investor from purchasing inappropriate investments. But let's face it—if I call a broker to make a purchase, the last thing most brokers are going to do is talk me out of the trade. Furthermore, it doesn't make sense that very soon I'll probably be able to buy a mutual fund simply by clipping a coupon from a newspaper advertisement and sending it to the fund along with my check, yet a firm offering a no-load stock is not even allowed to tell the investing public that its plan exists. Bottom line: there is no level playing field between stock and mutual-fund investing, which is a big reason that individual investors have made mutual funds their investment of choice.

Reasons for Optimism

Fortunately, I am encouraged by some recent developments that bode well for future applications of the "no-load" concept:

- **3DO Company**, a Redwood City, California-based maker of multimedia and interactive machines, had a program in 1994 in which the firm gave two shares of its stock to its machine manufacturers for every system sold. At the time of the offer, the stock was trading for roughly $25 per share. The two shares of stock were, in effect, a manufacturer's rebate of $50. The best part was that the company didn't have to come up with any cash and didn't anticipate any great dilution of stock from the program. While 3DO used the program to entice its manufacturers to sell more products, such a rebate program could easily be applied to the retail customer. Imagine General Motors offering a $2,000 rebate in the form of GM stock to Corvette buyers. The car buyer is happy because he or she is getting a kickback for the purchase, GM is happy because the shares can come out of treasury stock and don't cost the company anything, and the GM dealer is happy because the Corvette owner is now a GM shareholder, which may mean greater brand loyalty and repeat business.

- **Fidelity Trust**, a Salt Lake City bank owned by mutual-fund giant Fidelity Investments, offers a Visa or Mastercard that pays rebates good on purchases of Fidelity mutual funds. The credit card rebates 1 percent of your annual purchases on the card up to a maximum $100 per year. Those rebates go into a savings account run by the bank where they're held until $1,000 or more accrues, at which time the money is invested in either Fidelity's Puritan or Asset Manager fund. But before you get too excited, do the math. If the cap on the annual rebate is $100—meaning you charged at least $10,000—it will take you nearly 10 years—and roughly $100,000 in charges—to get to the $1,000 minimum. Obviously, you'd be better off paying off your credit card debt, tearing up your card, and taking the interest savings to buy Fidelity funds. However, the concept of rebates on a credit or debit card offers intriguing possibilities for no-load stock investors. Say you own an American Express charge card. Wouldn't it be neat to receive one share of American Express stock for every $500 in charges? The shares wouldn't necessarily cost American Express anything since it could be original issuance. And what a good way to maintain and build customer loyalty. Remember, I'm not saying that you purchase American Express stock by charging it on your credit card (the SEC frowns on this, although it's probably just a matter of time before stock can be purchased with a charge card). Rather, you receive American Express stock as a rebate for using the card.

■ **American Recreation Centers**, one of the no-load stocks profiled in this book, has in the past made available information for interested stock investors at its bowling alleys. You can't buy the shares. Still, it's a much quicker way to get the necessary information and application to buy the stock.

Market 2000

Another encouraging sign for the individual investor is the "Market 2000" report released by the Securities & Exchange Commission in 1994. Market 2000 represents the first major examination of the financial markets by the SEC since its report more than 20 years ago which led to, among other things, the elimination of fixed brokerage commissions and the creation of discount brokers.

While Market 2000 didn't contain anything as earth-shattering as the 1975 report—nor did it address at all the notion of no-load stocks—it did feature a few items that should make individual investors happy. Perhaps the biggest recommendation, as far as small investors are concerned, was the elimination of the "one-eighth" pricing system for stocks.

The practice of using eighths is said to have come from a centuries-old practice when Spanish pieces were the medium of exchange and those pieces could be broken into as many as eight parts. However, this practice makes little sense in today's markets. Interestingly, no exchange outside the United States trades in eighths. The report stated that the current system of using eights can cause artificially wide spreads and hinder quote competition by preventing offers to buy or sell at prices inside the prevailing quote. The current system may also contribute to the practice of payment for order flow by ensuring a dealer's spread that is large enough for a market maker to pay profitability a penny or two a share for order flow. And make no mistake—pennies count. Indeed, by some estimates, U.S. investors would have saved $1 billion in 1992 had stocks been priced just one penny cheaper. The report recommended a change to perhaps a one-sixteenth system, which is the current variation for stocks under $5 on the American Stock Exchange. Another alternative would be a decimal system, where prices are set in pennies. A decimal system is used in many overseas markets.

While the report favors a move to decimal pricing, it understands such a move could create increased costs for the markets. A move to sixteenths would not incur such extensive conversion costs. The report recommends that a conversion to a minimum variation of one-sixteenth occur as soon as possible.

Another part of the report that addressed small investors is in the disclosure of "soft-dollar" practices. A relationship involving soft dollars means that an investment adviser agrees to run trades through a particular broker. In return, the investment adviser receives a portion of the value of the commissions in the form of research and other services (soft-dollar deals were discussed in Chapter 3). Market 2000 stated that it believes advisers should disclose quantifiable information about soft-dollar arrangements to their clients, including specific information regarding the research and other services that an adviser receives.

Another recommendation of the report that may have an impact on small investors over time concerns companies moving their listings off the New York Stock Exchange. Currently, NYSE Rule 500 requires a company wishing to withdraw its securities from the New York Stock Exchange to submit the proposal to its shareholders. The rule requires that the proposal be approved by two-thirds of the outstanding shares, together with the failure of 10 percent of the individual shareholders to object. The report states that what once might have been a good rule is no longer justifiable given the high standards of other exchanges. While the report did not go as far as to call for the elimination of Rule 500, it did ask the New York Stock Exchange to submit a proposed rule change to modify the requirements, suggesting that new standards should rely on a determination by a company's board of directors rather than shareholder approval.

What does this mean for you and me? Not much right now. My guess is that most Big Board companies aren't going to want to jump to another exchange. However, 10 or 15 years from now, maybe there's an electronic exchange that's been established with less onerous listing fees for companies and much more reasonable trading costs and greater liquidity for investors. With the existence of such an electronic exchange, it might make sense for a firm, under certain circumstances, to delist from the New York Stock Exchange in order to join the new exchange. The study's recommendation to tone down Rule 500 would make this move easier to accomplish for companies.

Whether the recommendations of Market 2000 are adopted remains to be seen. A number of the recommendations will require action by the markets, not the SEC or Congress, and individuals representing the exchanges and the brokerage industry have been rather cool toward many of the recommendations. Still, the report reflects a sense that individual investors still matter to the SEC, which could ultimately lead to rulings making no-load stocks more available.

Developments Abroad

Not only is change occurring in this country, but developments abroad also bode well for individual investors and direct investment:

- Philippines' Silangan Airways is offering its passengers more than just jet lag and stale peanuts. The airline is giving passengers the choice of a 5 percent discount on a future flight or a 65 peso option on preferred stock in the airline. The options are convertible into nonvoting preferred shares paying an annual yield of 12 percent. Silangan Chairman Vicente Araneta was quoted in *The Wall Street Journal* as saying that he hopes passengers pick the investment since a customer base of shareholders enhances brand loyalty. Funny that the chairman of an airline with, at the time of this writing, only one plane and one route has figured out something that heads of much larger airlines still haven't figured out. Hey, Robert Crandall at American Airlines or Herbert Kelleher at Southwest Airlines, save your peanuts. Give us stock!

- In 1993, regulators of Japan's financial markets approved new investment products aimed at small investors. Regulators also waived certain taxes for companies that encourage small-scale stock purchases. Why do Japan's regulators want the small investor? For the same reasons that small investors are valued in this country—stability and liquidity. According to a *Wall Street Journal* article, there's a little over $9 trillion in Japanese private assets held by individuals. What those funds could do for Japanese stocks is amazing. Currently, wealthy speculators and foreigners, along with individual corporations, comprise the biggest stock holders. One factor keeping the small investor out of the market is that nearly all of Japan's blue-chip companies require a minimum purchase of 1,000 shares. The government has been waiving tax duties for companies that reduce minimum purchase requirements. But only a very small portion of the listed companies has lowered their minimums. Still, the Japanese investor, like the U.S. investor, has shown an interest in investments if the barriers to entry are reduced. A good example of this is the success of Japanese securities companies that launched stock funds aimed at small investors requiring investment of just 10,000 yen (roughly $100 U.S.) per month. Officials of these securities firms stated that they opened more than 300,000 of these accounts from February to May of 1993.

- Hungary is launching a "Small Investors Program" aimed at encouraging Hungarian participation in privatization and other projects, such as share issues on the Budapest Stock Exchange.

- The French Stock Exchange, in an attempt to boost participation by individuals, has implemented a number of "user-friendly" features. Perhaps the most noteworthy for small investors is a program that gives "low-income investors" the ability to pay for their newly acquired shares on a three-year installment basis, yet provides the ability to sell their shares during this period. Another feature is the creation of personal equity plans that will shelter capital gains on up to $100,000 in equity investments if shares are held for at least five years.

Why is what's going on in France or Hungary or Japan relevant to individual investors in the United States? With the globalization of today's financial markets and advances in electronic communications, one day it will be as easy for the little investor to buy stock on the French or Hungarian or Japanese stock exchanges as it is to buy on the New York Stock Exchange.

A Perfect World Revisited

You might recall that in this book's introduction, I talked about a perfect world for small investors, one in which you could go into a McDonald's or Wal-Mart and buy stock along with a hamburger or bug spray. Unfortunately, a perfect world does not exist in many regards. Today, investing for the small investor still means finding a broker and paying a hefty commission. Today, it's the institutional investors who get all the breaks from the brokers while individual investors are treated like second-class citizens.

But change is coming, and the emergence of no-load stocks is just one catalyst for change. The development of on-line trading systems that can easily be adapted to accommodate small investors, more responsive regulators, and growing awareness of the importance of the small investor abroad all point to an investing world that's changing for the better for small stock investors.

Even Wall Street may be changing its tune concerning the small investor. The following is a quote by Benjamin F. Edwards III, chairman of A.G. Edwards & Sons, a major brokerage firm, from *The Wall Street Journal:*

> I worry when we start doing things that help us but don't help the client. In a long bull market, you can charge clients fees, and if every month their account is worth more than the month before, they aren't upset about it. But you get a declining market and every month their accounts are worth less, and they see fees in there, they say, 'Why am I paying someone fees to lose my money?'

Of course, talk is cheap, and only time will tell whether the brokerage industry begins to respect the small investor. But if the number of no-load stocks grows as quickly as I expect, by the time brokers figure out that they need the individual investor, the individual investor may not need them.

Bibliography

Chapter One

Bloomberg, May 1994.
Business Week, December 21, 1992.
Business Week, June 6, 1994.
Currier, Chet, and David Smyth, *No Cost/Low Cost Investing*, Franklin Watts, New York, 1987.
First Trust Corporation, *Shareholder and Direct Purchase Program IRAs Market Research Evaluation*, 1994.
SmartMoney, June 1993.
The Wall Street Journal, July 23, 1993.
The Wall Street Journal, August 30, 1993.
The Wall Street Journal, November 22, 1993.
The Wall Street Journal, February 11, 1994.

Chapter Two

AAII Journal, August 1991.
Barron's, April 18, 1994.
Dick Davis Digest, May 23, 1994.
Directory of Dividend Reinvestment Plans, Standard & Poor, New York, 1994.
Investor's Business Daily, June 5, 1992.
Investor's Business Daily, April 26, 1994.
Lorie, James H., Peter Dodd, and Mary Hamilton Kimpton, *The Stock Market: Theories and Evidence*, 2d ed., Dow Jones-Irwin, Homewood, Illinois, 1985.
Mutual Fund News Service, May 18, 1994.
Radcliffe, Robert C., *Investment: Concepts, Analysis, and Strategy*, 2d ed., Scott, Foresman and Co., Chicago, 1987.
The Wall Street Journal, April 20, 1994.

Chapter Three

Barron's, April 12, 1993.
Barron's, January 10, 1994.
Bill Staton's Money Advisory, May 12, 1993.
Bogle, John C., *Bogle on Mutual Funds: New Perspectives for the Intelligent Investor* Irwin Professional Publishing, Burr Ridge, Illinois, 1994.
Business Week, January 31, 1994.

Business Week, February 14, 1994.
Business Week, April 4, 1994.
Business Week, May 23, 1994.
Chicago Tribune, March 23, 1993.
Chicago Tribune, May 19, 1993.
Chicago Tribune, March 6, 1994.
Chicago Tribune, April 6, 1994.
Chicago Tribune, May 11, 1994.
Daily Herald, March 31, 1992.
Donoghue's MONEYLETTER, May 1993.
5 Star Investor, December 1993.
5 Star Investor, March 1994.
Forbes, January 18, 1993.
Forbes, February 15, 1993.
Fortune, December 27, 1993.
FW, May 10, 1994.
In The Vanguard, Winter 1994.
Individual Investor, June 1993.
Individual Investor, March 1994.
Investment Company Institute, 1992 Annual Report.
Investor's Business Daily, May 1, 1992.
Investor's Business Daily, March 4, 1993.
Investor's Business Daily, May 28, 1993.
Investor's Business Daily, August 6, 1993.
Investor's Business Daily, December 14, 1993.
Investor's Business Daily, December 21, 1993.
Investor's Business Daily, March 4, 1994.
Investor's Business Daily, April 8, 1994.
Investor's Business Daily, April 21, 1994.
Investor's Business Daily, May 27, 1994.
Investor's Business Daily, June 10, 1994.
Investor's Business Daily, June 16, 1994.
Investor's Business Daily, June 20, 1994.
Kiplinger's Personal Finance Magazine, May 1994.
Money, September 1993.
Money, May 1994.
Mutual Fund News Service, October 4, 1989.
Mutual Fund News Service, September 2, 1993.
Mutual Fund News Service, February 10, 1994.
The New York Times, March 27, 1993.
The New York Times, January 22, 1994.
Press release from Investment Company Institute, February 16, 1994.
Press release from Investment Company Institute, March 8, 1994.
SmartMoney, February 1994.
SmartMoney, March 1994.
SmartMoney, April 1994.
Tax Wise Money, May 1994.

The Wall Street Journal, March 5, 1992.
The Wall Street Journal, March 19, 1993.
The Wall Street Journal, April 20, 1993.
The Wall Street Journal, August 16, 1993.
The Wall Street Journal, September 27, 1993.
The Wall Street Journal, November 10, 1993.
The Wall Street Journal, December 17, 1993.
The Wall Street Journal, January 17, 1994.
The Wall Street Journal, January 20, 1994.
The Wall Street Journal, January 21, 1994.
The Wall Street Journal, January 25, 1994.
The Wall Street Journal, January 28, 1994.
The Wall Street Journal, February 1, 1994.
The Wall Street Journal, February 11, 1994.
The Wall Street Journal, February 15, 1994.
The Wall Street Journal, February 17, 1994.
The Wall Street Journal, February 28, 1994.
The Wall Street Journal, March 2, 1994.
The Wall Street Journal, April 7, 1994.
The Wall Street Journal, May 17, 1994.
The Wall Street Journal, June 10, 1994.
The Wall Street Journal, June 23, 1994.
The Wall Street Journal, June 27, 1994.
Worth, July/August 1993.
Worth, October 1993.
Worth, March 1994.

Chapter Four

American Society of Corporate Secretaries, Inc., *Structuring and Administering A Dividend Reinvestment Plan*, 1993.
Barron's, June 21, 1993.
Barron's, April 11, 1994.
Business Week, Reinventing America 1992.
Capital Analytics Inc., *The Hidden Market: A Survey of Corporate Attitudes Toward Marketing To Shareholders*, ADP, New York, 1993.
Chairman of the U.S. Securities and Exchange Commission, *Report of the Bachmann Task Force on Clearance and Settlement Reform in U.S. Securities Markets*, May 1992.
Daily Local News (West Chester, PA), July 8, 1992.
Delaware County Daily Times, August 21, 1992.
Delaware County Daily Times, August 27, 1992.
Investor Relations Update, April 1992.
Investor's Business Daily, September 30, 1992.
Investor's Business Daily, December 31, 1992.
Investor's Business Daily, March 24, 1993.
Investor's Business Daily, April 12, 1994.

Kiplinger's Personal Finance Magazine, June 1992.

Main Line Times, September 3, 1992.

Management Accounting, September 1990.

Management Accounting, September 1993.

National Association of Investors Corporation, *A White Paper for the Individual Investor: a Four-Part Report Concerning the Individual Investor,* 1994.

The New York Times, July 31, 1993.

The New York Times, August 7, 1993.

The News & Observer, June 18, 1994.

The Output, January 1, 1994.

The Output, February 1, 1994.

The Philadelphia Inquirer, August 17, 1992.

The Philadelphia Inquirer, August 25, 1992.

The Philadelphia Inquirer, August 28, 1992.

The Philadelphia Inquirer, September 30, 1992.

Redemption Digest and Securities Industry Daily, April 18, 1994.

Redemption Digest and Securities Industry Daily, May 3, 1994.

Redemption Digest and Securities Industry Daily, May 4, 1994.

Redemption Digest and Securities Industry Daily, May 5, 1994.

Redemption Digest and Securities Industry Daily, May 6, 1994.

Redemption Digest and Securities Industry Daily, May 9, 1994.

Redemption Digest and Securities Industry Daily, May 10, 1994.

Redemption Digest and Securities Industry Daily, May 11, 1994.

Redemption Digest and Securities Industry Daily, May 12, 1994.

Redemption Digest and Securities Industry Daily, May 13, 1994.

Redemption Digest and Securities Industry Daily, May 16, 1994.

Redemption Digest and Securities Industry Daily, May 19, 1994.

Redemption Digest and Securities Industry Daily, May 20, 1994.

Redemption Digest and Securities Industry Daily, May 23, 1994.

Redemption Digest and Securities Industry Daily, May 24, 1994.

Redemption Digest and Securities Industry Daily, May 25, 1994.

Redemption Digest and Securities Industry Daily, May 26, 1994.

Redemption Digest and Securities Industry Daily, May 27, 1994.

Redemption Digest and Securities Industry Daily, May 31, 1994.

Redemption Digest and Securities Industry Daily, June 6, 1994.

Redemption Digest and Securities Industry Daily, June 24, 1994.

Scott, Mary, and Howard Rothman, *Companies With a Conscience: Intimate Portraits of Twelve Firms That Make a Difference,* Carol Publishing Group, New York, 1992.

The SEC Today, October 29, 1991.

Shareholder Communications Corporation Survey, March 18, 1993.

SmartMoney, May 1994.

Speech by Arthur Levitt, Chairman of the Securities and Exchange Commission, given before the Consumer Federation of America on March 10, 1994.

Trends, March/April 1992.

U.S. Working Committee-Group of Thirty Clearance and Settlement Project, *Discussion Document on Providing Alternatives to Certificates for the Retail Investor,* July 1991.

The Wall Street Journal, July 15, 1991.
The Wall Street Journal, April 27, 1992.
The Wall Street Journal, September 30, 1992.
The Wall Street Journal, December 29, 1992.
The Wall Street Journal, March 3, 1993.
The Wall Street Journal, May 5, 1993.
The Wall Street Journal, May 12, 1994.
The Wall Street Journal, June 7, 1994.

Chapter Five/Epilogue

Company quarterly and annual reports.
Value Line Investment Survey.
Standard & Poor's research reports.
Barron's, April 11, 1993.
Bureau of the Public Debt reports
Business Week, December 21, 1992.
Division of Market Regulation of the United States Securities and Exchange Commission, *Market 2000: An Examination of Current Equity Market Developments,* January 1994.
Financial Analysts Journal, January-February 1994.
Forbes, October 26, 1992.
FW, March 16, 1993.
FW, February 1, 1994.
FW, February 15, 1994.
Individual Investor, March 1994.
Investor's Business Daily, July 30, 1992.
Investor's Business Daily, January 28, 1994.
Investor's Business Daily, May 25, 1994.
Investor's Business Daily, June 9, 1994.
Kiplinger's Personal Finance Magazine, July 1994.
Management Accounting, September 1993.
National Association of Investors Corporation, *A White Paper for the Individual Investor: a Four-Part Report Concerning the Individual Investor,* 1994.
Press release from Uniform Capital Access Network, Inc., June 2, 1994.
Redemption Digest and Securities Industry Daily, May 17, 1994.
Redemption Digest and Securities Industry Daily, June 9, 1994.
Redemption Digest and Securities Industry Daily, June 10, 1994.
The Wall Street Journal, February 26, 1992.
The Wall Street Journal, March 6, 1992.
The Wall Street Journal, May 14, 1992.
The Wall Street Journal, September 8, 1992.
The Wall Street Journal, September 26, 1992.
The Wall Street Journal, October 2, 1992.
The Wall Street Journal, October 26, 1992.
The Wall Street Journal, January 14, 1993.

The Wall Street Journal, April 28, 1993.
The Wall Street Journal, May 18, 1993.
The Wall Street Journal, June 18, 1993.
The Wall Street Journal, September 1, 1993.
The Wall Street Journal, September 15, 1993.
The Wall Street Journal, December 23, 1993.
The Wall Street Journal, January 28, 1994.
The Wall Street Journal, January 31, 1994.
The Wall Street Journal, February 24, 1994.
The Wall Street Journal, March 15, 1994.
The Wall Street Journal, March 17, 1994.
The Wall Street Journal, April 26, 1994.
The Wall Street Journal, May 5, 1994.
The Wall Street Journal, May 6, 1994.
The Wall Street Journal, May 11, 1994.
The Wall Street Journal, May 16, 1994.
The Wall Street Journal, May 25, 1994.
The Wall Street Journal, May 27, 1994.
The Wall Street Journal, June 2, 1994.
Worth, March 1994.

Index

About the Author

Charles B. Carlson, CFA, is the author of the best-selling books *Buying Stocks Without a Broker* and *Free Lunch on Wall Street*, both published by McGraw-Hill. A Chartered Financial Analyst, he is also the editor of two widely followed investment newsletters: *Dow Theory Forecasts* and *DRIP Investor*. Mr. Carlson is often quoted in the media and frequently appears on radio and television.

Your Monthly Guide To
No-Load Stocks™ and
Dividend Reinvestment Plans

DRIP Investor, edited by Charles Carlson, CFA, author of *No-Load Stocks, Free Lunch on Wall Street,* best-selling *Buying Stocks Without A Broker,* and editor of the highly respected *Dow Theory Forecasts,* covers all aspects of no-load stocks and dividend reinvestment programs (DRIPs) — how to buy stocks without a broker, how to buy stocks at a discount, and how to buy blue-chips on the "installment plan" for as little as $10 a month. As a reader of *No-Load Stocks,* you may receive the Charter Rate of only $59 for a full year — a 25% savings. Money-back guarantee. You may cancel any time for a full refund.

With your subscription you will receive a *DRIP Investor* customized 3-ring storage binder, our 144-page, 1994-1995 *Directory of Dividend Reinvestment Plans,* plus our Special 12-page Report, *Why You Don't Need Wall Street.*

To take advantage of this generous offer, fill out the coupon below and mail today.

Introducing

DRIP *Investor*
Charter Rate Offer

❏ YES, start my subscription to *DRIP Investor* immediately at the Charter Rate of $59, a $20 savings. I may cancel any time for a full refund.

Payment Method
❏ Check or money order
❏ Please charge my   ❏ VISA   ❏ MC   ❏ American Express

Name (Please Print)	Credit Card Number
Address	Expiration Date
City State Zip	Signature

Mail today to: NLS

DRIP *Investor* • 7412 Calumet Ave. • Hammond, IN 46324-2692